instant WEB FORMS AND SURVEYS FOR CHILDREN'S/YA SERVICES AND SCHOOL LIBRARIES

GAIL JUNION-METZ AND DERREK L. METZ

NEAL-SCHUMAN NetGuide SERIES

NEAL-SCHUMAN PUBLISHERS, INC.
NEW YORK   LONDON

Published by Neal-Schuman Publishers, Inc.
100 Varick Street
New York, NY 10013

Copyright © 2002 by Gail Junion-Metz and Derrek L. Metz

All rights reserved.

Reproduction of this book, in whole or in part, without the permission of the publishers is prohibited.

Purchase of this book/CD-ROM entitles the purchaser and/or his institution to use, modify, and upload to one institution's Web server, the HTML forms, Perl scripts, and graphic files contained on the CD-ROM. Purchasers using the CD-based forms/surveys need not give copyright credit to the authors, nor bibliographic credit to this publication on every Web page that contains one of the forms/surveys. However, the authors require that copyright and bibliographic credit to this publication be cited, and be visible, somewhere on the purchaser's Web site. None of the content on the enclosed CD-ROM may be sold, transmitted, stored, or otherwise utilized outside the domain of the purchasing institution.

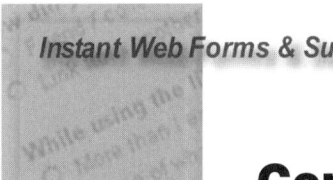

Contents

Preface — v

    What's On the CD? — vi
    What's In the Accompanying Manual? — x
    Sources for Further Help — xi

Acknowledgments — xiii

Introduction — 1
    Needed Skills — 1
    File Servers — A Brief Checklist — 2
    HTML Forms — A Brief Overview — 2
    Perl Scripts — A Brief Introduction — 9

SECTION 1 — HOW TO USE THE CD-ROM

Preview and Select a Form / Survey — 17

After You Download the Files to Your Desktop — 17
    Step 1 — Save the Downloaded Files — 17
    Step 2 — Check to See If Your Server Has a Perl Interpreter — 18
    Step 3 — Get the Paths to Your Server's E-mail Program and Perl Interpreter — 18
    Step 4 — Complete the Required Form Information — 18
    Step 5 — Complete the Required Script Information — 20
    Step 6 (optional) — Modify the HTML Forms — 21
    Step 7 (optional) — Modify the Form Colors — 22
    Step 8 (optional) — Modify the Perl Scripts — 23

Before You Upload the Files to Your Server — 25
    Step 1 — Test the Files Before They're Uploaded — 25
    Step 2 — Create Directories on Your Server to Hold the Forms/Scripts — 26
    Step 3 — Set Up Your Computers to View the Forms — 27
    Step 4 — Save the Files One Last Time . . . Just in Case — 28

Upload the Files to Your Server — 28
    FTP (file transfer) — A Brief Overview — 28
    Step 1 — Locate an FTP Program and Learn FTP Basics — 29
    Step 2 — Transfer the Files to Your Web Server — 29
    Step 3 — Test the Files After You've Uploaded Them — 29

SECTION 2 — FORMS, SURVEYS, AND SCRIPTS

Group 1 – Reference Forms	**35**
Ask a Reference Question form	36
Homework Assignment Alert form *(teachers/librarians/parents)*	44
Get Help Searching the Web form	53
Get Help Citing a Source form	61
Get Help With Your Homework form	70
Group 2 – Library Instruction Forms / Surveys	**79**
Meet With a Librarian form	80
Find a Class form	89
Training Interests Survey *(teachers/librarians/parents)*	97
"What Do You Want to Learn" Survey	105
Group 3 – Library Computer Forms / Surveys	**113**
Reserve a Library Computer form	114
Library Cybersurfer Survey	121
Home Cybersurfer Survey	134
Group 4 – Library Web Site Forms / Surveys	**147**
Suggest a New Web Link form	148
Report a Broken Link or Problem form	155
Sign Our Guest Book form	162
Library Web Site Survey	169
How to Evaluate a Web Site form	181
Group 5 – Collection Development Forms / Surveys	**193**
Recommend an Item form	194
Reading Interests Survey	201
Group 6 – Circulation Forms	**213**
Apply for a Library Card form	214
Hold / Recall / Renew form	223
Report a Missing Book form	231
Group 7– Miscellaneous Forms / Surveys	**239**
Incident Report form *(teachers/librarians/parents)*	240
Kids/Teens Program Interests Survey	248
Index	259
About the Authors	263

Preface

Designing usable and effective paper-based library forms and surveys has always been a challenge. As online technologies change the public and school library landscape, most public and school libraries now have the capability to add online forms and surveys to their Web sites in order to serve kids, teens, teachers, and parents. We created *Instant Web Forms and Surveys for Children's/YA Services and School Libraries* to help you upgrade your Web site . . . without spending hundreds of hours doing it . . . by providing you with many of the most popular and useful library forms and surveys for kids, teens, and staff in a ready-to-use format. Our major goal is to take the expense, work, and uncertainty out of online form and survey design and upload, and make it simple for public and school libraries to add these nifty tools to their Web sites.

The toolkit consists of a CD with ready-to-use forms and an accompanying manual with step-by-step instructions for using them.

The CD contains:

- Twenty-four ready-to-use online forms and surveys in HTML format.
- Twenty-four fully-tested and matching Perl scripts.
- A library of ready-to-select forms and surveys from which to choose.
- A choice of graphics in two different fonts (Times-Roman and Arial) and four different colors (red, blue, white, and black) that will help you "blend" the forms with your existing Web pages.
- A step-by-step tutorial that makes it simple to preview, select, and download just the right form or survey to your computer's desktop.
- Simple instructions to add your library's information to each form and its matching script.
- Step-by-step instructions to test the forms and scripts both before and after you upload them to your library's Web server.
- A backup copy of the printed manual instructions in PDF format just in case you misplace it or need an extra copy.

The accompanying manual contains:

- Step-by-step instructions to add your library's information to each form and the matching script.
- Step-by-step instructions to make simple (and optional) modifications to each of the forms and scripts.
- Step-by-step instructions to test the forms and scripts both before and after you upload them to your library's Web server.
- Printed copies of each of the 24 online forms and surveys.
- Printed copies of each of the 24 Perl scripts.

The forms and surveys in *Instant Web Forms and Surveys for Children's/YA Services and School Libraries* include "Ask a Reference Question form," "Homework Assignment Alert form," "Kids/Teens Program Interests Survey," "Homework Help form," "How to Evaluate a Web Site form" and many more. For a complete list be sure to read the next two sections: "What's On the CD?" and "What's In the Accompanying Manual?"

It's fascinating to receive feedback, opinions, and information from kids, teachers, and parents by adding online forms and surveys to your library's Web site. You will be surprised to discover how quickly you can preview, select, and download a form or survey to your computer's desktop. Without becoming an HTML expert you can add up to 24 online forms and surveys to your library's Web site. Kids, teens, and adults can easily complete each form and survey and e-mail the form's information to an appropriate staff member. Each form or survey automatically sends a "thank you" e-mail and screen message to the person who took the time to fill out the form or survey.

School libraries and public library children's/YA collections are the focus of our third CD. (Volumes for public libraries and academic libraries are also available.) Like other publications in Neal-Schuman's "How To" and "NetGuide" series, *Instant Web Forms and Surveys for Children's/YA Services and School Libraries* is designed for dedicated but busy library administrators, library professionals, and support staff. Our "instant" approach to online forms and script is evident throughout the CD and manual. Instead of teaching *you* how to create HTML forms and Perl scripts from scratch, *we* provide you with 24 fully-tested and functional forms and scripts that you can quickly and easily add to your library's Web site. You can choose to use the forms or surveys "as is" or make a few simple, optional modifications.

Perhaps you are not responsible for uploading the forms and surveys to your Web site, but you must converse with, and understand, the people who will do the job. You can use the toolkit to provide you with background information and instructions so you can work together more productively (and happily) with your technical staff.

This manual and CD grew out of the authors' differing, but in some ways also similar, experiences with the Web and Web sites. Gail is a former academic librarian and now full-time Web/Net trainer. Derrek is a college senior and real-life "techie" who designs and creates Web sites both for business and pleasure. While researching this CD we looked at lots of public library and school library Web sites and noticed that only a few provide kids, teens, teachers, parents, and staff with online forms and surveys. We e-mailed many public and school library Webmasters about why this was so and got the same answers again and again: All wanted to add forms and surveys to their Web sites, but few had the time and many did not possess the technical skills. By solving these two problems with *Instant Web Forms and Surveys for Children's/YA Services and School Libraries*, we hope it will be possible for more school libraries and public library children's/YA collections to easily access the views of their users by adding online forms and surveys to their Web sites.

What's On the CD?

The CD contains twenty-four forms and twenty-four surveys. It also contains a step-by-step tutorial that will let you preview and select just the right form from many different options. Finally, the CD contains a PDF version of this manual . . . just in case you need an extra copy. Read on to learn a few more details about what's on the CD.

The forms and surveys contained on the CD, and reproduced in the pages that follow, have been designed especially for school and public libraries. They're arranged on the CD, and in the manual, in seven general categories.

Each of the forms and surveys are described below.

Preface

Reference Forms

ASK A REFERENCE QUESTION

If students have a straightforward, factual question or reference question, they can fill in this form and e-mail it to your staff. Make sure you include a link to this form on your Web site's reference and home pages.

HOMEWORK ASSIGNMENT ALERT (TEACHERS/LIBRARIANS/PARENTS)

Help teachers, homeschooling parents, and other school staff help your students! Encourage them to use this form to let your staff know in advance about homework assignments that will require kids/teens to use your library's resources and services. Put a link to this form on your Web site's homework help and teacher pages.

GET HELP SEARCHING THE WEB

Do students need help searching the Web? Do they retrieve either too many or too few results? Do they want you to suggest ways they can focus their Web searches to retrieve better results? You can also use this form to find out the additional Web search classes you should be offering/developing. Add a link to this form to any of your Web site's Web search pages.

GET HELP CITING A SOURCE

Students often struggle to locate all the information they need to create complete citations for a bibliography. Put a link to this form on your reference and homework help Web pages so that students can e-mail you the information they have already located.

GET HELP WITH YOUR HOMEWORK

Do students need help with school assignments, research papers, or personal research projects but don't always have the time to meet with your staff? Now you can receive student requests for homework help via e-mail. Be sure to add a link to this form on your Web site's reference and homework help pages.

Library Instruction Forms / Surveys

MEET WITH A LIBRARIAN

Do students need help with school assignments, research papers, or personal research projects but you're often too busy to help them the moment they show up at your desk? Students can use this form to arrange, via e-mail or phone, to meet and talk with a librarian at a mutually agreeable time. Make sure to place a link to this form on your Web site's reference page.

FIND A CLASS

Do students want to take a class on how to use the library, search the Web, or use the library's computers but they don't know if the library offers the classes they're interested in on a date/at a time that's convenient for them? Have students fill out this form and then e-mail them a list of relevant library classes that are scheduled on (or close to) the dates/times they've indicated. Be sure to put a link to this form on your Web site's library instruction and home pages.

Training Interests Survey (teachers/librarians/parents)
Encourage teachers, homeschooling parents, and other librarians to fill out this brief survey to help you get an idea of how effective your current library training sessions are. You'll also be able to find out any new training sessions that they would like you to develop and when they'd like the classes offered. Finally, you can find out how teachers and parents learn about currently offered classes as well as how you can notify them of such opportunities in the future. Place a link to this survey periodically on your Web site's library instruction page.

What Do You Want to Learn Survey
Encourage students to fill out this short survey to help you get an idea of the kinds of learning needs your students have. Use the results to plan new training sessions and schedule them when students want them offered. Place a link to this survey periodically on your Web site's library instruction page.

Library Computers Forms / Surveys
Reserve a Library Computer
Do students hate to wait in line to use one of your library's computers? Provide them with this form so that they can ask to reserve a computer on a specific date and at a specific time. Put a link to this form on any of your Web site's Web search or technology pages.

Library Cybersurfer Survey
If you have students who use your library's computers to access the Internet and you'd like to know more about them so that you can help them better use your computers, the Internet, and your library's Web site, make sure you place a link to this survey periodically on your library's home page.

Home Cybersurfer Survey
If students use an Internet-connected computer at home, have them complete this brief survey so that you can learn how they use the Internet and your library's Web site when they're not in your library. Put a link to this survey periodically on your library's home page.

Library Web Site Forms / Surveys
Suggest a New Web Link
Encourage students to take a few minutes to recommend a new Web link they've found. Students can provide you with the site's URL, why they think you should add it your Web site, and even where on your site they think it should be located. Place a link to this form on any/all of your Web site's pages.

Report a Broken Link or Problem
It's a time-consuming job keeping all of your Web site links current. Students can help by reporting any changed or broken links they run into while using your Web site, any graphics/images that don't load properly, or any plug-ins that you need to acquire and/or update. Students can also let you know if they notice any typos, grammatical errors, or any other problems with your site. Put a link to this form on any/all of your Web site's pages.

Preface

SIGN OUR GUEST BOOK
Whether students are visiting your Web site from a distant country or from just down the street, encourage them to take a few minutes to add their name and comments to your virtual guest book. Post the most appropriate messages on your Web site so that your students and staff can see what other kids and teens think about your Web site. Put a link to the guest book on your library's home page.

LIBRARY WEB SITE SURVEY
If you'd like to know what your students, as well as long-distance student visitors, think of your library's Web site, have them complete this brief survey. Place a link to this survey periodically on your library's home page.

HOW TO EVALUATE A WEB SITE
Teaching students how to evaluate a Web site can be a daunting task. Use this form to help kids not only evaluate the Web sites they visit, but also learn some of the key questions they need to ask themselves about what they see and read on-line. Put a link to this form on your homework help and home pages.

Collection Development Forms / Surveys
RECOMMEND AN ITEM
Make it easy for students to suggest a book, videotape, DVD, or CD that they want you to purchase for your library collection. All students have to do is fill out the form and tell you why they think your library should purchase the item. Put a link to this form on your home page or library collections page.

READING INTERESTS SURVEY
One way to build your collection is have students help you to identify the types of materials that they read and the genres/subjects that interest them the most. Add a link to this survey periodically to your library collections page or home page.

Circulation Forms
APPLY FOR A LIBRARY CARD
If students haven't found the time to come to the library to get a library card, now they can apply for one on-line. If they are under 18, students must include information so that you can get in touch with their parents/guardians so they can complete the application and/or sign any permission forms. When their library card is ready to pick up, you can contact students via e-mail or phone to let them know where to pick up their new library card. Be sure to put a link to this form on your circulation Web page.

HOLD / RECALL / RENEW
Students can use this form to extend the due date of an item they've already checked out, to ask that an item checked out by another person be returned to the library so that they can use it, or to place a hold on an item that has been returned, or is about to be returned, by another person. You can contact students via e-mail or phone to let them know when they can pick up the item or when a renewed item is due. Put a link to this form on all of your circulation pages.

REPORT A MISSING BOOK
Make it easy for students to let you know that they can't locate an item that is not checked out. You can also use the information on this form to contact students via e-mail or phone if you locate the item. Place a link to this form on your home page, your circulation page, and your library collections pages.

Miscellaneous Forms

INCIDENT REPORT (TEACHERS/LIBRARIANS/PARENTS)
Teachers, staff, and parents can help you make the library a more user-friendly and safe place. They can use this nifty online form to alert you to any situation or problem that you need to know and do something about. Put a link to this form on your Web site's reference, circulation, or administration pages.

KIDS/YA/TEEN PROGRAM INTERESTS SURVEY
Kids and teens often are looking for things to do and get involved in. Use this survey to find out the types of programs and clubs your library can offer them after school, after supper, on weekends, or during the summer. Put a link to this survey periodically on your library's home page.

The Preview/Selection Tutorial
Once you decide which of the forms or surveys you want to add to your Web site, use the step-by-step tutorial on the CD to:

1. Preview the forms so that you can see what they will look like when they're on your Web site.
2. Select a form to download to your computer's desktop.
3. Preview the two possible form fonts (Arial or Times-Roman).
4. Select the form font.
5. Preview the four different form color choices (black, blue, red, and white).
6. Select the form color.
7. Review the selections you've made and preview the form you've selected.
8. Download the form (along with its matching Perl script) to your computer's desktop.

If you want to exit the tutorial, click on the "Back to Table of Contents" link at the bottom of many of the tutorial screens.

The PDF Files
In addition to the printed manual that accompanies the CD, there is also an Acrobat (PDF) copy of Section 1 of the manual on the CD. If you misplace your manual, or if you need an additional copy for your library's technical person, all you have to do is print a copy from the CD.

You will find hypertext links to each of the PDF manual sections on the CD version of this page. To view and print the manual, you must have the Adobe Acrobat reader installed on your computer. If you need to download the free reader software, connect to *www.adobe.com/*.

What's In the Accompanying Manual?

The manual is available in three formats. There is a printed version that accompanies the CD. There is an abbreviated and linked version on the CD, and there is an Acrobat (PDF) version of the printed manual on the CD.

Overviews, Introductions
Included in the manual is a brief introduction to HTML form tags. We've also included an introduction to Perl scripts. These basic introductions should suffice to get you started if you've never worked with HTML form tags or Perl scripts before.

Step-By-Step Instructions

Once you've used the CD's preview/selection tutorial to download an HTML form and its matching Perl script to your computer's desktop, you'll want to use the manual's step-by-step instructions to help you:

1. Fill in the required information on both the form and script.
2. Optionally, customize the form and script.
3. Test the form and script before you upload them to your server.
4. Test how the form/script pair works together after you've uploaded both files to your server.

Printed Forms / HTML Documents / Perl Scripts

We've included printed examples of every form in the printed manual. All examples use the Arial (sans-serif) font. If you want to see what a form looks like with the Times-Roman (serif) font, use the preview/selection tutorial and view the form when you get to the "Review the Selections You've Made" step at the end of the tutorial. Use the printed form examples to help you:

1. Decide which form(s) to add to your Web site.
2. Examine the individual form fields included on each form.
3. Decide which form features you might want to modify.
4. Test the form before you upload it to your server.
5. Test the form after it's uploaded to your Web server.

We also included printed examples of every form's HTML code. Use the code examples to help you:

1. Learn about HTML form tags, element types, and attributes.
2. Complete the required information in each form.
3. Optionally, modify the form.
4. Test the form before you upload it to your server.
5. Test the form/script pair after it's uploaded to your server.

Finally, we included printed examples of the Perl scripts that match the forms. Use the printed Perl script examples to help you:

1. Identify the different part of a Perl script.
2. Complete the required information in each script.
3. Optionally, modify the script.
4. Test the script before you upload it to your server.
5. Test the form/script pair after it's uploaded to your server.

Sources for Further Help

Books

Castro. Elizabeth. 1998. *Perl and CGI for the World Wide Web.* Visual Quickstart Guide. Berkeley, CA: Peachpit Press.
Castro, Elizabeth. 2000. *HTML 4 for the World Wide Web.* Visual Quickstart Guide. Berkeley, CA: Peachpit Press.
Guthrie, Malcolm. 1998. *Forms: Interactivity for the World Wide Web.* San Jose, CA: Adobe Press.
Hoffman, Paul. 2000. *Perl for Dummies (with CD-ROM).* 3rd ed. New York: Hungry Minds.
Levine, John R., and Margaret L. Young. 1998. *UNIX for Dummies.* 4th ed. New York: Hungry Minds.
Multer, Kent. 2000. *The Official Miva Web-Scripting Book.* Lakewood, CO: Top Floor Publishing.

Oliver, Dick. 2001. *Sams Teach Yourself HTML 4 in 24 Hours.* Indianapolis, IN: Sams.
Tittel, Ed, Mary Madden, and James Michael Stewart (contributors). 1999. *Windows NT Server 4 for Dummies.* New York: Hungry Minds.

Web Sites

Acrobatics: A Tutorial on Adobe Acrobat and the Portable Document Format (PDF) [Online]. Available: scout.cs.wisc.edu/addserv/toolkit/enduser/archive/1997/euc–9712.html
Bare Bones Guide to HTML [Online]. Available: werbach.com/barebones/
CuteFTP [Online]. Available: www.cuteftp.com/
Fetch [Online]. Available: fetchsoftworks.com
FTPplanet.com [Online]. Available: www.FTPplanet.com/
HTML Form Testing Home Page [Online]. Available: server3.pa-x.dec.com/nsl/formtest/home.html
HTML Goodies [Online]. Available: htmlgoodies.earthweb.com/
The HTML Station [Online]. Available: www.december.com/html/
HTML Tag List [Online]. Available: www.home.zonnet.nl/robschluter/htmltaglist/
Perl Language Home Page [Online]. Available: www.perl.com/
Two4U's Color Page [Online]. Available: www.two4u.com/color/
UNIX Help For Users [Online]. Available: www.mcsr.olemiss.edu/unixhelp/
UNIX Reference Desk [Online]. Available: www.geek-girl.com/unix.html
Unix Wizards [Online]. Available: www.unix-wizards.com/
WDVL: The Illustrated Encyclopedia of Web Technology [Online]. Available: wdvl.internet.com/
Web Builder's Toolkit [Online]. Available: hiwaay.net/~crispen/kellys_place/web_tools.html
Web Diner Forms Tutorial [Online]. Available: www.webdiner.com/annexe/forms/wdform1.htm
Webmaster's Reference Library [Online]. Available: www.webreference.com/
Web Style Guide [Online]. Available: info.med.yale.edu/caim/manual/contents.html
Writing for the Web: A Primer for Librarians [Online]. Available: bones.med.ohio-state.edu/eric/papers/primer/webdocs/html

Introduction

This section will give you an idea of who can, and should, use this CD and its accompanying manual. It will also provide you with brief introductions to servers and to the two types of files that are found on the CD and printed in the manual.

* * * * *

Thank you for purchasing *Instant Web Forms and Surveys for Children's/YA Services and School Libraries*. We hope you'll find working with the CD's preview/selection tutorial, the printed and online manuals, and the forms and scripts themselves, relatively simple and straightforward.

We've done everything we can to make the CD and its manual as non-technical as possible; however, there are a few unavoidable technical details that require you, or your technical person, to have some basic skills.

Needed Skills

Here are some of the assumptions we've made about you and your library's technical person, and the skills you both need to possess to successfully use this product.

We assume that you are involved with creating and maintaining your library's Web site.

We assume that you have a working knowledge of HTML and have either created a home page from scratch or used an HTML editing program like FrontPage, PageMill, or DreamWeaver, and have had experience with editing HTML documents to resolve problems and to fix broken links.

We assume that you've enhanced your Web site to the extent that you've added some graphics, tables, imagemaps, or frames to individual Web pages, and are now ready to take the next step and get involved in the world of HTML forms and Perl scripts. (You may even have a little form/script experience . . . if you do, this CD and manual will probably seem basic.)

We assume that either you are one of two people: you are a staff member who works closely with your technical person or you are the library's technical/Web/Internet person.

If you are the staff member who works closely with your technical person, you should be able to save files, rename files, and have some experience transferring files either to/from your server, or to/from another site. (In order to get the files from the CD to your computer you, or your technical counterpart, will need to download files to your computer's desktop, modify them minimally, save/archive them, then upload them to your server.)

If you are the technical/Web/Internet server person you should have a basic knowledge of either UNIX or NT (depending on your server type), be familiar with your server's directory structure and be able to locate the directory paths to your e-mail system, cgi-bin directory, and Perl interpreter. (If your server doesn't have a Perl interpreter you must have the skills to download a version from the Web and install it on your server.) You also must be able to access your server's directories, make directories, and set up server/directory permissions for staff members who will be adding, editing, and deleting HTML forms and Perl scripts on your server.

This list of assumptions might, at first glance, seem a bit daunting. Before you give up before you've even started — or before you start previewing, selecting, downloading, editing, and uploading the files on this CD — we strongly recommend that you meet with any/all staff who possess any of the above-listed skills to see who can/will do what.

If after you've met, you still find that you lack some of the technical skills necessary to successfully use this product, we recommend that you locate an outside person (perhaps a technical expert from your city or county government, a local company technical person, or your school district technology coordinator) who can help you with the technical preparations and steps that you can't handle yourself.

File Servers — A Brief Checklist

Servers are computers that store different types of files. The forms and scripts on this CD must be loaded onto a server to make them work. Generally, technical staff handles the details that are necessary to get and keep a server up and running. Therefore if you are a staff member who works with your technical/server person, now might be a perfect time to meet with him/her and get an introduction to your server and some of its basic technical details.

Since you already have a Web site, we assume that you either own a server or have access to someone else's Web server. Either way, you already have individual HTML documents stored in some identifiable directory on your/someone else's server.

The forms and scripts on this CD will eventually wind up in different directories on your server. You'll load the HTML forms into the same directory that contains your Web site's other HTML documents. You'll load the Perl scripts into a separate cgi-bin directory that is designed especially for such programs.

The following are things you should know in advance about your library's server:

If your library has its own server you, or your local technical person, probably already know what type of server it is. If you have your Web site's files stored on someone else's computer, you may or may not know whether it is a UNIX or NT server — now is the time to find out.

Find out if the server has a cgi-bin directory already set up on it. If not, your technical person will need to create one.

Find out if the server has a Perl interpreter program already stored somewhere on it. If not, you or your technical person will need to download and install one. (Later we list a Web site where you can download the correct Perl interpreter program for your server type.)

Locate and note the directory paths to your library's e-mail system, to its Perl interpreter program, and to your server's cgi-bin directory.

Find out who has "permissions" to access the different areas of the server. ("Permissions" are virtual keys that give or deny access to different server directories and functions. Check with the technical person in charge of your server to get a list of permissions related to the e-mail and cgi-bin directories.

HTML Forms — A Brief Overview

There are 24 different HTML forms on this CD. We designed them so that you'll only need to change a few things to get them to work when online and match your other Web site content. The CD-ROM will allow you to use the forms in two ways. You can use them "as is"(adding only the required information to make them work), making only cosmetic textual changes (editing the introductory paragraphs or slightly re-wording the form's questions/statements, or modifying the form's colors and fonts). We designed the CD and manual to be used primarily this way.

You can also, if you choose, add new elements to the forms or reorder the fields. However, this will require you to also modify the matching Perl script. We don't recommend you do this unless you are

Introduction

already familiar with script coding. Remember that these forms/scripts were designed as a simple/quick/non-technical alternative for librarians who may not have the time/expertise to create their own forms and matching scripts.

If you are not already familiar with HTML form tags, please take a few minutes to read the following brief introduction. It will familiarize you with the tags that you'll find on each of the forms.

Form Basics

Standard Web page HTML documents can function independently of any/all other HTML documents. Form HTML documents won't function unless there is a matching Perl script also loaded somewhere on the same server. This pairing of two interrelated, but differently formatted files makes creating and working with HTML forms/Perl scripts more challenging and also more fun.

When you visit a Web site and fill in an online form you're only interacting with the HTML form document until you press the "Submit Form" button . . . then you're interacting with the form's matching script that handles/responds to the information patrons submit via the HTML form.

The <form> Tag

The <form> tag is the first tag in every form and the </form> tag is the last tag. Inside the opening tag are the two tag attributes, method= and **action**=. The method= attribute tells a patron's computer how to send the form's information to your library's Web server. The action= attribute tells a patron's computer where the form's matching Perl script is located on your Web server, so that the script can process and react to the information submitted via the HTML form.

```
<form method="post" action="http://www.yourLibrary.org/cgi-bin/crg4.pl">
```

Form Tag Elements

All forms are made up of elements and most form elements have two attributes **name**= and **type**= (see below for examples of the **name**= and **type**= attributes). Form elements identify the form's different types of information and methods for delivering information. Each form element must have a unique name so that a Web server will be able to identify every piece of form information. Form element names are also case sensitive and shouldn't include spaces or punctuation marks (other than an underscore character).

Every form on the CD uses one or more of the following types of form elements. There are additional form element types besides the ones listed below, but since they are not used on any of the forms, we didn't include them. For a complete list and description of every possible form element type, see any of the HTML texts listed in the bibliography at the end of this manual.

Form element types provide patrons with different methods for getting their questions, requests, comments, and personal/contact information to you and your staff. Some form element types allow patrons to type text information into an open text area, while other form elements allow patrons to select from a number/variety of pre-structured responses. To learn about the various elements you'll see on every form, read on. If you'll be customizing the CD's forms or creating your own forms from scratch, the following brief explanation will serve to get you started.

SINGLE LINE TEXT BOX
This element produces a text box that allows patrons to enter a single line of text.

input type= set to "text"
size= the number of characters (size=10 will hold 10 characters and/or spaces)

name= name of the form element

    <input type ="text" name="state" size=10>

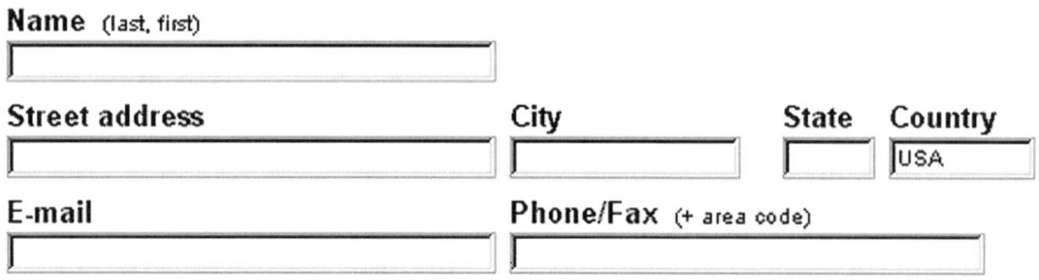

MULTIPLE-LINE TEXT BOX
This element produces a text box that allows patrons to enter more than one line of text.

opening <textarea> tag
name= of your text area
number of cols (columns) and rows
text that will appear inside the box
closing </textarea> tag

    <textarea name="zip_code" cols=40 rows=5>Your zip code</textarea>

Subject of your message

RADIO BUTTON
This element produces a yes/no, multiple-choice button feature.

input type= set to "radio"
name= all answer choices for the same question have the same name
value= either yes or no

    <input type="radio" name="type" value="comment">
    <input type="radio" name="type" value="suggestion">

Type of your message

Introduction

CHECK BOX
This element produces a square box that a patron can select by clicking in it.

input type= set to "checkbox"
name= of the form element
value= either on or off

> Books<input type ="checkbox" name ="books" value="on">
> Magazines<input type ="checkbox" name ="magazines" value=on">
> Newspapers<input type ="checkbox" name ="newspapers" value="on">

Which three library resouces do you use the most? (check 3)

☐ Books ☐ Magazines ☐ Newspapers ☐ Audiotapes/CDs

☐ Videos/DVDs ☐ Reference materials ☐ The Web

SUBMIT BUTTON
This element sends the information in the form to your Web server.

input type= set to "submit"
value= text that shows up on the face of the button

> <input type="submit" value="Send Message">

[Send Message]

RESET BUTTON
This element puts all of your form's fields back to the way they were before a patron started to fill out the form.

input type= set to "reset"
value= text that shows up on the face of the button

> <input type="reset" value="Clear Form">

[Clear Form]

HIDDEN FORM FIELDS
Hidden form fields hold the behind-the-scenes instructions that are sent to the script along with the information/selections that a patron provides you via a form/survey. Below is an example of the three hidden

fields that can be found in each of the HTML form documents. You must add information to two of the three hidden fields in order for them to work.

input type= set to "hidden"
name= name of the form element
value= your e-mail address, the URL of your home page, the name of the form/survey

```
<input type="hidden" name="LibraryEmail" value="you@yourLibrary.org">
<input type="hidden" name="LibraryURL" value="http://www.yourLibrary.org">
<input type="hidden" name="Form" value="Ask a Reference Question">
```

Sample Form
We've highlighted some form fields in a form so that you can familiarize yourself with what the fields look like. The bold printed text below explains the form elements immediately following them.

```
<html>
<head><title>Comments, Suggestions</title></head>
<body bgcolor="#FFFFFF">
<table width="700" border="0" height="85" bgcolor="#003399">
<tr valign="middle" align="center"><td>
<p><font halign=center color="#FFFFFF" face="Arial, Helvetica, sans-serif" size="+3"> <b><i>Comments, Suggestions </i></b></font></p>
</td></tr></table>
```

Here is the HTML code for the start of the form. Note the attributes method= and action=

```
<form method="post" action="http://www.yourLibrary.org/cgi-bin/crg4.pl">
```

```
<p> </p>
<p><font face="Arial, Helvetica, sans-serif" size="2"><b>Please take a few minutes to send us your comments about, and suggestions for, improving our library <br>and its resources/services. We'd also like to know what you think of our Web site and Web links.</b></font></p>
<p> </p>
```

Here is the HTML code for the hidden elements of the form that communicate with the script

```
<input type="hidden" name="LibraryEmail" value="you@yourLibrary.org">
<input type="hidden" name="LibraryURL" value="http://www.yourLibrary.org">
<input type="hidden" name="Form" value="Comments, Suggestions"></p>
```

```
<table width="500" border="0" cellspacing="4" cellpadding="1">
<tr> <td width="187">
<b><font face="Arial, Helvetica, sans-serif" size="2">Name</font></b>  <font size="1" face="Arial, Helvetica, sans-serif">(last, first)</font><br><font face="Arial, Helvetica, sans-serif" size="2"><input type="text" name="Name" size="25"></font></td>
```

Introduction

```html
<td width="121"> </td><td width="33"> </td><td width="131"> </td></tr>
<tr><td width="187">
```

Here is the HTML code for a single text box. Note the input type="text" and the matching name= field.

```html
<b><font face="Arial, Helvetica, sans-serif" size="2">Street address<br></font></b>
<font face="Arial, Helvetica, sans-serif" size="2"><input type="text" name="StreetAddress" size="25"></font>
</td>

<td width="121">
<b><font face="Arial, Helvetica, sans-serif" size="2">City<br></font></b><font face="Arial, Helvetica, sans-serif" size="2"><input type="text" name="City" size="10"></font></td>
<td width="33">
<b><font face="Arial, Helvetica, sans-serif" size="2">State<br></font></b><font face="Arial, Helvetica, sans-serif" size="2"><input type="text" name="State" size="2" maxlength="2">
</font></td>
<td width="131">
<b><font face="Arial, Helvetica, sans-serif" size="2">Country <br></font></b><font face="Arial, Helvetica, sans-serif" size="2"><input type="text" name="Country" size="5" value="USA">
</font></td></tr>
<tr><td width="187">
<b><font face="Arial, Helvetica, sans-serif" size="2">E-mail<br></font></b><font face="Arial, Helvetica, sans-serif" size="2"><input type="text" name="Email" size="25"></font></td>
<td colspan="3">
<b><font face="Arial, Helvetica, sans-serif" size="2">Phone/Fax</font></b>  <font size="1" face="Arial, Helvetica, sans-serif">(+ area code)</font><br><font face="Arial, Helvetica, sans-serif" size="2">
<input type="text" name="Phone/Fax" size="24"></font>
</td></tr></table>
<p>
```

Here is the HTML code for a series of radio buttons. Note that the name= tag is the same for each option, but the value= tag for each option is different.

```html
<b><font face="Arial, Helvetica, sans-serif" size="2">Type of your message<br></font></b>
<font face="Arial, Helvetica, sans-serif" size="2">
<input type="radio" name="Type" value="Comment">Comment    
<input type="radio" name="Type" value="Suggestion">Suggestion    
<input type="radio" name="Type" value="New idea">New idea   
<input type="radio" name="Type" value="Compliment">Compliment   
<input type="radio" name="Type" value="Complaint">Complaint</font></p>

<p>
<b><font face="Arial, Helvetica, sans-serif" size="2">Subject of your message </font></b>
<br><font face="Arial, Helvetica, sans-serif" size="3"><textarea name="Subject" cols="40" rows="2">
```

\</textarea>\</font>\</p>
\<p>

Here is the HTML code for a multi-line text box. Note the difference in tagging from the single line text box.

\<b>\<font face="Arial, Helvetica, sans-serif" size="2">Your message\</font>\</b>\
\<font face="Arial, Helvetica, sans-serif" size="3">\<textarea name="Message" cols="40" rows="10">\</textarea>
\</font>\</p>

\<p> \</p>
\<table width="700" border="0" cellspacing="10" cellpadding="1">\<tr>\<td width="255">
\<div align="right">

Here is the HTML code for the form's submit button.

\<input type="submit" name="send" value="Send Message">

\</div>\</td>
\<td width="192"> \</td>\<td width="207">\<div align="left">

Here is the HTML code for the form's reset button.

\<input type="reset" name="clear" value="Clear Form">
\</div>\</td>
\</tr>\<tr colspan=3>\<td colspan=3>
\<table width="500" border="0" height="2" align="center" cellpadding="0" cellspacing="0" bgcolor="#003399">\<tr>\<td>\<font size="1" color="#003399">.\</font>\</td>\</tr>\</table>
\</td>\</tr>
\<tr>\<td colspan=3>\<div align="center">

Here is the HTML code for the form's footer information, including the URL and "mailto" link.

\<font face="Arial, Helvetica, sans-serif" size="1">\<b>http://\</b>\</font>\
\<font face="Arial, Helvetica, sans-serif" size="1">\<b>© 2002\</b>\</font>
\<font face="Arial, Helvetica, sans-serif" size="2">\<a href="mailto:">
\<b>\<font size="1">Contact Webmaster\</font>\</b>\</a> \</font>\</div>

Here is the HTML code for the end of the form.

\</td>\</tr>\</table>\</form>

\</body>
\</html>

Perl Scripts — A Brief Introduction

Perl (Practical Extraction and Reporting Language) is a programming language. The scripts (or mini-programs) on the CD are written in Perl. Perl scripts look somewhat intimidating at first glance, but they're not so hard to figure out after you've seen a few. (Remember how difficult HTML documents looked when you first started to work with them?)

There are 24 different Perl scripts on the CD. As with the HTML versions of these forms and surveys, there are two ways that you can use the scripts on this CD. Firstly, you can use the scripts "as is" (adding only the required information to make them work), or you can make minor changes to them (like editing the on-screen response or e-mail message a patrons sees when s/he presses the "Submit Form" button). You can find directions for making minor changes to the scripts later in this manual.

Secondly, you can add new form elements to any of the forms. This approach will require you to add new lines of Perl code to the script. We don't recommend you do this unless you are already familiar with script coding. Remember that these forms/scripts were designed as a simple/quick/non-technical alternative for librarians who may not have the time/expertise to create their own forms and matching scripts.

If you are not familiar with Perl scripts, please take a few minutes to read the following brief introduction. It will familiarize you with a few of the "coding bits" that you'll need to locate and complete in order to get the scripts to work.

Perl Basics

HTML forms can be loaded onto your library's Web server, but they won't function unless there is a matching Perl script also loaded somewhere on the same server. This pairing of two interrelated, but differently formatted files, makes creating and working with HTML forms/Perl scripts more challenging and also more fun.

When you visit a Web site and fill in an online form you're only interacting with the HTML form document until you press the "Submit Form" button . . . then you're interacting with the form's matching Perl script.

You can write or edit Perl scripts using any simple text editor (such as WordPad or NotePad) as long as you save the script in ASCII (plain text) format. All Perl programs are case sensitive. Every Perl script has to have a .pl file extension.

Below is a brief introduction to Perl and Perl scripts. It is designed to help you understand a bit about the scripts that are included on the CD and the part of the script that you'll have to modify in order to get them to function. If you want to learn more about Perl and scripts so that you can add additional form/script fields or make major changes to the forms/scripts, you'll need to purchase one of the excellent Perl texts cited in this manual's bibliography.

PERL HEADERS

Every Perl script begins with what is called a header. The header contains instructions that tell each Perl script how it will function and where it can locate necessary programs (like your server's Perl interpreter).

PERL VARIABLES

All the Perl scripts on the CD contain variables. Variables link to and do something with the information that a patron types/selects on a form.

When a patron submits a form by clicking the "Submit" button, it activates the matching Perl script that is stored on your Web server. The data from the HTML form, which is sent to the matching PERL script, will match up its matching script variable.

HTML Form Element	PERL variable
NAME	$in{'NAME'}
DATE	$in{'DATE'}

The following example will make this even clearer. The "Library Purchase Request" HTML form contains a single-line text box that is named "TITLE." A patron types "Geek Love" into the form text box and submits the form to the library's Web server. The Web server will receive this information and the matching script will create a variable that looks like this:

$in{'TITLE'} = "Geek Love"

THE PRINT FUNCTION

All the Perl scripts on the CD contain print functions. Print functions allow scripts to send messages to patrons automatically. The messages can either display on a patron's or your library's computer, or be sent as messages directly to a patron's e-mail address. Here are some examples that will help to familiarize you with what a print function looks like.

The PERL script below will display "Thanks for filling out our survey" on a patron's computer screen:

print ("Thanks for filling out our survey");

The bit of Perl script below will display "Thanks for recommending the title Geek Love. You'll be notified if we decide to purchase it." The first line contains the variable. Note also that each line of text is in a separate print function.

$in{'TITLE'} = "Geek Love";
print ("Thanks for recommending the title $in{'TITLE'}.");
print ("You'll be notified if we decide to purchase it.");

Sample Script

We've highlighted the various sections and fields of one of the scripts so that you can familiarize yourself with what each part looks like and does.

This section of the script is called the header:

Here is where you must specify the directory path to the Perl interpreter program on your server.

#!/usr/local/bin/perl

Here are the basic instructions for how the script will interact with the form data. (The spacing/indentions are necessary for the script to function properly.)

```
if ($ENV{'REQUEST_METHOD'}eq"GET"){$buffer = $ENV{'QUERY_STRING'};}
    elsif($ENV{'REQUEST_METHOD'}eq"POST"){
      read(STDIN,$buffer,$ENV{'CONTENT_LENGTH'});
    }
```

Introduction 11

```
$bufferb = $buffer;
#separate the name of the input from its value.
@forminputs = split(/&/, $bufferb);

foreach $forminput (@forminputs)
{
    #separate the name of the input from its value
    ($name, $value) = split(/=/, $forminput);

    #Un-Webify plus signs and %-encoding
    $value =~ tr/+/ /;
    $value =~ s/%([a-fA-F0-9][a-fA-F0-9])/pack("C", hex($1))/eg;

    #stick them in the in array
    $in{$name} = $value;
}
print "Content-type: text/html\n\n";
```

This section of the script contains instructions for e-mailing the form information to the appropriate staff member:

Here is where you must specify the directory path to your library's e-mail program.

```
open (LMAIL, "|/usr/sbin/sendmail-t");
```

Here is a list of script fields that match the form fields. Also included are instructions for how to send the form information via e-mail to the appropriate staff member.

```
print LMAIL ("To: $in{LibraryEmail}\n");
print LMAIL ("From: $in{Email}\n");
print LMAIL ("Subject: $in{Form} —patron submission\n");

print LMAIL ("————————\nPatron information\n\n");
print LMAIL ("Name:\n $in{Name}\n\n");
print LMAIL ("Street address:\n $in{StreetAddress}\n\n");
print LMAIL ("City:\n $in{City}\n\n");
print LMAIL ("State:\n $in{State}\n\n");
print LMAIL ("Country:\n $in{Country}\n\n");
print LMAIL ("E-mail:\n $in{Email}\n\n");
print LMAIL ("Phone / fax:\n $in{PhoneFax}\n\n");

print LMAIL ("————————\nSubmitted information \n\n");

print LMAIL ("Type of message:\n $in{Type}\n\n");
print LMAIL ("Message subject:\n $in{Subject}\n\n");
```

print LMAIL ("My message:\n $in{Message}\n\n");
print LMAIL ("\n.\n");

This section of the script contains instructions for e-mailing a "thank you" message to the patron who filled out the form/survey:

Here is where you must specify the directory path to your library's e-mail program.

open (MAIL, "|/usr/sbin/sendmail-t");

Here is the text of the "thank you" e-mail message that will be sent to the patron. Also included in the script are instructions for how to send the message. (You may modify the text of this message if you wish.)

print MAIL<<toEnd;
To: $in{Email}
From: $in{LibraryEmail}
Subject: $in{Form}

Thanks for sending us your comments and suggestions.\n\n
We are always looking for new ideas and ways we can make the library better!

toEnd
 print MAIL ("\n.\n");

This section of the script contains instructions for displaying a "thank you" screen message to the patron who filled out the form/survey and a link back to your Web site:

Here are instructions for setting up the display on the patron's computer screen.

print ("<html><head><title>$in{Form}</title></head>");
print ("<body bgcolor=\"ffffff\">");

Here is the text of the "thank you" message that will display after a patron has submitted the form. Also included in the script are instructions for how to send the message. (You may modify the text of this message if you wish.)

print ("Thanks for sending us your comments and suggestions.<p>
We are always looking for new ideas and ways we can make the library better!");

Here is the text of the hypertext link that will display after a patron has submitted the form. (You may modify the text of the link if you wish.)

print ("<p> <a href=$in{LibraryURL}>Return to our main page.</a> ");

This is the end of the script.

print ("</body></html>");

SECTION 1
How to Use the CD-ROM

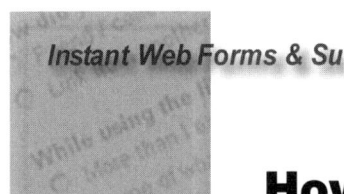

How to Use the CD-ROM

Preview and Select a Form / Survey

Once you decide which of the forms or surveys you want to add to your Web site, use the simple, step-by-step tutorial on the CD to:

1. Preview all the forms, so that you can know what they'll look like when they're on your Web site.
2. Select a specific form to download.
3. Preview the two possible form fonts (Arial or Times-Roman).
4. Select the form's font.
5. Preview the four different form color choices (black, blue, red, and white).
6. Select the form's color.
7. Review the selections you've made and preview the form you've selected.
8. Download the form (along with its matching Perl script) to your computer's desktop. (We've included step-by-step instructions for both Windows PC and Macintosh users.)

To start using the preview/selection tutorial, launch the CD. When you get to the "Table of Contents" page, click on the link that says "Preview and Select a Form/Survey."

If you want to exit the tutorial, click on any of the "Back to Table of Contents" links that can be found at the bottom of many of the tutorial screens.

After You Download the Files to Your Desktop

This section will provide you with step-by-step instructions to help you edit the HTML forms and Perl scripts so that they will work when placed on your library's server. There are eight steps (five are required and three are optional). Every task is explained in detail and includes examples from the forms/scripts.

This section will also provide you with instructions to help you modify, in a limited way, the HTML forms and Perl scripts. Every modification step is explained in detail and includes examples from the forms/scripts.

Step 1 — Save the Downloaded Files

The first thing you must to do after you've finished downloading the HTML form and the Perl script to your desktop is to save/archive them so that you don't lose them. (We assume you already know how to save files.) We suggest that you make multiple saved copies. First, save both files somewhere on your computer's hard drive. Next, save both files to a floppy/Zip disk.

After saving the files, store the floppy disk or Zip disk in a safe place, take it home, or give it to a colleague to ensure that if something happens to your office area, or to your library, you still have the files. (Consider archiving the rest of your Web site's HTML documents offsite, if you haven't already done so.)

Step 2 — Check to See If Your Server Has a Perl Interpreter
In order to get the Perl scripts to function, your server must have a Perl interpreter program loaded on it. With any luck, your server already has a Perl interpreter on it. Follow the instructions below to see if a Perl interpreter is already installed on your server.

UNIX servers   At the command prompt type which perl
NT servers   At the command prompt type dir /s perl.exe

If your server doesn't currently have a Perl interpreter program loaded on it, don't despair. You or a technical staff member can easily FTP a free copy of the interpreter software from one of two Web sites.

If you need a UNIX/Linux Perl interpreter, connect to *www.perl.org/* and download the version appropriate for your version of UNIX or Linux. If you need an NT Perl interpreter, connect to *www.activestate.com/* and download the version appropriate for your NT server.

Step 3 — Get the Paths to Your Server's E-mail Program and Perl Interpreter
In order to complete the required information on the forms and scripts you'll need to locate two directory paths on your Web server.

UNIX SERVERS
At the command prompt:

Type which perl to locate the path to your Perl interpreter. If you don't have an interpreter program yet, have a technical staff person provide you with its directory path.

Type which sendmail (or the name of another UNIX e-mail program). The server will display its directory path.

NT SERVERS
You can search for an e-mail program and its directory path on an NT server the same way you search for a program and its directory path on any Windows PC. Just open up Windows NT Explorer and browse through the menu structure until you locate your server's e-mail program and its Perl interpreter. Once you locate them, the directory path should display in the dialog window at the top of the Explorer screen. Copy it down and you're all set!

Step 4 — Complete the Required Form Information
In order to get the forms to function you *must* add a few pieces of information to each form that you download. The simple instructions and HTML code samples that follow will make this process easy and fast.

LINK UP THE FORM AND SCRIPT
You *must* link up the HTML form with its Perl script. Below (in bold text) is where you'll add the URL for your library's Web server and the path through your server's directories to the cgi-bin directory where the form's matching Perl script is stored.

Note: The text you need to change on the actual forms will not be in bold.

How to Use the CD-ROM

```
<font halign=center color="#FFFFFF" face="Arial, Helvetica, sans-serif" size="+3">
<b><i>Reserve a Library Computer</i></b></font></p>
</td></tr></table>
<form method="post" action="http://www.yourLibrary.org/cgi-bin/clc1.pl"><p> </p>
<p><font face="Arial, Helvetica, sans-serif" size="2"><b>Do you hate to wait in line to use one of the library's computers? Just fill out the form below to reserve <br>a computer on a specific date and at a specific time. All reservations must be made in advance and <br>dates/times are assigned on a first-come-first-serve basis. We'll call or send you an e-mail message <br> letting you know if a computer is available when you want/need it.</b></font></p>
```

COMPLETE THE LINK BACK TO YOUR LIBRARY'S HOMEPAGE

You *must* provide a way for patrons to return to your Web site after they've sent you a form or survey. Below (in bold text) is where you'll add the URL for the link that will return patrons back to a specified Web page (like your library's homepage) after they've filled out a form/survey.

Note: The text you need to change on the actual forms will not be in bold.

```
<p> </p>
<input type="hidden" name="LibraryEmail" value="you@yourLibrary.org">
<input type="hidden" name="LibraryURL" value="http://www.yourLibrary.org">
<input type="hidden" name="Form" value="Reserve a Library Computer"></p>
<table width="500" border="0" cellspacing="4" cellpadding="1">
<tr><td width="187">
```

SPECIFY THE E-MAIL ADDRESS OF THE PERSON WHO'LL RECEIVE THE FORM INFORMATION

You *must* provide the e-mail address of the staff member whose job it is to collect/process the information submitted by patrons via the form/survey. (If you wish, circulation forms can be e-mailed to circulation staff, and reference forms can be e-mailed to reference staff.) Below (in bold text) is where you add a staff e-mail address to the HTML code.

Note: The text you need to change on the actual forms will not be in bold.

```
<p> </p>
<input type="hidden" name="LibraryEmail" value="you@yourLibrary.org">
<input type="hidden" name="LibraryURL" value="http://www.yourLibrary.org">
<input type="hidden" name="Form" value="Reserve a Library Computer"></p>
<table width="500" border="0" cellspacing="4" cellpadding="1">
<tr><td width="187">
```

ADD THE URL FOR THE FORM

It's good Web design and a good idea to include the URL for every Web page in the footer information. (That way patrons can make a note of it so they can return to it again. Also when/if patrons print the page, the URL always prints on the page.) Below (in bold text) is where you *must* add the URL to the HTML code.

Note: The text you need to add to the actual forms will not be in bold.

```
<font face="Arial, Helvetica, sans-serif" size="1"><b>http://</b></font><br>  <font face="Arial, Helvetica, sans-serif" size="1"><b>&copy; 2002</b></font>
<font face="Arial, Helvetica, sans-serif" size="2"><a href="mailto:">
<b><font size="1">Contact Webmaster</font></b></a> </font></div>
</td></tr></table></form>
</body>
</html>
```

ADD A "MAILTO" LINK TO YOUR WEBMASTER

It's also good Web design and a good idea to include an e-mail link to your library's Webmaster on every page so that patrons have a way to let him/her know about broken links or any other errors that might be found on your Web site. To get the mailto link to work, you *must* add the e-mail address of your Webmaster after the colon and before the closing quotation marks (in bold text). Optionally, you can rename the text of the link, just change the bold text below.

Note: The text you need to add to/change on the actual forms will not be in bold.

```
<font face="Arial, Helvetica, sans-serif" size="1"><b>http://</b></font><br>  <font face="Arial, Helvetica, sans-serif" size="1"><b>&copy; 2002</b></font>
<font face="Arial, Helvetica, sans-serif" size="2"><a href="mailto:">
<b><font size="1">Contact Webmaster</font></b></a> </font></div>
```

Step 5 — Complete the Required Script Information

In order to get the scripts to function, you *must* add a few pieces of information to each script you download. The simple instructions and Perl code samples that follow will make this process simple and fast.

SPECIFY THE PATH TO YOUR SERVER'S PERL INTERPRETER

You *must* tell the Perl script where the Perl interpreter is located on your Web server. Below (in bold text) is where you add the path through your server's directories to where the Perl interpreter is stored.

Note: The text instructions below are included in each Perl script so that you can more quickly and easily locate the correct line of coding to complete. However, the text to change in the actual scripts is not bold.

#!/usr/local/bin/perl

```
# ****************************************************************
# ABOVE is where you MUST specify the path to your
# perl interpreter on your Web server.
# Replace /usr/local/bin/perl with your path.
# ****************************************************************
#
```

How to Use the CD-ROM

SPECIFY THE PATH TO YOUR SERVER'S E-MAIL PROGRAM (SO THAT YOU CAN GET FORM INFORMATION E-MAILED TO YOU)

You *must* tell the Perl script where your library's e-mail program is located on your server so that the script will be able to locate the e-mail program in order to e-mail the form information to the staff member whose job it is to collect/process it. Below (in bold text) is where you add the path through your server's directories to where your e-mail program is stored.

Note: The text instructions below are included in each Perl script so that you can more quickly and easily locate the correct line of coding to complete. However the text to change in the actual scripts is not bold.

```
# ******************************************************************
# Here's where you MUST specify the path to your
# email program (probably sendmail) ON your Web server.
# Replace /usr/sbin/sendmail with your path.
# ******************************************************************
```

open (LMAIL, "I/**usr/sbin/sendmail** -t");

SPECIFY THE PATH TO YOUR SERVER'S E-MAIL PROGRAM (SO THAT THE SCRIPT CAN SEND AN E-MAIL RESPONSE TO THE PATRON)

You *must* tell the Perl script where your library's e-mail program is located on your server so that the script will be able to locate the e-mail program in order to send an e-mail "thank you" message to the patron who filled out the form/survey. Below (in bold text) is where you add the path through your server's directories to where your e-mail system is stored.

Note: The text instructions below are included in each Perl script so that you can more quickly and easily locate the correct line of coding to complete. However, the text to change in the actual scripts is not bold.

```
# ******************************************************************
# Here's where you MUST specify the path to your
# email program ON your Web server.
# Replace /usr/sbin/sendmail with your path.
# ******************************************************************
```

open (MAIL, "I/**usr/sbin/sendmail**-t");

Step 6 (Optional) — Modify the HTML Forms

If you wish, you can make the following changes to any/all of the forms. All the changes below are very basic and only affect the HTML forms. (In other words, they don't involve making major changes to any of the HTML documents nor do they require that you make any changes to the matching Perl scripts.)

If you want to make changes to the forms that also require you to change the Perl scripts (like renaming form element names), you'll need more knowledge about Perl scripts than we assume you have. Please make sure you get, and read, one of the Perl script texts that are cited in the bibliography at the end of this manual before you make any changes other than those listed below.

MAKE MINOR CHANGES TO FORM TEXT

You can make minor changes to the text that displays on the form. Limit your editing to minor changes in wording, not changes in meaning. For instance, if you want to change the text "Junior High" to "Middle School" edit the bold text below.

What a patron will see on the form will then be "Middle School," but the e-mail form response that your staff member receives will still say "Junior High." (To make the text the same on the form and e-mail message, you would have to also change the HTML form value and the matching variable on the Perl script.)

Note: The text you need to change on the actual forms will not be in bold.

\<input type="radio" name="EducationLevel" value="Elementary"\>**Elementary**
\<input type="radio" name="EducationLevel" value="Junior High"\>**Junior High**
\<input type="radio" name="EducationLevel" value="High School"\>**High School**

CHANGE THE FORM FONTS

We've provided you with forms that contain the two most common Web site fonts, a serif font (Times-Roman) and a sans-serif font (Arial). If your Web site uses another font, you can change the fonts on any/all of the forms/surveys so that they blend in with your other Web pages. First, you'll need to decide which font you want to substitute (by looking at the HTML code on your Web pages), then you'll have to change all of the font tags on the form . . . there are lots of them!

Tip: Use the "find/replace" feature of any full-featured word-processing package to quickly make all the changes.

Note: The text you need to change on the actual forms will not be in bold.

\<p\>**\<font face="Arial, Helvetica, sans-serif" size="2"\>**\<b\>Would you like help searching the Internet/Web for information and facts? Do you retrieve either too \<br\>many or too few results from the Web? Would you like our librarians to suggest ways you can focus your \<br\>Web searches to retrieve highly relevant results? We'll send you an e-mail message or call you to help \<br\>you use/search the Web more effectively.\</b\>\</font\>\</p\>

Step 7 (Optional) — Modify the Form Colors

If you wish, you can make the following changes to any/all of the forms. All the changes below are very basic and only affect the HTML forms. (In other words, they don't involve making major changes to any of the HTML documents nor do they require that you make any changes to the matching Perl scripts.)

CHANGE THE COLOR OF THE HEADER AND BOTTOM LINE

You can easily change the background colors of the colored header and the bottom line on each form/survey to match your Web site colors. All you need to do is locate a list of browser-safe, six-digit/character hexadecimal color codes (connect to *www.two4u.com/colors/* for an online list). Once you've found a color you like (or a color that matches the graphics you use already on your Web site) and you've determined what its hexadecimal color code is, just substitute the new color code for the two color codes below (in bold text).

How to Use the CD-ROM 23

Tip: Please be aware that colors display differently on PC and Macintosh computers. Be sure to check to see that the color you've selected looks good on both types of machines.

Note: The text you need to change on the actual forms will not be in bold.

HEADER GRAPHIC
```
<html>
<head><title>Internet Search Help</title></head>
<body bgcolor="#FFFFFF">
<table width="700" border="0" height="85" bgcolor="#003399">
<tr valign="middle" align="center"><td>
<p><font halign=center color="#FFFFFF" face="Arial, Helvetica, sans-serif" size="+3">
```

BOTTOM LINE
```
<tr colspan=3> <td colspan=3>
<table width="500" border="0" height="2" align="center" cellpadding="0" cellspacing="0" bgcolor="#003399"><tr><td><font size="1" color="#003399">.</font></td></tr></table>
</td></tr>
```

CHANGE THE COLOR OF THE HEADER TEXT
You also can easily change the color of the text inside the colored header on each form/survey. (For instance, you might want to switch from white text to black text.) Once you've found a color you like (or a color that matches the text you use already in your Web site graphics) and you've determined what its hexadecimal color code is, just substitute the new color code for the color code below (in bold text).

Tip: Please be aware that colors display differently on PC and Macintosh computers. Be sure to check to see that the color you've selected looks good on both types of machines.

Note: The text you need to change on the actual forms will not be in bold.

```
<table width="700" border="0" height="85" bgcolor="#003399">
<tr valign="middle" align="center"><td>
<p><font halign=center color="#FFFFFF" face="Arial, Helvetica, sans-serif" size="+3">
```

Step 8 (Optional) — Modify the Perl Scripts
If you wish, you can make the following changes to any/all of the scripts. All the changes below are very basic and only affect the Perl scripts. (In other words, they don't involve making major changes to any of the scripts nor do they require that you make any changes to the matching HTML forms.)

RE-WORD THE "THANK YOU" SCREEN MESSAGE
We've included an appropriate and patron-friendly screen message with each form. If you like, you can change the wording of the screen message . . . just edit the text (displayed in bold).

Note: The text instructions below are included in each Perl script so that you can more quickly and easily locate the correct line of coding to complete. However, the text to change in the actual scripts is not bold.

```
#  ************************************************************
#  Here's where you MAY change the screen response
#  the user sees after submitting the form. You may
#  reword the message.
#  ************************************************************
```

print ("**Thanks for sending us a library computer reservation.<p>
A librarian will contact you in the next couple of days to let you know if a computer
is available on the day and at the time you requested.**");

RE-WORD THE "THANK YOU" E-MAIL MESSAGE

We've also included an appropriate e-mail message with each form (it's identical to the screen message). If you like, you can change the wording of the e-mail message . . . just edit the text (displayed in bold).

Note: The text instructions below are included in each Perl script so that you can more quickly and easily locate the correct line of coding to complete. However the text to change in the actual scripts is not bold.

```
#  ************************************************************
#  Here's where you MAY customize the email
#  response to the user. You may change any wording
#  on the two lines
#  ************************************************************
```

print MAIL<<toEnd;
To: $in{Email}
From: $in{LibraryEmail}
Subject: $in{Form}

**Thanks for sending us your comments and suggestions.\n\n
We are always looking for new ideas and ways we can make the library better!**
toEnd
 print MAIL ("\n.\n");

RE-WORD THE LINK BACK TO YOUR LIBRARY'S HOME PAGE

We've included a generic "Return to Our Main Page" link with each form. If you like, you can change the wording of the link . . . just edit the text (displayed in bold).

Note: The text instructions below are included in each Perl script so that you can more quickly and easily locate the correct line of coding to complete. However, the text to change in the actual scripts is not bold.

```
#  ************************************************************
#  Here's where you MAY change the wording of the link
#  back to your main page. You may replace "Return
#  to our main page" with your own wording.
#  ************************************************************
```

print ("<p> <a href=$in{LibraryURL}>**Return to our main page.**</a> ");
print ("</body></html>");

Before You Upload the Files to Your Server

This section will provide you with step-by-step instructions and lists of the things to check when you test the forms and scripts prior to uploading them to your server. It will remind you to create the necessary directories to hold the Perl scripts and your HTML forms. In addition, it will help you set up your library's computers so that the forms/scripts will look their best when patrons view them.

Step 1 — Test the Files Before They're Uploaded

Once you've finished adding the required information to both the forms and scripts, you *must* test them before you upload them to your server. Below are instructions for testing your forms and scripts (and lists of the things that need to be tested).

HOW TO TEST AN HTML FORM

To test the forms, start your library's Web browser (Internet Explorer or Netscape). If your library provides both browsers to staff and patrons, start both and check your HTML on each one.

First, you'll need to see if the *visible* changes you made to the form are correct. To do this:

1. Click on word "File" which is located in the top left corner of both browsers.
2. If you are using Netscape, select and click on the "Open Page" option. If you are using Internet Explorer, select and click on the "Open" option.
3. Use the "Browse" button and the directory dialog boxes to locate your computer's desktop. Then click until the files for that directory display . . . one of them should be your form.
4. Once you've located the form, highlight it, and then click on it.
5. Both Netscape and Internet Explorer will then ask you if you want to open the form. Confirm that you do by clicking on the "Open" or "OK" button.
6. You should now be viewing the form from your desktop.

Here is a list of the visible text on a form that you should check:

> Check to see that the page URL in the footer displays correctly.
> Check to see that the "mailto" link in the footer goes to the correct address (click on it).
> If you've modified any of the form text (the introduction, any minor re-wording of form element text), check to see it displays correctly.
> If you've modified the color of the form header (and/or the color of the header text) and color of the bottom line, check to see it displays correctly.
> If you've modified the fonts, check to see that the whole form displays in the new font.

Next, you'll need to see if the changes you made, that are *not visible*, are correct. To do this:

1. If you are using Netscape or Internet Explorer, click on the "View" menu and click on either the "Page Source" or "Source" option from the pull-down menu.
2. An additional window with the HTML coding for your form will appear on your screen.

3. Use this display to make sure that the hidden HTML coding changes you made are correct. (When you are finished checking the form, click on the "X" box in the upper right corner of the screen, if using a PC, or the square in the upper left corner of the screen, if using a Macintosh.)

Here is a list of the coding-level HTML on a form that you should check:

> Check to see that the form action contains the correct URL and directory path to where you will be storing the Perl script once you upload it.
> Check to see that there is a link in one of the hidden fields to your home page (or whichever page you want a patron to return to after they've finished filling out a form or survey).
> Check to see that you've also put the correct e-mail address into one of the hidden fields.

HOW TO TEST A PERL SCRIPT

To test the scripts, open a simple word-processing program. If you are using a PC, open either NotePad or WordPad. If you are using a Macintosh, open SimpleText. Don't use a full-featured word-processing program like Word, WordPerfect, ClarisWorks, or Microsoft Works, as they can add unwanted formatting to the script.

To test a script:

1. Open either NotePad, WordPad, or SimpleText.
2. Click on the "File" option in the upper left corner of the window, and then click on the "Open" option.
3. Use the "Browse" button and the directory dialog boxes to locate your computer's desktop. Then click until the files for that directory display . . . one of them should be your script.
4. Once you've located the script, highlight it, and then double click on it.
5. You should now be viewing the script from your desktop.

Here is a list of script items that you should check:

> Check to see that the correct path to your Web server's Perl interpreter is in the first line of code.
> Check to see that the correct path to your Web server's e-mail program is in the script in two places.
> Check to see that the e-mail address of the person who'll receive the e-mailed form input is correct.
> If you re-worded the screen response message, check to see that it is correct.
> If you re-worded the e-mail response message, check to see that it is correct.
> If you re-worded the "Return to Your Main Page" link, check to see that it is correct.

Step 2 — Create Directories on Your Server to Hold the Forms/Scripts

Before you upload the first Perl script to your Web server, you must have, or must create, a cgi-bin directory. If your Web server does not already have a cgi-bin directory, ask the person in charge of your server to create one. (This is not generally something you can do, not because it is so difficult, but because you probably don't have "permission" to make this type of directory on your server.) Make sure your technical person provides you with the path to the cgi-bin directory and sets up the server's permissions so that when you are ready to upload the script to the server you can go ahead and put it in the correct directory. Once you've found your server's cgi-bin directory or created one, make a note of the directory path so that you can load any other of the CD's Perl scripts into it.

If you already have a Web site, you've probably created a directory for your Web page HTML files. You don't have to create a new directory to hold the forms and scripts, just put them into the directory with your other Web HTML documents. (You might want to make a note of the directory path to your HTML files, so that when you get ready to upload the forms or scripts you'll know right where they go.)

Step 3 — Set Up Your Computers to View the Forms

All of the forms on the CD are designed for computer monitors with a screen resolution set to 800 × 600 pixels. This is so that the formatting of each form remains consistent from one monitor setting to another. If your monitor resolution is set at 640 × 480 pixels, the forms may appear a bit large for the screen. This means that patrons might have to use the horizontal scroll bar, located at the bottom of your Web browser's window, to view all of the form's content. If your monitor resolution is set at 1024 × 768 pixels the forms will probably not fill up the whole screen and will not be centered on screen.

CHANGING MONITOR RESOLUTIONS — WINDOWS PC

If you don't know the resolution setting of the computer monitors in your library, or if you wish to change the resolution to the optimal 800 × 600 setting, just follow these simple instructions:

1. Click on the "Start" button in the bottom left corner of your computer screen.
2. Locate the "Settings" option from the pop-up menu. (If you are using a computer that is connected to an NT server, this option may or may not appear on the pop-up menu. If it does not appear, contact your NT technical person so that they can change the monitor resolution for you.)
3. Select on the "Settings" option and then click on the "Control Panel" option from the additional menu that pops open.
4. A free-floating "Control Panel" window will open up. Locate and click on the "Display" icon and double click on it.
5. You will see a window display with a number of tabs at the top of the screen. What exactly you will see will depend on which version of Windows you are using (95/98/NT). Locate the "Settings" tab and click on it
6. Somewhere on the screen you will see what your current screen resolution is. It should look something like 640 × 480 (but may actually be another set of numbers). Using the method supplied on the screen (either a movable tab or pull-down menu), select the 800 × 600 pixels option.
7. To apply this change to the monitor resolution you will need to restart your computer. Just click on "Yes" when Windows asks you if you want to restart.

CHANGING MONITOR RESOLUTIONS — MACINTOSH

If you don't know the resolution setting of the computer monitors in your library, or if you wish to change the resolution to the optimal 800 × 600 setting, just follow these simple instructions:

1. Click on the apple icon on the top left corner of your computer screen.
2. Click on the "Control Panel" option from the pull-down menu.
3. Click on either the "Monitors" or "Display" or "Appearance" option (the name will depend on which version of MacOS your computer is running).
4. Somewhere on the screen that pops up you will see what your current screen resolution is. It should look something like 640 × 480 (but may actually be another set of numbers). Using the method supplied on the screen (either a movable tab or a pull-down menu), select the 800 × 600 pixels option.

To apply the change to the monitor resolution you will need to restart your computer. Depending on your version of MacOS, your computer may or may not ask you if you want it to restart itself. If it doesn't, be sure you manually shut down and restart.

INTERNET-BASED LIBRARY PATRONS
It's also important that you let your patrons with home/school/business computers know that to optimally view the forms they might want to reset their monitors to 800 × 600 pixels. Consider putting a brief message to this effect on your home page and also on any page that contains a link to one of the forms or surveys.

Step 4 — Save the Files One Last Time . . . Just In Case
Once you've selected and downloaded a form/script pair to your desktop and once you've taken the time to complete/modify the form and script, you'll want to save them one last time. (We recommend saving copies on floppy or Zip drive and storing one copy offsite.)

Upload the Files to Your Server

The next-to-last stage involves transferring (uploading) the files from your desktop to your library's server. If you're not familiar with file transfer (FTP), we've included a brief overview to help you get started or to help you understand better what your technical staff member will need to do to upload the files. The last stage involves testing the forms and scripts one more time. This time, though, you'll be checking to make sure that the form and script work together properly.

FTP (File Transfer) — A Brief Overview
To get the forms/surveys onto your Web server, you'll have to FTP (upload) them. Transferring files used to be a complex task; nowadays, all you have to do to transfer a file is:

1. Locate your FTP software, download free FTP software, or purchase FTP software.
2. Get the permissions set up on your server so that you can upload (FTP) files to them.
3. Know a bit about how the directories and files are arranged on your server.
4. Know a tiny bit about file extensions.
5. Know how to use your FTP software to actually transfer (upload) the forms and scripts to your Web server.

If the above list of what you need to do/know in order to transfer the files to your server is a bit overwhelming, consider asking your technical counterpart to set up the required server directories and do the file transfers for you.

If your technical staff person will be handling the directory setup and uploading tasks . . . all *you'll* have to do is:

1. Select a form or survey using the Preview/Selection Tutorial on the CD.
2. Download it to your computer's desktop.
3. Complete the required parts on each HTML form and Perl script and/or modify it.
4. Save the form and script to a floppy disk.
5. Hand the floppy to your technical person so they can upload the files for you!

Step 1 – Locate an FTP Program and Learn the FTP Basics

The first thing you must do is to locate or purchase a copy of some FTP software. If you need FTP software and you use a Windows PC (or have an NT server), there should be a generic FTP program (with the filename FTP) located in the Windows directory on your computer's hard drive. It's not the most user-friendly piece of software, but with a little reading and practice you can master it fairly quickly. If you don't have FTP software and want some that is easy to learn and use, try either CuteFTP, if you're a Windows user, or Fetch, if you're a Macintosh user. You can either download free/demo versions of them or download/purchase them.

Computers store individual files (like the CD's individual HTML and Perl script files) in directories and sub-directories. Depending on the FTP software you use, a directory will either look like a folder icon, or it will indicate by code/word that it is a directory. Clicking on a folder icon (or supplying the correct keystroke/command) will "open" a folder so that you can see the files and/or sub-directories inside it. Files look either like pieces of paper with different things written on them, or they are identifiable as files by their textual file extensions.

File extensions let you know a file's format and probable content. There are only three file extensions you'll need to learn and work with. The extensions are:

.htm	HTML file
.pl	Perl script
.pdf	PDF (Acrobat) file

All the forms on the CD have an .htm file extension. All the Perl scripts have a .pl file extension. All the Acrobat-formatted sections of this manual have a .pdf file extension.

Step 2 — Transfer the Files to Your Web Server

Which keys you press or commands you type to transfer (upload) the forms and scripts to your server depend entirely on the FTP software program you use. Since there are so many possible variations/looks to the actual transfer process and so many different types/brands of FTP software, we cannot explain how you will actually transfer the files from your computer's desktop to your Web server.

If your technical staff person will transfer the files for you, you don't have to worry about this step at all. If you are the person who will be transferring the files and you don't have much experience doing it, we recommend that you read the help/readme files that accompany your FTP software and/or purchase a book that explains how to use your FTP software. We've listed some excellent FTP resources in the "Sources for Further Help" section of the Preface.

Step 3 — Test the Files After You've Uploaded Them

Once you've finished uploading the forms and scripts to your server you *must* test them again. This time you'll be checking to see if the HTML forms and Perl scripts work together correctly and output e-mail data to a staff member and a "Thank You" message to a patron. Below are instructions for testing your forms and scripts.

CHECK TO SEE IF THE FORM/SCRIPT PAIR WORKS TOGETHER CORRECTLY

To test the form/script pair, fire up your library's Web browser (Internet Explorer or Netscape).

1. Type in the URL for the form. It should display on your computer screen. Make sure that the URL in

the footer displays correctly. Check to make sure that the "mailto" link in the footer goes to the correct address (click on it). If you've modified any of the form text (the introduction, any minor re-wording of form element text), check to make sure it displays correctly. If you've modified the color of the form header (and/or the color of the header text) and the color of the bottom line, check to make sure it displays correctly. If you've modified the fonts, check to make sure that the whole form displays in the new font.

If the form doesn't display, you might have transferred the HTML form into the wrong directory, or you might have copied down the URL incorrectly. Check to see where the HTML form is located (and move the file to the correct directory if necessary) or copy down the correct URL/path and try typing the URL again.

If anything in the form doesn't display correctly, take out your saved copy on disk, make the necessary corrections, test it before you upload it, and then upload/overwrite the form or have your technical person upload/overwrite it for you . . . and then retest it again!

2. Once the form displays on your screen, fill out the form just like a patron would (including *your* real e-mail address) and click on the "Send" button. If the form/script are working together correctly you should see a "Thank You" message on your computer screen, along with a working link back to your library's home page (or whatever page you designated). Make sure that the message is correct and that the link takes you back to the correct Web page.

If the message or URL is incorrect, correct the information on your server. Use a server text editor like Emacs or PICO to make the necessary changes to the message or URL. If you don't want to make the changes online, just pull out the saved copy of the Perl script, go back into NotePad, WordPad, or SimpleWrite, and change the message or URL. Then re-save the script (and back it up again), upload it, and overwrite/replace the existing script, or hand it to your techie to upload and overwrite/replace. Then test it again.

3. Once you've seen the "Thank You" message on the screen and made sure that the link below it works, it's time to check your e-mail. If the form/script is working correctly you should receive an e-mail message (depending on your e-mail system, this could take a while to receive) with the form name in the subject line. The message will be identical to the "Thank You" message that displayed on your computer screen.

If you didn't receive an e-mail message, check to see that the correct path to your e-mail program was added to the Perl script. If you did receive an e-mail but the message was incorrect, correct it. You can correct both of these errors in the Perl script by opening up a simple word processor, making the corrections, and uploading the script to your server again.

4. Finally, you should ask the staff member who is assigned to collect/process the form information if they've received an e-mail message containing the form information. (The subject line on the e-mail message will be the form name.) If they received the e-mail message, print it out and check to make sure that all the fields on the e-mail and on the form match. (The wording won't match exactly, but each form field should correspond to one on the e-mail message.)

If the staff member didn't receive an e-mail message, check to see if their correct e-mail address was added to the HTML form. If it wasn't, correct the HTML form using a simple word processor (or make the correction by using a server text editor like Emacs or PICO). If the staff member does receive an e-mail but the form data on it is incorrect, this isn't easily fixed. If this happens, find someone in your community who knows how to troubleshoot Perl scripts and ask them to change/correct it for you.

Congratulations!!!
You've just successfully added a working form to your library's Web site. If you've never done anything like this before, give yourself credit for what you've just accomplished. Now all that's left to do is to let your library patrons know that "you've got forms!"

SECTION 2
Forms, Surveys, and Scripts

Instant Web Forms & Surveys

Group 1 — Reference Forms

In this section you'll find Web-based forms that will enable students to contact library staff to get help with basic reference questions, research projects, and class assignments. In this section you'll also find a handy form so that teachers and parents can alert your staff to upcoming homework assigments that will require students to use your library's resources.

Ask a Reference Question
If students have a straightforward, factual question or reference question, they can fill in this form and e-mail it to your staff. Make sure you include a link to this form on your Web site's reference and home pages.

Homework Assignment Alert *(teachers/librarians/parents)*
Help teachers, homeschooling parents and other school staff help your students! Encourage them to use this form to let your staff know in advance about homework assignments that will require kids/teens to use your library's resources and services. Put a link to this form on your Web site's homework help and teacher pages.

Get Help Searching the Web
Do students need help searching the Web? Do they retrieve either too many or too few results? Do they want you to suggest ways they can focus their Web searches to retrieve better results? You can also use this form to find out the additional Web search classes you should be offering/developing. Add a link to this form to any of your Web site's Web search pages.

Get Help Citing a Source
Students often struggle to locate all the information they need to create complete citations for a bibliography. Put a link to this form on your reference and homework help Web pages so that students can e-mail you the information they have already located.

Get Help With Your Homework
Do students need help with school assignments, research papers, or personal research projects but don't always have the time to meet with your staff? Now you can receive student requests for homework help via e-mail. Be sure to add a link to this form on your Web site's reference and homework help pages.

Ask a Reference Question

If you'd like an answer to a reference question fill in the form below. We will provide you with an answer (and references to books / Web sites) as soon as possible via e-mail. For a quicker answer, visit the library's reference desk.

Name (first, last)

E-mail address

Home address (+ city)

School you attend

Home phone/fax (+ areacode)

Teacher's name

What grade are you in?
- ○ 3   ○ 4   ○ 5   ○ 6   ○ 7
- ○ 8   ○ 9   ○ 10   ○ 11   ○ 12

What is your question? (give us as many details as you can)

How would you like us to contact you?
○ E-mail   ○ Phone (when is the best day/time to call?)

I need an answer before... (eg. Oct. 2nd)
○ Anytime is fine

I would like to receive
○ Facts / Specific information   ○ Reference to books / Web sites   ○ Both facts and references

For sources I have to use (select any/all)
○ Books   ○ Magazines   ○ Web sites   ○ Pictures / Maps
○ Other (explain)

[Send Question]   [Clear Form]

http://

© 2002 Contact Webmaster

Ask a Reference Question — HTML Form

```
<html>
<head><title>Ask a Reference Question</title></head>
<body bgcolor="#FFFFFF">
<table width="700" border="1" height="85" bgcolor="ffffff">
<tr valign="middle" align="center"><td>
<p><font halign=center color="#000000" face="Arial, Helvetica, sans-serif" size="+3">
<b><i>Ask a Reference Question</i></b></font></p>
</td></tr></table>
<form method="post" action="http://www.yourLibrary.org/cgi-bin/crg1.pl"><p> </p>
<p>
<b><font size="2" face="Arial, Helvetica, sans-serif">If you'd like an answer to a reference question fill in the form below. We will provide you with an answer <br>(and references to books / Web sites) as soon as possible via e-mail. For a quicker answer, visit the library's <br>reference desk.</font></b></p>
<p> </p>
<input type="hidden" name="LibraryEmail" value="you@yourLibrary.org">
<input type="hidden" name="LibraryURL" value="http://www.yourLibrary.org">
<input type="hidden" name="Form" value="Ask a Reference Question">
<p></p>
<table width="407" border="0" cellspacing="4" cellpadding="1">
<tr><td width="202">
<b><font face="Arial, Helvetica, sans-serif" size="2">Name</font></b><font face="Arial, Helvetica, sans-serif" size="1">  (first, last)</font><br><font face="Arial, Helvetica, sans-serif" size="2">
<input type="text" name="Name" size="25"></font></td>
<td width="189">
<b><font face="Arial, Helvetica, sans-serif" size="2">E-mail address<br></font></b><font face="Arial, Helvetica, sans-serif" size="2"><input type="text" name="Email" size="25"></font></td></tr>
<tr><td width="202" height="2">
<b><font face="Arial, Helvetica, sans-serif" size="2">Home address</font> </b><font face="Arial, Helvetica, sans-serif" size="1"> (+ city)</font><br><font face="Arial, Helvetica, sans-serif" size="2">
<input type="text" name="HomeAddr" size="25"></font></td>
<td width="189" height="2">
<b><font face="Arial, Helvetica, sans-serif" size="2">School you attend<br></font></b><font face="Arial, Helvetica, sans-serif" size="2"><input type="text" name="School" size="25"></font></td></tr>
<tr><td width="202" height="2">
<b><font face="Arial, Helvetica, sans-serif" size="2">Home phone/fax</font> </b><font face="Arial, Helvetica, sans-serif" size="1"> (+ areacode)</font><br><font face="Arial, Helvetica, sans-serif" size="2"><input type="text" name="HomePhone" size="25"></font></td>
<td width="189" height="2">
<b><font face="Arial, Helvetica, sans-serif" size="2">Teacher's name<br></font></b><font face="Arial, Helvetica, sans-serif" size="2"><input type="text" name="Teacher" size="25"></font></td></tr>
<tr><td width="391" colspan="2" height="48">
<b><font face="Arial, Helvetica, sans-serif" size="2">What grade are you in?</font></b><br><font face= "Arial, Helvetica, sans-serif" size="2"></font>
```

Group 1—Reference Forms

```html
<table width="87%" border="0" cellspacing="4" cellpadding="0"><tr><td height="8" width="16%">
<font face="Arial, Helvetica, sans-serif" size="2"><input type="radio" name="EducationLevel" value="3">
3</font></td>
<td height="8" width="16%">
<font face="Arial, Helvetica, sans-serif" size="2"><input type="radio" name="EducationLevel" value="4">
4</font></td>
<td height="8" width="16%">
<font face="Arial, Helvetica, sans-serif" size="2"><input type="radio" name="EducationLevel" value="5">
5</font></td>
<td height="8" width="16%">
<font face="Arial, Helvetica, sans-serif" size="2"><input type="radio" name="EducationLevel" value="6">
6</font></td>
<td height="8" width="36%">
<font face="Arial, Helvetica, sans-serif" size="2"><input type="radio" name="EducationLevel" value="7">
7</font></td></tr>
<tr><td height="2" width="16%">
<font face="Arial, Helvetica, sans-serif" size="2"><input type="radio" name="EducationLevel" value="8">
8</font></td>
<td height="2" width="16%">
<font face="Arial, Helvetica, sans-serif" size="2"><input type="radio" name="EducationLevel" value="9">
9</font></td>
<td height="2" width="16%">
<font face="Arial, Helvetica, sans-serif" size="2"><input type="radio" name="EducationLevel" value="10">
10</font></td>
<td height="2" width="16%">
<font face="Arial, Helvetica, sans-serif" size="2"><input type="radio" name="EducationLevel" value="11">
11</font></td>
<td height="2" width="36%">
<font face="Arial, Helvetica, sans-serif" size="2"><input type="radio" name="EducationLevel" value="12">
12</font></td></tr></table>
</td></tr></table>
<p><br>
<b><font face="Arial, Helvetica, sans-serif" size="2">What is your question?</font></b><font face="Arial, Helvetica, sans-serif" size="1">  (give us as many details as you can)</font><br><font face="Arial, Helvetica, sans-serif" size="3"><textarea name="Question" cols="40" rows="10"></textarea> </font></p>
<p>
<font face="Arial, Helvetica, sans-serif" size="2"><b>How would you like us to contact you?</b></font>
<br><font face="Arial, Helvetica, sans-serif" size="3">
<input type="radio" name="Reply" value="Email"></font><font face="Arial, Helvetica, sans-serif" size="2">
E-mail</font>   
<input type="radio" name="Reply" value="Phone"><font face="Arial, Helvetica, sans-serif" size="2"> Phone
</font>  <font face="Arial, Helvetica, sans-serif" size="1">(when is the best day/time to call?)
</font><font face="Arial, Helvetica, sans-serif" size="2"> <input type="text" name="BestTime" size="10">
</font></p>
<p>
```

```html
<b><font face="Arial, Helvetica, sans-serif" size="2">I need an answer before...  </font></b>
<font face="Arial, Helvetica, sans-serif" size="1">(eg. Oct. 2nd) <font size="3"><br><input type="text" name="NeedBefore" size="15"></font></font>      <input type="radio" name="TimeIssue" value="Time is not an issue"><font face="Arial, Helvetica, sans-serif" size="2"> Anytime is fine</font></p>
<p>
<b><font face="Arial, Helvetica, sans-serif" size="2">I would like to receive<br></font></b>
<input type="radio" name="Answer" value="Facts / Specific information"><font face="Arial, Helvetica, sans-serif" size="2">Facts / Specific information   
<input type="radio" name="Answer" value="References to books / Web sites">Reference to books / Web sites   
<input type="radio" name="Answer" value="Both facts and references">Both facts and references</font>
</p><p>
<b><font face="Arial, Helvetica, sans-serif" size="2">For sources I have to use  </font></b>
<font face="Arial, Helvetica, sans-serif" size="1">(select any/all)</font><br><font face="Arial, Helvetica, sans-serif" size="2">
<input type="radio" name="B" value="Books">Books  
<input type="radio" name="M" value="Magazines">Magazines   
<input type="radio" name="WS" value="Web sites">Web sites   
<input type="radio" name="PM" value="Pictures / Maps">Pictures / Maps</font>   
<br><input type="radio" name="O" value="Other">Other<b><font face="Arial, Helvetica, sans-serif" size="2"> </font></b><font face="Arial, Helvetica, sans-serif" size="1">(explain)<font size="3">
 <input type="text" name="OtherSources" size="15"></font></font></font></p>
<p> </p>
<table width="700" border="0" cellspacing="10" cellpadding="1"><tr><td width="247"><div align="right">
<input type="submit" name="send" value="Send Question"></div></td><td width="200"> </td>
<td width="207"> <div align="left"><input type="reset" name="clear" value="Clear Form"></div></td></tr>
<tr colspan=3><td colspan=3>
<table width="500" border="1" height="2" align="center" cellpadding="0" cellspacing="0" bgcolor="ffffff"><tr><td><font size="1" color="#ffffff">.</font></td></tr></table></td></tr>
<tr><td colspan=3><div align="center">
<font face="Arial, Helvetica, sans-serif" size="1"><b>http://  </b></font><br><font size="2"> 
<font face="Arial, Helvetica, sans-serif" size="1"><b>&copy; 2002</b></font></font>
<font face="Arial, Helvetica, sans-serif" size="2"><a href="mailto:">
<b><font size="1">Contact Webmaster</font></b></a></font></div></td></tr>
</table></form>
</body>
</html>
```

Group 1—Reference Forms

Ask a Reference Question — Perl Script

```perl
#!/usr/local/bin/perl

# *************************************************************
# ABOVE is where you MUST specify the path to your
# perl interpreter on your Web server.
# Replace /usr/local/bin/perl with your path.
# *************************************************************

if ($ENV{'REQUEST_METHOD'}eq"GET"){$buffer = $ENV{'QUERY_STRING'};}
    elsif($ENV{'REQUEST_METHOD'}eq"POST"){
        read(STDIN,$buffer,$ENV{'CONTENT_LENGTH'});
    }
$bufferb = $buffer;
#separate the name of the input from its value.
@forminputs = split(/&/, $bufferb);

foreach $forminput (@forminputs)
{
    #separate the name of the input from its value
    ($name, $value) = split(/=/, $forminput);

    #Un-Webify plus signs and %-encoding
    $value =~ tr/+/ /;
    $value =~ s/%([a-fA-F0-9][a-fA-F0-9])/pack("C", hex($1))/eg;

    #stick them in the in array
    $in{$name} = $value;
}
print "Content-type: text/html\n\n";

####################################################
# ABOVE is the required header for a perl script   #
####################################################

#######################################################
# (Below) Email received by library containing user-entered information #
#######################################################

# *************************************************************
# Here's where you MUST specify the path to your
# email program (probably sendmail) ON your Web server.
# Replace /usr/sbin/sendmail with your path.
# *************************************************************
```

```perl
open (LMAIL, "|/usr/sbin/sendmail -t");
print LMAIL ("To: $in{LibraryEmail}\n");
print LMAIL ("From: $in{Email}\n");
print LMAIL ("Subject: $in{Form} - patron submission\n");

print LMAIL ("-------------------\nPatron information\n\n");


print LMAIL ("Name:\n $in{Name}\n\n");
print LMAIL ("E-mail Address:\n $in{Email}\n\n");
print LMAIL ("Home Address:\n $in{HomeAddr}\n\n");
print LMAIL ("School:\n $in{School}\n\n");
print LMAIL ("Home Phone/Fax:\n $in{HomePhone}\n\n");
print LMAIL ("Teacher's Name:\n $in{Teacher}\n\n");
print LMAIL ("Grade:\n $in{EducationLevel}\n\n");

print LMAIL ("-------------------\nSubmitted information \n\n");

print LMAIL ("My question:\n $in{Question}\n\n");
print LMAIL ("My preferred reply method:\n $in{Reply}\n\n");
print LMAIL ("Best day/time to reach me:\n $in{BestTime}\n\n");
print LMAIL ("I need an answer before:\n $in{NeedBefore} $in{TimeIssue}\n\n");
print LMAIL ("I would like to receive:\n $in{Answer}\n\n");
print LMAIL ("Sources I would like:\n $in{B}, $in{M}, $in{WS}, $in{PM}, $in{O}\n\n");
print LMAIL ("Other sources: $in{OtherSources}\n\n");
print LMAIL ("\n.\n");

##############################################
# Email received by the user confirming form submission #
##############################################

# ***********************************************
# Here's where you MUST specify the path to your
# email program ON your Web server.
# Replace /usr/sbin/sendmail with your path.
# ***********************************************

open (MAIL, "|/usr/sbin/sendmail -t");

# ***********************************************
# Here's where you MAY customize the email
# response to the user. You may change any wording
# on the form.
# ***********************************************
print MAIL<<toEnd;
```

Group 1—Reference Forms

To: $in{Email}
From: $in{LibraryEmail}
Subject: $in{Form}

Thanks for sending us your reference question.\n\n
A librarian will contact you in the next couple of days with either an answer to your question or a list of resources that will help you answer the question yourself.

toEnd
   print MAIL ("\n.\n");

```
##########################################
# Screen response to user after submitting the form  #
##########################################
```

print ("<html><head><title>$in{Form}</title></head>");
print ("<body bgcolor=\"ffffff\">");

```
# ***********************************************************
# Here's where you MAY change the screen response
# the user sees after submitting the form. You may
# change any wording between the quotation marks.
# ***********************************************************
```

print ("Thanks for sending us your reference question.<p>
A librarian will contact you in the next couple of days with either an answer to your question or a list of resources that will help you answer the question yourself. ");

```
# ***********************************************************
# Here's where you MAY change the name of the link
# back to your main page. You may replace Return
# to our main page with your own wording.
# ***********************************************************
```

print ("<p> <a href=$in{LibraryURL}>Return to our main page.</a> ");
print ("</body></html>");

Homework Assignment Alert

Teachers / Librarians / Parents

Help us help your students! Use this form to let our staff know in advance about homework assignments that will require kids/teens to use the library's resources and services.

Name (first, last)

E-mail address

Address (+ city)

Name of school

Phone/Fax (+ areacode)

Grade(s) you teach

I am a...
- ○ Classroom teacher
- ○ Librarian / Media specialist
- ○ School staff / Administrator
- ○ Parent
- ○ Other (explain)

Describe the assignment (give us as many details as you can)

Grade level

Number of students

Number of sources required

Date assigned

Date due

Number of pages required

Types of resources required (select any/all)
- ○ Books
- ○ Magazines
- ○ Web sites
- ○ Dictionaries
- ○ Encyclopedias
- ○ Newspapers
- ○ Maps
- ○ Pictures
- ○ Other (explain)

Types of resources that can't be used

Suggest one or two related books / Web sites

Will you give this assignment again? ○ Yes ○ No

[Send Alert] [Clear Form]

http://
© 2002 Contact Webmaster

Homework Assignment Alert — HTML Form

```
<html>
<head><title>Homework Assignment Alert</title></head>
<body bgcolor="#FFFFFF">
<table width="700" border="1" height="85" bgcolor="ffffff">
<tr valign="middle" align="center"><td>
<p>
<font halign=center color="#000000" face="Arial, Helvetica, sans-serif" size="+3">
<b><i>Homework Assignment Alert</i></b></font></p>
</td></tr></table>
<form method="post" action="http://www.yourLibrary.org/cgi-bin/crg1.pl"><p> </p>
<p>
<b><font size="2" face="Arial, Helvetica, sans-serif"><i>Teachers / Librarians / Parents</i>
</font></b></p><p>
<b><font size="2" face="Arial, Helvetica, sans-serif">Help us help your students! Use this form to let our staff know in advance about homework assignments <br>that will require kids/teens to use the library's resources and services.</font></b></p>
<p> </p>
<input type="hidden" name="LibraryEmail" value="you@yourLibrary.org">
<input type="hidden" name="LibraryURL" value="http://www.yourLibrary.org">
<input type="hidden" name="Form" value="Homework Assignment Alert">
<p></p>
<table width="426" border="0" cellspacing="4" cellpadding="1">
<tr><td width="202">
<b><font face="Arial, Helvetica, sans-serif" size="2">Name</font></b><font face="Arial, Helvetica, sans-serif" size="1">  (first, last)</font><br><font face="Arial, Helvetica, sans-serif" size="2">
<input type="text" name="Name" size="25"></font></td>
<td width="205">
<b><font face="Arial, Helvetica, sans-serif" size="2">E-mail address<br></font></b><font face="Arial, Helvetica, sans-serif" size="2"><input type="text" name="Email" size="25"></font></td></tr>
<tr><td width="202" height="2">
<b><font face="Arial, Helvetica, sans-serif" size="2">Address</font>  </b><font face="Arial, Helvetica, sans-serif" size="1">(+ city)</font><br><font face="Arial, Helvetica, sans-serif" size="2">
<input type="text" name="Addr" size="25"></font></td>
<td width="205" height="2">
<b><font face="Arial, Helvetica, sans-serif" size="2">Name of school<br></font></b><font face="Arial, Helvetica, sans-serif" size="2"><input type="text" name="School" size="25"></font></td></tr>
<tr><td width="202" height="2">
<b><font face="Arial, Helvetica, sans-serif" size="2">Phone/Fax</font>  </b><font face="Arial, Helvetica, sans-serif" size="1">(+ areacode)</font><br><font face="Arial, Helvetica, sans-serif" size="2">
<input type="text" name="Phone" size="25"></font></td>
<td width="205" height="2">
<b><font face="Arial, Helvetica, sans-serif" size="2">Grade(s) you teach<br></font></b><font face= "Arial, Helvetica, sans-serif" size="2"><input type="text" name="Grade" size="25"></font></td></tr>
```

```html
<tr><td colspan="2" height="2">
<p>
<b><font face="Arial, Helvetica, sans-serif" size="2">I am a...</font></b><br>
<table width="100%" border="0" cellpadding="0" cellspacing="4"><tr><td width="51%">
<font face="Arial, Helvetica, sans-serif" size="2"><input type="radio" name="Iama" value="Classroom teacher">Classroom teacher</font></td>
<td width="49%">
<font face="Arial, Helvetica, sans-serif" size="2"><input type="radio" name="Iama" value="Librarian / Media specialist"> Librarian / Media specialist</font></td></tr>
<tr><td width="51%">
<font face="Arial, Helvetica, sans-serif" size="2"><input type="radio" name="Iama" value="School staff / Administrator">School staff / Administrator</font></td>
<td width="49%">
<font face="Arial, Helvetica, sans-serif" size="2"><input type="radio" name="Iama" value="Parent"> Parent</font></td></tr>
<tr><td colspan="2" height="2">
<font face="Arial, Helvetica, sans-serif" size="2"><input type="radio" name="Iama" value="Other">Other<b>
<font face="Arial, Helvetica, sans-serif" size="1">  </font></b><font face="Arial, Helvetica, sans-serif" size="1">(explain)</font><b><font size="2"> <input type="text" name= "IamaOther" size="15"></font></b></font>
</td></tr></table>
</td></tr></table>
<p><br>
<b><font face="Arial, Helvetica, sans-serif" size="2">Describe the assignment</font></b><font face= "Arial, Helvetica, sans-serif" size="1">  (give us as many details as you can)</font><br>
<font face="Arial, Helvetica, sans-serif" size="3"><textarea name="Describe" cols="40" rows="10">
</textarea></font></p>
<table width="694" border="0" cellspacing="0" cellpadding="0">
<tr><td width="128">
<font face="Arial, Helvetica, sans-serif" size="2"><b>Grade level</b></font><font face="Arial, Helvetica, sans-serif" size="3"><br><input type="text" name="GradeLevel" size="5"></font></td>
<td width="148">
<font face="Arial, Helvetica, sans-serif" size="2"><b>Number of students</b></font><font face="Arial, Helvetica, sans-serif" size="3"><br><input type="text" name="NumberStudents" size="5"></font></td>
<td width="418">
<font face="Arial, Helvetica, sans-serif" size="2"><b>Number of sources required</b></font><font face="Arial, Helvetica, sans-serif" size="3"><br><input type="text" name="NumberResources" size="5">
</font></td></tr>
<tr><td width="128" height="2">
<font face="Arial, Helvetica, sans-serif" size="2"><b>Date assigned</b></font><font face="Arial, Helvetica, sans-serif" size="3"><br><input type="text" name="DateGiven" size="5"></font></td>
<td width="148" height="2">
<font face="Arial, Helvetica, sans-serif" size="2"><b>Date due</b></font><font face="Arial, Helvetica, sans-serif" size="3"><br><input type="text" name="DateDue" size="5"></font></td>
<td width="418" height="2">
```

```html
<font face="Arial, Helvetica, sans-serif" size="2"><b>Number of pages required</b><font face="Arial, Helvetica, sans-serif" size="3"><br><input type="text" name="Length" size="5"></font></font>
</td></tr></table>
<p>
<b><font face="Arial, Helvetica, sans-serif" size="2">Types of resources required</font></b><font face="Arial, Helvetica, sans-serif" size="1">  (select any/all)</font><br>
<table width="544" border="0" cellspacing="0" cellpadding="0"><tr><td width="140">
<font face="Arial, Helvetica, sans-serif" size="2"><input type="radio" name="T1" value="Books">
Books</font></td>
<td width="127">
<font face="Arial, Helvetica, sans-serif" size="2"><input type="radio" name="T2" value="Magazines">
Magazines</font></td>
<td width="107">
<font face="Arial, Helvetica, sans-serif" size="2"><input type="radio" name="T3" value="Web sites">
Web sites</font></td>
<td width="170">
<font face="Arial, Helvetica, sans-serif" size="2"><input type="radio" name="T4" value="Dictionaries">
Dictionaries</font></td></tr>
<tr><td width="140">
<font face="Arial, Helvetica, sans-serif" size="2"><input type="radio" name="T5" value="Encyclopedias">
Encyclopedias</font></td>
<td width="127">
<font face="Arial, Helvetica, sans-serif" size="2"><input type="radio" name="T6" value="Newspapers">
Newspapers</font></td>
<td width="107">
<font face="Arial, Helvetica, sans-serif" size="2"><input type="radio" name="T7" value="Maps">Maps
</font></td>
<td width="170">
<font face="Arial, Helvetica, sans-serif" size="2"><input type="radio" name="T8" value="Pictures">
Pictures</font></td></tr>
<tr><td colspan="4">
<font face="Arial, Helvetica, sans-serif" size="2"><input type="radio" name="T9" value="Other">
Other  <font face="Arial, Helvetica, sans-serif" size="1">(explain)</font><font size="2">
<input type="text" name="TypeROther" size="15"></font></font>
</td></tr></table>
<p>
<b><font face="Arial, Helvetica, sans-serif" size="2">Types of resources that can't be used<br>
</font></b><font size="3" face="Arial, Helvetica, sans-serif"><input type="text" name="CantUse" size="20">
</font></p>
<p>
<b><font face="Arial, Helvetica, sans-serif" size="2">Suggest one or two related books / Web sites<br>
</font></b><font size="3" face="Arial, Helvetica, sans-serif"><input type="text" name="Suggest" size="20">
</font></p>
<p>
<b><font face="Arial, Helvetica, sans-serif" size="2">Will you give this assignment again? 
```

Group 1—Reference Forms

```html
  </font></b><font face="Arial, Helvetica, sans-serif" size="2">
<input type="radio" name= "Again" value="Yes">Yes   
<input type="radio" name="Again" value="No">No</font></p><p> </p>
<p>
<table width="700" border="0" cellspacing="10" cellpadding="1"><tr><td width="215"><div align="right">
<input type="submit" name="send" value="Send Alert"></div></td><td width="232"> </td><td width="207">
<div align="left"><input type="reset" name="clear" value= "Clear Form"></div></td></tr><tr colspan=3>
<td colspan=3>
<table width="500" border="1" height="2" align="center" cellpadding="0" cellspacing="0"
bgcolor="ffffff"><tr><td><font size="1" color="#ffffff">.</font></td></tr></table></td></tr><tr>
<td colspan=3><div align="center">
<font face="Arial, Helvetica, sans-serif" size="1"><b>http://</b></font><br><font size="2"> 
<font face="Arial, Helvetica, sans-serif" size="1"><b>&copy; 2002</b></font></font>
<font face="Arial, Helvetica, sans-serif" size="2"><a href="mailto:">
<b><font size="1">Contact Webmaster</font></b></a></font></div></td></tr>
</table></form>
</body>
</html>
```

Homework Assignment Alert — Perl Script

```perl
#!/usr/local/bin/perl

# ****************************************************************
# ABOVE is where you MUST specify the path to your
# perl interpreter on your Web server.
# Replace /usr/local/bin/perl with your path.
# ****************************************************************

if ($ENV{'REQUEST_METHOD'}eq"GET"){$buffer = $ENV{'QUERY_STRING'};}
    elsif($ENV{'REQUEST_METHOD'}eq"POST"){
        read(STDIN,$buffer,$ENV{'CONTENT_LENGTH'});
    }
$bufferb = $buffer;
#separate the name of the input from its value.
@forminputs = split(/&/, $bufferb);

foreach $forminput (@forminputs)
{
    #separate the name of the input from its value
    ($name, $value) = split(/=/, $forminput);

    #Un-Webify plus signs and %-encoding
    $value =~ tr/+/ /;
    $value =~ s/%([a-fA-F0-9][a-fA-F0-9])/pack("C", hex($1))/eg;

    #stick them in the in array
    $in{$name} = $value;
}
print "Content-type: text/html\n\n";

################################################
# ABOVE is the required header for a perl script    #
################################################


#####################################################
# (Below) Email received by library containing user-entered information #
#####################################################


# ****************************************************************
# Here's where you MUST specify the path to your
# email program (probably sendmail) ON your Web server.
# Replace /usr/sbin/sendmail with your path.
# ****************************************************************
```

Group 1—Reference Forms

```
open (LMAIL, "|/usr/sbin/sendmail -t");
print LMAIL ("To: $in{LibraryEmail}\n");
print LMAIL ("From: $in{Email}\n");
print LMAIL ("Subject: $in{Form} - patron submission\n");

print LMAIL ("-------------------\nPatron information\n\n");
print LMAIL ("Name:\n $in{Name}\n\n");
print LMAIL ("E-mail Address:\n $in{Email}\n\n");
print LMAIL ("Home Address:\n $in{HomeAddr}\n\n");
print LMAIL ("School:\n $in{School}\n\n");
print LMAIL ("Home Phone/Fax:\n $in{HomePhone}\n\n");
print LMAIL ("Teacher's Name:\n $in{Teacher}\n\n");
print LMAIL ("Grade:\n $in{EducationLevel}\n\n");

print LMAIL ("-------------------\nSubmitted information \n\n");

print LMAIL ("Describe the assignment:\n $in{Describe}\n\n");

print LMAIL ("Grade level:\n $in{GradeLevel}\n\n");
print LMAIL ("Number of students:\n $in{NumberStudents}\n\n");
print LMAIL ("Date assignment given:\n $in{DateGiven}\n\n");
print LMAIL ("Date due:\n $in{DateDue}\n\n");
print LMAIL ("Length of assignment (no. of pages):\n $in{Length}\n\n");
print LMAIL ("Number of resources required:\n $in{NumberResources}\n\n");

print LMAIL ("Types of resources required:\n $in{T1}, $in{T2}, $in{T3}, $in{T4}, $in{T5}, $in{T6}, $in{T7}, $in{T8}, $in{T9}, $in{TypeROther}\n\n");

print LMAIL ("Types of resources that can't be used:\n $in{CantUse}\n\n");

print LMAIL ("Suggest one or two related books / Web sites:\n $in{Suggest}\n\n");

print LMAIL ("Will you give this assignment again?\t $in{Again}\n");
print LMAIL ("\n.\n");

###############################################
# Email received by the user confirming form submission #
###############################################

# ***********************************************************
# Here's where you MUST specify the path to your
# email program ON your Web server.
# Replace /usr/sbin/sendmail with your path.
# ***********************************************************
```

```
open (MAIL, "|/usr/sbin/sendmail -t");

# ***************************************************
# Here's where you MAY customize the email
# response to the user. You may change any wording
# on the form.
# ***************************************************

print MAIL<<toEnd;
To: $in{Email}
From: $in{LibraryEmail}
Subject: $in{Form}

Thanks for taking the time to fill out our Homework Assignment Alert.

toEnd
    print MAIL ("\n.\n");


#########################################
# Screen response to user after submitting the form  #
#########################################

print ("<html><head><title>$in{Form}</title></head>");
print ("<body bgcolor=\"ffffff\">");

# ***************************************************
# Here's where you MAY change the screen response
# the user sees after submitting the form. You may
# change any wording between the quotation marks.
# ***************************************************

print ("Thanks for taking the time to fill out our Homework Assignment Alert.");

# ***************************************************
# Here's where you MAY change the name of the link
# back to your main page. You may replace Return
# to our main page with your own wording.
# ***************************************************

print ("<p><center><a href=$in{LibraryURL}>Return to our main page.</a></center>");
print ("</body></html>");
```

Get Help Searching the Web

Would you like help searching the Web? Do you find either too many or too few results? Would you like to focus your Web searches to locate really great results? We'll e-mail or phone you to help you use and search the Web more effectively.

Name (first, last)

E-mail address

Home address (+ city)

School you attend

Home phone/fax (+ areacode)

Teacher's name

What grade are you in?
- ○ 3   ○ 4   ○ 5   ○ 6   ○ 7
- ○ 8   ○ 9   ○ 10   ○ 11   ○ 12

What did you search the Web for? (give us as many details as you can)

What word(s) or phrase(s) did you use to search? (eg. tigers, "Tiger Woods")

Which Web search tools did you use? (eg. Yahooligans, KidsClick)

Type of help you need
- ○ I couldn't find what I was searching for
- ○ I found too many results
- ○ I'd like to get fewer results
- ○ I'd like to improve my search
- ○ I'm not really sure if I searched correctly
- ○ I'd like to learn how to search better
- ○ Other (explain)

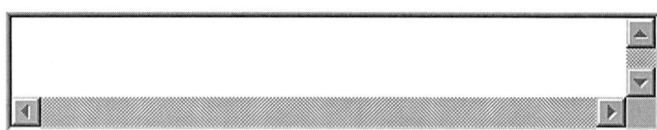

Send Request   Clear Form

http://
© 2002 Contact Webmaster

Group 1—Reference Forms

Get Help Searching the Web — HTML Form

```
<html>
<head><title>Get Help Searching the Web</title></head>
<body bgcolor="#FFFFFF">
<table width="700" border="1" height="85" bgcolor="ffffff">
<tr valign="middle" align="center"><td>
<p>
<font halign=center color="#000000" face="Arial, Helvetica, sans-serif" size="+3">
<b><i>Get Help Searching the Web</i></b></font></p>
</td></tr></table>
<form method="post" action="http://www.yourLibrary.org/cgi-bin/crg5.pl"><p> </p>
<p>
<font face="Arial, Helvetica, sans-serif" size="2"><b>Would you like help searching the Web? Do you find either too many or too few results? Would you like <br>to focus your Web searches to locate really great results? We'll e-mail or phone you to help you use <br>and search the Web more effectively.</b></font>
</p><p> </p><input type="hidden" name="LibraryEmail" value="you@yourLibrary.org">
<input type="hidden" name="LibraryURL" value="http://www.yourLibrary.org">
<input type="hidden" name="Form" value="Get Help Searching the Web">
<p></p>
<table width="407" border="0" cellspacing="4" cellpadding="1">
<tr><td width="202">
<b><font face="Arial, Helvetica, sans-serif" size="2">Name</font></b><font face="Arial, Helvetica, sans-serif" size="1">  (first, last)</font><br><font face="Arial, Helvetica, sans-serif" size="2">
<input type="text" name="Name" size="25"></font></td>
<td width="189">
<b><font face="Arial, Helvetica, sans-serif" size="2">E-mail address<br></font></b><font face="Arial, Helvetica, sans-serif" size="2"><input type="text" name="Email" size="25"></font></td></tr>
<tr><td width="202" height="2">
<b><font face="Arial, Helvetica, sans-serif" size="2">Home address</font><font face="Arial, Helvetica, sans-serif" size="1"> </b> (+ city)</font><br><font face="Arial, Helvetica, sans-serif" size="2">
<input type="text" name="HomeAddr" size="25"></font></td>
<td width="189" height="2">
<b><font face="Arial, Helvetica, sans-serif" size="2">School you attend<br></font></b><font face="Arial, Helvetica, sans-serif" size="2"><input type="text" name="School" size="25"></font></td></tr>
<tr><td width="202" height="2">
<b><font face="Arial, Helvetica, sans-serif" size="2">Home phone/fax</font><font face="Arial, Helvetica, sans-serif" size="1">  (+ areacode)</font><br><font face="Arial, Helvetica, sans-serif" size="2">
<input type="text" name="HomePhone" size="25"></font></td>
<td width="189" height="2">
<b><font face="Arial, Helvetica, sans-serif" size="2">Teacher's name<br></font></b><font face="Arial, Helvetica, sans-serif" size="2"><input type="text" name="Teacher" size="25"></font></td></tr>
<tr><td width="391" colspan="2" height="48">
<b><font face="Arial, Helvetica, sans-serif" size="2">What grade are you in?</font></b><br>
<table width="87%" border="0" cellspacing="4" cellpadding="0"><tr><td height="8" width="16%">
```

```html
<font face="Arial, Helvetica, sans-serif" size="2"><input type="radio" name="EducationLevel" value="3">
3</font></td>
<td height="8" width="16%">
<font face="Arial, Helvetica, sans-serif" size="2"><input type="radio" name="EducationLevel" value="4">
4</font></td>
<td height="8" width="16%">
<font face="Arial, Helvetica, sans-serif" size="2"><input type="radio" name="EducationLevel" value="5">
5</font></td>
<td height="8" width="16%">
<font face="Arial, Helvetica, sans-serif" size="2"><input type="radio" name="EducationLevel" value="6">
6</font></td>
<td height="8" width="36%">
<font face="Arial, Helvetica, sans-serif" size="2"><input type="radio" name="EducationLevel" value="7">
7</font></td></tr>
<tr><td height="2" width="16%">
<font face="Arial, Helvetica, sans-serif" size="2"><input type="radio" name="EducationLevel" value="8">
8</font></td>
<td height="2" width="16%">
<font face="Arial, Helvetica, sans-serif" size="2"><input type="radio" name="EducationLevel" value="9">
9</font></td>
<td height="2" width="16%">
<font face="Arial, Helvetica, sans-serif" size="2"><input type="radio" name="EducationLevel" value="10">
10</font></td>
<td height="2" width="16%">
<font face="Arial, Helvetica, sans-serif" size="2"><input type="radio" name="EducationLevel" value="11">
11</font></td>
<td height="2" width="36%">
<font face="Arial, Helvetica, sans-serif" size="2"><input type="radio" name="EducationLevel" value="12">
12</font>
</td></tr></table>
</td></tr></table>
<p><br>
<b><font face="Arial, Helvetica, sans-serif" size="2">What did you search the Web for?  
</font></b><font face="Arial, Helvetica, sans-serif" size="1">(give us as many details as you can)</font>
<br><font face="Arial, Helvetica, sans-serif" size="3"><textarea name="Search" cols="40" rows="2">
</textarea></font></p>
<p>
<b><font face="Arial, Helvetica, sans-serif" size="2">What word(s) or phrase(s) did you use to search?
</font> </b><font face="Arial, Helvetica, sans-serif" size="1">(eg., tigers, &quot;Tiger Woods&quot;)
</font><br><font face="Arial, Helvetica, sans-serif" size="3"><textarea name="Words" cols="40" rows= "2">
</textarea></font></p>
<p>
<b><font face="Arial, Helvetica, sans-serif" size="2">Which Web search tools did you use? </font>
</b><font face="Arial, Helvetica, sans-serif" size="1"> (eg. Yahooligans, KidsClick)</font><br>
<font face="Arial, Helvetica, sans-serif" size="3"><textarea name="Tools" cols="40" rows="2"> </textarea>
```

Group 1—Reference Forms

```html
</font></p>
<p>
<b><font face="Arial, Helvetica, sans-serif" size="2">Type of help you need</font></b><br>
<dl><dt><dd><font face="Arial, Helvetica, sans-serif" size="2"><input type="radio" name="Help" value="I couldn't find what I was searching for"> I couldn't find what I was searching for</font>
<dd><font face="Arial, Helvetica, sans-serif" size="2"><input type="radio" name="Help" value="I found too many results">I found too many results</font>
<dd><font face="Arial, Helvetica, sans-serif" size="2"><input type="radio" name="Help" value="I'd like to get fewer results">I'd like to get fewer results</font>
<dd><font face="Arial, Helvetica, sans-serif" size="2"><input type="radio" name="Help" value="I'd like to improve my search">I'd like to improve my search</font>
<dd><font face="Arial, Helvetica, sans-serif" size="2"><input type="radio" name="Help" value="I'm not really sure if I searched correctly">I'm not really sure if I searched correctly</font>
<dd><font face="Arial, Helvetica, sans-serif" size="2"><input type="radio" name="Help" value="I'd like to learn how to search better">I'd like to learn how to search better</font>
<br><font face="Arial, Helvetica, sans-serif" size="2"><input type="radio" name="Help" value="Other">
Other  <font size="1">(explain)<br>      
<font size= "3"><textarea name= "HelpOther" cols="30" rows="2"></textarea></font></font></font></dl>
<p> </p>
<table width="700" border="0" cellspacing="10" cellpadding="1"><tr><td width="243"><div align="right"><input type="submit" name="send" value="Send Request"></div></td><td width="204">  
</td><td width="207"><div align="left"><input type="reset" name="clear" value="Clear Form"></div></td></tr>
<tr colspan=3> <td colspan=3>
<table width="500" border="1" height="2" align="center" cellpadding="0" cellspacing="0" bgcolor="ffffff"><tr><td><font size="1" color="#ffffff">.</font></td></tr></table></td></tr><tr>
<td colspan=3><div align="center">
<font face="Arial, Helvetica, sans-serif" size="1"><b>http://</b></font><br> 
<font face="Arial, Helvetica, sans-serif" size="1"><b>&copy; 2002</b></font>
<font face="Arial, Helvetica, sans-serif" size="2"><a href="mailto:">
<b><font size="1">Contact Webmaster</font></b></a></font></div></td></tr>
</table></form>
</body>
</html>
```

Get Help Searching the Web — Perl Script

```perl
#!/usr/local/bin/perl

# ***************************************************************
# ABOVE is where you MUST specify the path to your
# perl interpreter on your Web server.
# Replace /usr/local/bin/perl with your path.
# ***************************************************************

if ($ENV{'REQUEST_METHOD'}eq"GET"){$buffer = $ENV{'QUERY_STRING'};}
    elsif($ENV{'REQUEST_METHOD'}eq"POST"){
        read(STDIN,$buffer,$ENV{'CONTENT_LENGTH'});
    }
$bufferb = $buffer;
#separate the name of the input from its value.
@forminputs = split(/&/, $bufferb);

foreach $forminput (@forminputs)
{
    #separate the name of the input from its value
    ($name, $value) = split(/=/, $forminput);

    #Un-Webify plus signs and %-encoding
    $value =~ tr/+/ /;
    $value =~ s/%([a-fA-F0-9][a-fA-F0-9])/pack("C", hex($1))/eg;

    #stick them in the in array
    $in{$name} = $value;
}
print "Content-type: text/html\n\n";

###############################################
# ABOVE is the required header for a perl script    #
###############################################


#################################################################
# (Below) Email received by library containing user-entered information #
#################################################################

# ***************************************************************
# Here's where you MUST specify the path to your
# email program (probably sendmail) ON your Web server.
# Replace /usr/sbin/sendmail with your path.
# ***************************************************************
```

Group 1—Reference Forms

```perl
open (LMAIL, "|/usr/sbin/sendmail -t");
print LMAIL ("To: $in{LibraryEmail}\n");
print LMAIL ("From: $in{Email}\n");
print LMAIL ("Subject: $in{Form} - patron submission\n");

print LMAIL ("-------------------\nPatron information\n\n");
print LMAIL ("Name:\n $in{Name}\n\n");
print LMAIL ("E-mail Address:\n $in{Email}\n\n");
print LMAIL ("Home Address:\n $in{HomeAddr}\n\n");
print LMAIL ("School:\n $in{School}\n\n");
print LMAIL ("Home Phone/Fax:\n $in{HomePhone}\n\n");
print LMAIL ("Teacher's Name:\n $in{Teacher}\n\n");
print LMAIL ("Grade:\n $in{EducationLevel}\n\n");

print LMAIL ("-------------------\nSubmitted information \n\n");

print LMAIL ("What did you search the Web for?\n $in{Search}\n\n");
print LMAIL ("What word(s) or phrases did you use to search?\n $in{Words}\n\n");
print LMAIL ("Which Web search tools did you use?\n $in{Tools}\n\n");
print LMAIL ("Type of help needed:\n $in{Help}\n\n");
print LMAIL ("Other type of help:\t $in{HelpOther}\n");
print LMAIL ("\n.\n");

###############################################
# Email received by the user confirming form submission #
###############################################

# ************************************************************
# Here's where you MUST specify the path to your
# email program ON your Web server.
# Replace /usr/sbin/sendmail with your path.
# ************************************************************

open (MAIL, "|/usr/sbin/sendmail -t");

# ************************************************************
# Here's where you MAY customize the email
# response to the user. You may change any wording
# on the form.
# ************************************************************

print MAIL<<toEnd;
To: $in{Email}
From: $in{LibraryEmail}
Subject: $in{Form}
```

A librarian will get in contact with you shortly with help for searching the Web.

toEnd
   print MAIL ("\n.\n");

###
Screen response to user after submitting the form
###

print ("<html><head><title>$in{Form}</title></head>");
print ("<body bgcolor=\"ffffff\">");

***
Here's where you MAY change the screen response
the user sees after submitting the form. You may
change any wording between the quotation marks.
***

print ("A librarian will get in contact with you shortly with help for searching the Web.");

***
Here's where you MAY change the name of the link
back to your main page. You may replace Return
to our main page with your own wording.
***

print ("<p> <a href=$in{LibraryURL}>Return to our main page.</a> ");
print ("</body></html>");

Get Help Citing a Source

If you need a citation to a book or magazine article for a bibliography and are having trouble finding all the information, fill in the information you've already found on the form below. We'll do our best to find the missing information for you.

Name (first, last)

E-mail address

Home address (+ city)

School you attend

Home phone/fax (+ areacode)

Teacher's name

What grade are you in?

- ○ 3
- ○ 4
- ○ 5
- ○ 6
- ○ 7
- ○ 8
- ○ 9
- ○ 10
- ○ 11
- ○ 12

Fill in as much information as you can

Title

Author / Artist

Edition

ISBN number

Publisher

Date published

If a magazine article...

Magazine title

Magazine date   **Volume number**   **Issue number**

I found this information cited in... (name of book/magazine)

I need help before... (eg. Oct. 2nd)   ○ Anytime is fine

[Send Request]   [Clear Form]

http://
© 2002 Contact Webmaster

Group 1—Reference Forms

Get Help Citing a Source — HTML Form

```html
<html>
<head><title>Get Help Citing a Source</title></head>
<body bgcolor="#FFFFFF">
<table width="700" border="1" height="85" bgcolor="#ffffff" bordercolor="#000000">
<tr valign="middle" align="center">
<td>
<p>
<font halign=center color="#FFFFFF" face="Arial, Helvetica, sans-serif" size="+3">
<b><i><font color="#000000">Get Help Citing a Source</font></i></b></font></p>
</td></tr></table>
<form method="post" action="http://www.yourLibrary.org/cgi-bin/crg6.pl "><p> </p>
<p>
<font face="Arial, Helvetica, sans-serif" size="2"><b>If you need a citation to a book or magazine article for a bibliography and are having trouble finding <br>all the information, fill in the information you've already found on the form below. We'll do our best <br>to find the missing information for you.</b></font></p>
<p> </p>
<input type="hidden" name="LibraryEmail" value="you@yourLibrary.org">
<input type="hidden" name="LibraryURL" value="http://www.yourLibrary.org">
<input type="hidden" name="Form" value="Get Help Citing a Source">
<p></p>
<table width="407" border="0" cellspacing="4" cellpadding="1">
<tr><td width="202">
<b><font face="Arial, Helvetica, sans-serif" size="2">Name</font></b><font face="Arial, Helvetica, sans-serif" size="1">  (first, last)</font><br><font face="Arial, Helvetica, sans-serif" size="2">
<input type="text" name="Name" size="25"></font></td>
<td width="189">
<b><font face="Arial, Helvetica, sans-serif" size="2">E-mail address<br></font></b><font face="Arial, Helvetica, sans-serif" size="2"><input type="text" name="Email" size="25"></font></td></tr>
<tr><td width="202" height="2">
<b><font face="Arial, Helvetica, sans-serif" size="2">Home address</font> </b><font face="Arial, Helvetica, sans-serif" size="1"> (+ city)</font><br><font face="Arial, Helvetica, sans-serif" size= "2">
<input type="text" name="HomeAddr" size="25"></font></td>
<td width="189" height="2">
<b><font face="Arial, Helvetica, sans-serif" size="2">School you attend<br></font></b><font face="Arial, Helvetica, sans-serif" size="2"><input type="text" name="School" size="25"></font></td></tr>
<tr><td width="202" height="2">
<b><font face="Arial, Helvetica, sans-serif" size="2">Home phone/fax</font><font face="Arial, Helvetica, sans-serif" size="1">  (+ areacode)</font><br><font face="Arial, Helvetica, sans-serif" size= "2">
<input type="text" name="HomePhone" size="25"></font></td>
<td width="189" height="2">
<b><font face="Arial, Helvetica, sans-serif" size="2">Teacher's name<br></font></b><font face="Arial, Helvetica, sans-serif" size="2"><input type="text" name="Teacher" size="25"></font></td></tr>
<tr><td width="391" colspan="2" height="48">
```

```html
<b><font face="Arial, Helvetica, sans-serif" size="2">What grade are you in?</b><br></font>
<table width="87%" border="0" cellspacing="4" cellpadding="0"><tr><td height="8" width="16%">
<font face="Arial, Helvetica, sans-serif" size="2"><input type="radio" name="EducationLevel" value="3">
3 </font></td>
<td height="8" width="16%">
<font face="Arial, Helvetica, sans-serif" size="2"><input type="radio" name="EducationLevel" value="4">
4</font></td>
<td height="8" width="16%">
<font face="Arial, Helvetica, sans-serif" size="2"><input type="radio" name="EducationLevel" value="5">
5</font></td>
<td height="8" width="16%">
<font face="Arial, Helvetica, sans-serif" size="2"><input type="radio" name="EducationLevel" value="6">
6</font></td>
<td height="8" width="36%">
<font face="Arial, Helvetica, sans-serif" size="2"><input type="radio" name="EducationLevel" value="7">
7</font></td></tr>
<tr><td height="2" width="16%">
<font face="Arial, Helvetica, sans-serif" size="2"><input type="radio" name="EducationLevel" value="8">
8</font></td>
<td height="2" width="16%">
<font face="Arial, Helvetica, sans-serif" size="2"><input type="radio" name="EducationLevel" value="9">
9</font></td>
<td height="2" width="16%">
<font face="Arial, Helvetica, sans-serif" size="2"><input type="radio" name="EducationLevel" value="10">
10</font></td>
<td height="2" width="16%">
<font face="Arial, Helvetica, sans-serif" size="2"><input type="radio" name="EducationLevel" value="11">
11</font></td>
<td height="2" width="36%">
<font face="Arial, Helvetica, sans-serif" size="2"><input type="radio" name="EducationLevel" value="12">
12</font>
</td></tr></table>
</td></tr></table>
<p><br><p>
<font face="Arial, Helvetica, sans-serif" size="3"><b>Fill in as much information as you can</b></font></p><p>
<font face="Arial, Helvetica, sans-serif" size="2"><b>Title</b><br><font size="3"><input type="text"
name="Title" size="40"></font></font></p>
<p>
<font face="Arial, Helvetica, sans-serif" size="2"><b>Author / Artist</b><br><font size="3">
<input type="text" name="Author" size="40"></font></font></p>
<table width="209" border="0" cellpadding="0" cellspacing="0">
<tr><td width="92">
<font face="Arial, Helvetica, sans-serif" size="2"><b>Edition</b><br><font size="3"><input type="text"
name="Edition" size="10"></font></font></td>
<td width="107">
<font face="Arial, Helvetica, sans-serif" size="2"><b>ISBN number</b><br><font size="3"><input type= "text"
```

```html
name="ISBN" size="10"></font></font>
</td></tr></table>
<p>
<font face="Arial, Helvetica, sans-serif" size="2"><b>Publisher</b><br><font size="3"><input type= "text"
name="Publisher" size="40"></font></font></p>
<p>
<font face="Arial, Helvetica, sans-serif" size="2"><b>Date published</b><br><font size="3"><input type= "text"
name="PublisherDate" size="40"></font></font></p>
<p> </p><p>
<font face="Arial, Helvetica, sans-serif" size="3"><b>If a magazine article...</b></font></p>
<p>
<font face="Arial, Helvetica, sans-serif" size="2"><b>Magazine title</b><br><font size="3"><input type= "text"
name="MagName" size="40"></font></font></p>
<table width="600" border="0" cellspacing="0" cellpadding="0">
<tr><td width="115" height="11">
<font face="Arial, Helvetica, sans-serif" size="2"><b>Magazine date</b><br><font size="3"><input type="text"
name="MagazineDate" size="10"></font></font></td>
<td width="125" height="11">
<font face="Arial, Helvetica, sans-serif" size="2"><b>Volume number</b><br><font size="3">
<input type="text" name="VolNum" size="10"></font></font></td>
<td width="360" height="11">
<font face="Arial, Helvetica, sans-serif" size="2"><b>Issue number</b><br><font size="3"><input  type="text"
name="IssueNum" size="10"></font></font>
</td></tr></table>
<p> </p>
<p>
<font face="Arial, Helvetica, sans-serif" size="2"><b>I found this information cited in... </b>
<font face="Arial, Helvetica, sans-serif" size="1"> (name of book/magazine)</font><b><br></b>
<font  face="Arial, Helvetica, sans-serif" size="3"><textarea name= "Cited" cols="40" rows="2"></textarea>
</font></font><br></p>
<p>
<font face="Arial, Helvetica, sans-serif" size="2"><b>I need help before... </b><font face="Arial, Helvetica,
sans-serif" size="1"> (eg. Oct. 2nd)</font><br><font size="3"><input type="text" name="NeedBefore"
size="15">      </font><input type="radio" name="TimeIssue" value="Time is not
an issue">Anytime is fine</font></p>
<p> </p>
<table width="700" border="0" cellspacing="10" cellpadding="1"><tr><td width="249"><div align="right">
<input type="submit" name="send" value="Send Request"></div></td><td width="198"> </td>
<td width="207"><div align="left"><input type="reset" name="clear" value="Clear Form"></div></td></tr>
<tr colspan=3><td colspan=3>
<table width="500" border="1" height="2" align="center" cellpadding="0" cellspacing="0" bgcolor="#ffffff"
bordercolor="#000000"><tr><td><font size="1" color="#ffffff">.</font></td></tr></table></td></tr><tr>
<td colspan=3><div align="center">
<font face="Arial, Helvetica, sans-serif" size="1"><b>http://</b></font><br><font size="2"> 
<font face="Arial, Helvetica, sans-serif" size="1"><b>&copy; 2002</b></font></font>
```

```html
<font face="Arial, Helvetica, sans-serif" size="2"><a href="mailto:">
<b><font size="1">Contact Webmaster</font></b></a><font></div></td></tr>
</table></form>
</body>
</html>
```

Group 1—Reference Forms

67

Get Help Citing a Source — Perl Script

```perl
#!/usr/local/bin/perl

# ***************************************************
# ABOVE is where you MUST specify the path to your
# perl interpreter on your Web server.
# Replace /usr/local/bin/perl with your path.
# ***************************************************

if ($ENV{'REQUEST_METHOD'}eq"GET"){$buffer = $ENV{'QUERY_STRING'};}
    elsif($ENV{'REQUEST_METHOD'}eq"POST"){
        read(STDIN,$buffer,$ENV{'CONTENT_LENGTH'});
    }
$bufferb = $buffer;
#separate the name of the input from its value.
@forminputs = split(/&/, $bufferb);

foreach $forminput (@forminputs)
{
    #separate the name of the input from its value
    ($name, $value) = split(/=/, $forminput);

    #Un-Webify plus signs and %-encoding
    $value =~ tr/+/ /;
    $value =~ s/%([a-fA-F0-9][a-fA-F0-9])/pack("C", hex($1))/eg;

    #stick them in the in array
    $in{$name} = $value;
}
print "Content-type: text/html\n\n";

#############################################
# ABOVE is the required header for a perl script    #
#############################################


###################################################
# (Below) Email received by library containing user-entered information #
###################################################


# ***************************************************
# Here's where you MUST specify the path to your
# email program (probably sendmail) ON your Web server.
# Replace /usr/sbin/sendmail with your path.
# ***************************************************
```

```perl
open (LMAIL, "|/usr/sbin/sendmail -t");
print LMAIL ("To: $in{LibraryEmail}\n");
print LMAIL ("From: $in{Email}\n");
print LMAIL ("Subject: $in{Form} - patron submission\n");

print LMAIL ("-------------------\nPatron information\n\n");


print LMAIL ("Name:\n $in{Name}\n\n");
print LMAIL ("E-mail Address:\n $in{Email}\n\n");
print LMAIL ("Home Address:\n $in{HomeAddr}\n\n");
print LMAIL ("School:\n $in{School}\n\n");
print LMAIL ("Home Phone/Fax:\n $in{HomePhone}\n\n");
print LMAIL ("Teacher's Name:\n $in{Teacher}\n\n");
print LMAIL ("Grade:\n $in{EducationLevel}\n\n");

print LMAIL ("-------------------\nSubmitted information \n\n");

print LMAIL ("Title:\n $in{Title}\n\n");
print LMAIL ("Author / Artist:\n $in{Author}\n\n");
print LMAIL ("Edition:\n $in{Edition}\n\n");
print LMAIL ("ISBN number:\n $in{ISBN}\n\n");
print LMAIL ("Publisher:\n $in{Publisher}\n\n");
print LMAIL ("Date of publication:\n $in{PublisherDate}\n\n");
print LMAIL ("-------------------\nIf a Magazine Article... \n\n");
print LMAIL ("Magazine title:\n $in{MagName}\n\n");
print LMAIL Magazine date:\n $in{MagazineDate}\n\n");
print LMAIL ("Volume number:\n $in{VolNum}\n\n");
print LMAIL ("Issue number:\n $in{IssueNum}\n\n");
print LMAIL ("The above information was cited in:\n $in{Cited}\n\n");
print LMAIL ("I need it before:\n $in{NeedBefore} $in{TimeIssue}\n\n");
print LMAIL ("\n.\n");

################################################
# Email received by the user confirming form submission #
################################################

# **********************************************************
# Here's where you MUST specify the path to your
# email program ON your Web server.
# Replace /usr/sbin/sendmail with your path.
# **********************************************************

open (MAIL, "|/usr/sbin/sendmail -t");
```

Group 1—Reference Forms

```
# **************************************************
# Here's where you MAY customize the email
# response to the user. You may change any wording
# on the form.
# **************************************************

print MAIL<<toEnd;
To: $in{Email}
From: $in{LibraryEmail}
Subject: $in{Form}

Thanks for sending us your citation request.\n\n
We'll do our best to send you a completed citation within 48 hours.

toEnd
    print MAIL ("\n.\n");



##########################################
# Screen response to user after submitting the form  #
##########################################

print ("<html><head><title>$in{Form}</title></head>");
print ("<body bgcolor=\"ffffff\">");

# **************************************************
# Here's where you MAY change the screen response
# the user sees after submitting the form. You may
# change any wording between the quotation marks.
# **************************************************

print ("Thanks for sending us your citation request.<p>
We'll do our best to send you a completed citation within 48 hours.");

# **************************************************
# Here's where you MAY change the name of the link
# back to your main page. You may replace Return
# to our main page with your own wording.
# **************************************************

print ("<p><center><a href=$in{LibraryURL}>Return to our main page.</a></center>");
print ("</body></html>");
```

69

Get Help With Your Homework

Do you need help with homework, research papers, or personal projects but don't have the time to meet with a librarian? We'll provide you with factual information and help you cite your sources correctly... all via e-mail.

Name (first, last)

E-mail address

Home address (+ city)

School you attend

Home phone/fax (+ areacode)

Teacher's name

What grade are you in?
- ○ 3   ○ 4   ○ 5   ○ 6   ○ 7
- ○ 8   ○ 9   ○ 10 ○ 11 ○ 12

What type of assignment do you need help with?
- ○ Homework   ○ School research paper   ○ Non-school personal research
- ○ Other (explain)

What is your assignment? (give us as many details as you can)

For sources, do you need to use? (select any/all)
- ○ Books   ○ Magazines   ○ Web sites   ○ Pictures / Maps
- ○ Other (explain)

Type of help you need
- ○ I'm not quite sure how to start
- ○ I'd like to find specific facts / information
- ○ I'd like to find relevant books / magazines / Web sites
- ○ I'd like to organize the information I find
- ○ I'd like to create a bibliography
- ○ I'd like to learn how to do homework assignments faster and easier
- ○ Other (explain)

I need help before... (eg. Oct. 2nd)

○ Anytime is fine

Send Request   Clear Form

http://
© 2002 Contact Webmaster

Get Help With Your Homework — HTML Form

```html
<html>
<head><title>Get Help With Your Homework</title>
</head>
<body bgcolor="#FFFFFF">
<table width="700" border="1" height="85" bgcolor="ffffff"><tr valign="middle" align="center"><td>
<p>
<font halign=center color="#000000" face="Arial, Helvetica, sans-serif" size="+3">
<b><i>Get Help With Your Homework</i></b></font></p>
</td></tr></table>
<form method="post" action="http://www.yourLibrary.org/cgi-bin/crg2.pl"><p> </p>
<p>
<b><font size="2" face="Arial, Helvetica, sans-serif">Do you need help with homework, research papers, or personal projects but don't have the time to meet<br> with a librarian? We'll provide you with factual information and help you cite your sources <br>correctly... all via e-mail.</font></b></p>
<p> </p>
<input type="hidden" name="LibraryEmail" value="you@yourLibrary.org">
<input type="hidden" name="LibraryURL" value="http://www.yourLibrary.org">
<input type="hidden" name="Form" value="Get Help With Your Homework">
<p></p>
<table width="407" border="0" cellspacing="4" cellpadding="1">
<tr><td width="202">
<b><font face="Arial, Helvetica, sans-serif" size="2">Name</font></b><font face="Arial, Helvetica, sans-serif" size="1">  (first, last)</font><br><font face="Arial, Helvetica, sans-serif" size="2">
<input type="text" name="Name" size="25"></font></td>
<td width="189">
<b><font face="Arial, Helvetica, sans-serif" size="2">E-mail address<br></font></b><font face="Arial, Helvetica, sans-serif" size="2"><input type="text" name="Email" size="25"></font></td></tr>
<tr><td width="202" height="2">
<b><font face="Arial, Helvetica, sans-serif" size="2">Home address</font> </b><font face="Arial, Helvetica, sans-serif" size="1"> (+ city)</font><br><font face="Arial, Helvetica, sans-serif" size="2">
<input type="text" name="HomeAddr" size="25"></font></td>
<td width="189" height="2">
<b><font face="Arial, Helvetica, sans-serif" size="2">School you attend<br></font></b><font face="Arial, Helvetica, sans-serif" size="2"><input type="text" name="School" size="25"></font></td></tr>
<tr><td width="202" height="2">
<b><font face="Arial, Helvetica, sans-serif" size="2">Home phone/fax</font> </b><font face="Arial, Helvetica, sans-serif" size="1"> (+ areacode)</font><br><font face="Arial, Helvetica, sans-serif" size="2"><input type="text" name="HomePhone" size="25"></font></td>
<td width="189" height="2">
<b><font face="Arial, Helvetica, sans-serif" size="2">Teacher's name<br></font></b><font face="Arial, Helvetica, sans-serif" size="2"><input type="text" name="Teacher" size="25"></font></td></tr>
<tr><td width="391" colspan="2" height="48">
<b><font face="Arial, Helvetica, sans-serif" size="2">What grade are you in?<br></font>
```

Group 1—Reference Forms

```html
<table width="87%" border="0" cellspacing="4" cellpadding="0"><tr><td height="8" width="16%">
<font face="Arial, Helvetica, sans-serif" size="2"><input type="radio" name="EducationLevel" value="3">
3</font></td>
<td height="8" width="16%">
<font face="Arial, Helvetica, sans-serif" size="2"><input type="radio" name="EducationLevel" value="4">
4</font></td>
<td height="8" width="16%">
<font face="Arial, Helvetica, sans-serif" size="2"><input type="radio" name="EducationLevel" value="5">
5</font></td>
<td height="8" width="16%">
<font face="Arial, Helvetica, sans-serif" size="2"><input type="radio" name="EducationLevel" value="6">
6</font></td>
<td height="8" width="36%">
<font face="Arial, Helvetica, sans-serif" size="2"><input type="radio" name="EducationLevel" value="7">
7</font></td></tr>
<tr><td height="2" width="16%">
<font face="Arial, Helvetica, sans-serif" size="2"><input type="radio" name="EducationLevel" value="8">
8</font></td>
<td height="2" width="16%">
<font face="Arial, Helvetica, sans-serif" size="2"><input type="radio" name="EducationLevel" value="9">
9</font></td>
<td height="2" width="16%">
<font face="Arial, Helvetica, sans-serif" size="2"><input type="radio" name="EducationLevel" value="10">
10</font></td>
<td height="2" width="16%">
<font face="Arial, Helvetica, sans-serif" size="2"><input type="radio" name="EducationLevel" value="11">
11</font></td>
<td height="2" width="36%">
<font face="Arial, Helvetica, sans-serif" size="2"><input type="radio" name="EducationLevel" value="12">
12</font>
</td></tr></table>
</td></tr></table>
<p><br>
<b><font face="Arial, Helvetica, sans-serif" size="2">What type of assignment do you need help with?<br>
</b></font>
<input type="radio" name="ResearchType" value="Homework">Homework   
<input type="radio" name="ResearchType" value="School research paper">School research paper
   
<input type="radio" name="ResearchType" value="Non-school personal research">Non-school personal
research   <br>
<input type="radio" name="ResearchType" value="Other">Other   <font size="1">(explain)
 <font size="2"><input type="text" name="OtherResearchType" size="10"></font></font></font></p>
<p>
<font face="Arial, Helvetica, sans-serif" size="2"><b>What is your assignment?  </b><font
face="Arial, Helvetica, sans-serif" size="1">(give us as many details as you can)<br><font size="3">
```

```html
<textarea name="Topic" cols="40" rows="10"></textarea></font></font></font></p>
<p>
<b><font face="Arial, Helvetica, sans-serif" size="2">For sources, do you need to use?</font></b>
<font face="Arial, Helvetica, sans-serif" size="2">  <font face="Arial, Helvetica, sans-serif" size="1"> (select any/all)</font><br>
<input type="radio" name="B" value="Books">Books   
<input type="radio" name="M" value="Magazines">Magazines   
<input type="radio" name="WS" value="Web sites">Web sites   
<input type="radio" name="PM" value="Pictures / Maps">Pictures / Maps   <br>
<input type="radio" name="Sources" value="Other">Other   <font size="1">(explain)
 <font size="2"><input type="text" name="OtherSources" size="10"></font></font></font></p>
<p>
<b><font face="Arial, Helvetica, sans-serif" size="2">Type of help you need</font></b></p>
<dl><dt>
<dd><font face="Arial, Helvetica, sans-serif" size="2"><input type="radio" name="Help" value="I'm not quite sure how to start">I'm not quite sure how to start</font>
<dd><font face="Arial, Helvetica, sans-serif" size="2"><input type="radio" name="Help" value="I'd like to find specific facts / information">I'd like to find specific facts / information</font>
<dd><font face="Arial, Helvetica, sans-serif" size="2"><input type="radio" name="Help" value="I'd like to find relevant books / magazines / Web sites">I'd like to find relevant books / magazines / Web sites</font><br>
<dd><font face="Arial, Helvetica, sans-serif" size="2"><input type="radio" name="Help" value="I'd like to organize the information I find">I'd like to organize the information I find</font>
<dd><font face="Arial, Helvetica, sans-serif" size="2"><input type="radio" name="Help" value="I'd like to create a bibliography">I'd like to create a bibliography</font>
<dd><font face="Arial, Helvetica, sans-serif" size="2"><input type="radio" name="Help" value="I'd like to learn how to do homework assignments faster and easier">I'd like to learn how to do homework assignments faster and easier</font><br>
<dd><font face="Arial, Helvetica, sans-serif" size="2"><input type="radio" name="Help" value="Other">
Other  <font size="1">(explain)<br><font size="2">        
<font size="3"><textarea name="HelpOther" cols="30" rows="2"></textarea></font> </font></font></font></dl>
<dl><dt><font face="Arial, Helvetica, sans-serif" size="2"><b>I need help before... </b><font face="Arial, Helvetica, sans-serif" size="1"> (eg. Oct. 2nd)</font><br><font size="3"><input type="text" name="NeedBefore" size="15">     </font><input type="radio" name="TimeIssue" value="Time is not an issue">Anytime is fine</font></dt>
</dl>
<p> </p>
<table width="700" border="0" cellspacing="10" cellpadding="1"><tr><td width="240"><div align="right">
<input type="submit" name="send" value="Send Request"></div></td><td width="207"> </td>
<td width="207"><div align="left"><input type="reset" name="clear" value="Clear Form"></div></td></tr>
<tr colspan=3><td colspan=3>
<table width="500" border="1" height="2" align="center" cellpadding="0" cellspacing="0"
bgcolor="ffffff"><tr><td><font size="1" color="#ffffff">.</font></td></tr></table></td></tr><tr>
<td colspan=3><div align="center">
<font face="Arial, Helvetica, sans-serif" size="1"><b>http://</b></font><br><font size="2"> 
<font face="Arial, Helvetica, sans-serif" size="1"><b>&copy; 2002</b></font></font>
```

```html
<font face="Arial, Helvetica, sans-serif" size="2"><a href="mailto:">
<b><font size="1">Contact Webmaster</font></b></a></font></div></td></tr>
</table></form>
</body>
</html>
```

Get Help With Your Homework — Perl Script

```perl
#!/usr/local/bin/perl

# ***************************************************************
# ABOVE is where you MUST specify the path to your
# perl interpreter on your Web server.
# Replace /usr/local/bin/perl with your path.
# ***************************************************************

if ($ENV{'REQUEST_METHOD'}eq"GET"){$buffer = $ENV{'QUERY_STRING'};}
    elsif($ENV{'REQUEST_METHOD'}eq"POST"){
        read(STDIN,$buffer,$ENV{'CONTENT_LENGTH'});
    }
$bufferb = $buffer;
#separate the name of the input from its value.
@forminputs = split(/&/, $bufferb);

foreach $forminput (@forminputs)
{
    #separate the name of the input from its value
    ($name, $value) = split(/=/, $forminput);

    #Un-Webify plus signs and %-encoding
    $value =~ tr/+/ /;
    $value =~ s/%([a-fA-F0-9][a-fA-F0-9])/pack("C", hex($1))/eg;

    #stick them in the in array
    $in{$name} = $value;
}
print "Content-type: text/html\n\n";

###############################################
# ABOVE is the required header for a perl script    #
###############################################


#####################################################
# (Below) Email received by library containing user-entered information #
#####################################################


# ***************************************************************
# Here's where you MUST specify the path to your
# email program (probably sendmail) ON your Web server.
# Replace /usr/sbin/sendmail with your path.
# ***************************************************************
```

Group 1—Reference Forms

```
open (LMAIL, "|/usr/sbin/sendmail -t");
print LMAIL ("To: $in{LibraryEmail}\n");
print LMAIL ("From: $in{Email}\n");
print LMAIL ("Subject: $in{Form} - patron submission\n");

print LMAIL ("------------------\nPatron information\n\n");


print LMAIL ("Name:\n $in{Name}\n\n");
print LMAIL ("E-mail Address:\n $in{Email}\n\n");
print LMAIL ("Home Address:\n $in{HomeAddr}\n\n");
print LMAIL ("School:\n $in{School}\n\n");
print LMAIL ("Home Phone/Fax:\n $in{HomePhone}\n\n");
print LMAIL ("Teacher's Name:\n $in{Teacher}\n\n");
print LMAIL ("Grade:\n $in{EducationLevel}\n\n");

print LMAIL ("------------------\nSubmitted information \n\n");

print LMAIL ("What type of assignment do you need help with?\n $in{ResearchType}\n\n");
print LMAIL ("Other type:\n $in{OtherResearchType}\n\n");
print LMAIL ("What is your homework assignment?\n $in{Topic}\n\n");
print LMAIL ("For sources you need to use:\n $in{B}, $in{M}, $in{WS}, $in{PM}, $in{Sources},
$in{OtherSources}\n\n");

print LMAIL ("Type of help needed:\n $in{Help}\n\n");
print LMAIL ("Other type of help:\n $in{HelpOther}\n\n");
print LMAIL ("I need help before:\n $in{NeedBefore} $in{TimeIssue}\n\n");
print LMAIL ("\n.\n");

##############################################
# Email received by the user confirming form submission #
##############################################

# ***********************************************************
# Here's where you MUST specify the path to your
# email program ON your Web server.
# Replace /usr/sbin/sendmail with your path.
# ***********************************************************

open (MAIL, "|/usr/sbin/sendmail -t");

# ***********************************************************
# Here's where you MAY customize the email
# response to the user. You may change any wording
# on the form.
```

```
# **************************************************

print MAIL<<toEnd;
To: $in{Email}
From: $in{LibraryEmail}
Subject: $in{Form}

Thanks for sending us your request for homework help. A librarian will contact you shortly.
toEnd
    print MAIL ("\n.\n");

##########################################
# Screen response to user after submitting the form  #
##########################################

print ("<html><head><title>$in{Form}</title></head>");
print ("<body bgcolor=\"ffffff\">");


# **************************************************
# Here's where you MAY change the screen response
# the user sees after submitting the form. You may
# change any wording between the quotation marks.
# **************************************************

print ("Thanks for sending us your request for homework help. A librarian will contact you shortly");

# **************************************************
# Here's where you MAY change the name of the link
# back to your main page. You may replace Return
# to our main page with your own wording.
# **************************************************

print ("<p><center><a href=$in{LibraryURL}>Return to our main page.</a></center>");
print ("</body></html>");
```

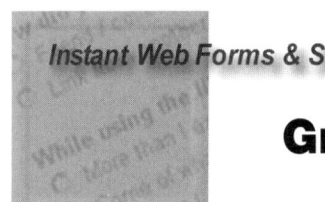

Group 2 — Library Instruction Forms / Surveys

In this section you'll find two Web-based forms and two surveys. One form lets students request a face-to-face meeting with library staff in order to get help with their school assignments. The second form helps students learn about library classes that are being offered on days, and at times, they can attend. The surveys will enable teachers, parents, and students to give your staff feedback on the current training sessions you offer as well as input on new training sessions that they need you to develop.

Meet With a Librarian
Do students need help with school assignments, research papers, or personal research projects but you're often too busy to help them the moment they show up at your desk? Students can use this form to arrange, via e-mail or phone, to meet and talk with a librarian at a mutually agreeable time. Make sure to place a link to this form on your Web site's reference page.

Find a Class
Do students want to take a class on how to use the library, search the Web, or use the library's computers but they don't know if the library offers the classes they're interested in on a date/at a time that's convenient for them? Have students fill out this form and then e-mail them a list of relevant library classes that are scheduled on (or close to) the dates/times they've indicated. Be sure to put a link to this form on your Web site's library instruction and home pages.

Training Interests Survey *(teachers/librarians/parents)*
Encourage teachers, homeschooling parents, and other librarians to fill out this brief survey to help you get an idea of how effective your current library training sessions are. You'll also be able to find out any new training sessions that they would like you to develop and when they'd like the classes offered. Finally, you can find out how teachers and parents learn about currently offered classes as well as how you can notify them of such opportunities in the future. Place a link to this survey periodically on your Web site's library instruction page.

"What Do You Want to Learn?" Survey
Encourage students to fill out this short survey to help you get an idea of the kinds of learning needs your students have. Use the results to plan new training sessions and schedule them when students want them offered. Place a link to this survey periodically on your Web site's library instruction page.

Meet With a Librarian

Do you need help with homework, research papers, or personal projects? We'll arrange, via e-mail or phone, to meet with you.

Name (first, last)

E-mail address

Home address (+ city)

School you attend

Home phone/fax (+ areacode)

Teacher's name

What grade are you in?
- ○ 3 ○ 4 ○ 5 ○ 6 ○ 7
- ○ 8 ○ 9 ○ 10 ○ 11 ○ 12

Dates / times you are able to meet

Date _____ Time _____
Date _____ Time _____
Date _____ Time _____

We need to meet before... (eg. Oct. 2nd)

_____ ○ Anytime is fine

How can we help you? (give us as many details as you can)

What library resources have you already used / checked? (select any/all)
- ○ Online / Card catalog ○ Reference materials ○ Books
- ○ Magazine articles ○ CD-ROMs / Online databases ○ Other (explain) _____

[Send Request] [Clear Form]

http://

© 2002 Contact Webmaster

Meet With a Librarian — HTML Form

```html
<html>
<head><title>Meet With a Librarian</title></head>
<body bgcolor="#FFFFFF">
<table width="700" border="1" height="85" bgcolor="ffffff"><tr valign="middle" align="center"><td>
<p>
<font halign=center color="#000000" face="Arial, Helvetica, sans-serif" size="+3">
<b><i>Meet With a Librarian</i></b></font></p>
</td></tr></table>
<form method="post" action="http://www.yourLibrary.org/cgi-bin/cli1.pl"><p> </p>
<p>
<font face="Arial, Helvetica, sans-serif" size="2"><b>Do you need help with homework, research papers, or personal projects? We'll arrange, via e-mail or phone, <br>to meet with you.</b></font></p>
<p> </p>
<input type="hidden" name="LibraryEmail" value="you@yourLibrary.org">
<input type="hidden" name="LibraryURL" value="http://www.yourLibrary.org">
<input type="hidden" name="Form" value="Meet With a Librarian"><p></p>
<table width="407" border="0" cellspacing="4" cellpadding="1">
<tr><td width="202">
<b><font face="Arial, Helvetica, sans-serif" size="2">Name</font></b><font face="Arial, Helvetica, sans-serif" size="1">  (first, last)</font><br><font face="Arial, Helvetica, sans-serif" size="2">
<input type="text" name="Name" size="25"></font></td>
<td width="189">
<b><font face="Arial, Helvetica, sans-serif" size="2">E-mail address<br></font></b><font face="Arial, Helvetica, sans-serif" size="2"><input type="text" name="Email" size="25"></font></td></tr>
<tr><td width="202" height="2">
<b><font face="Arial, Helvetica, sans-serif" size="2">Home address</font>  </b><font face="Arial, Helvetica, sans-serif" size="1">(+ city)</font><br><font face="Arial, Helvetica, sans-serif" size="2">
<input type="text" name="HomeAddr" size="25"></font></td>
<td width="189" height="2">
<b><font face="Arial, Helvetica, sans-serif" size="2">School you attend<br></font></b><font face="Arial, Helvetica, sans-serif" size="2"><input type="text" name="School" size="25"></font></td></tr>
<tr><td width="202" height="2">
<b><font face="Arial, Helvetica, sans-serif" size="2">Home phone/fax</font></b><font face="Arial, Helvetica, sans-serif" size="1">  (+ areacode)</font><br><font face="Arial, Helvetica, sans-serif" size="2"><input type="text" name="HomePhone" size="25"></font></td>
<td width="189" height="2">
<b><font face="Arial, Helvetica, sans-serif" size="2">Teacher's name<br></font></b><font face="Arial, Helvetica, sans-serif" size="2"><input type="text" name="Teacher" size="25"></font></td></tr>
<tr><td width="391" colspan="2" height="48">
<b><font face="Arial, Helvetica, sans-serif" size="2">What grade are you in?</font></b><br><font face= "Arial, Helvetica, sans-serif" size="2"> </font>
<table width="87%" border="0" cellspacing="4" cellpadding="0"><tr><td height="8" width="16%">
<font face="Arial, Helvetica, sans-serif" size="2"><input type="radio" name="EducationLevel" value="3">
```

```html
3</font></td>
<td height="8" width="16%">
<font face="Arial, Helvetica, sans-serif" size="2"><input type="radio" name="EducationLevel" value="4">
4</font></td>
<td height="8" width="16%">
<font face="Arial, Helvetica, sans-serif" size="2"><input type="radio" name="EducationLevel" value="5">
5</font></td>
<td height="8" width="16%">
<font face="Arial, Helvetica, sans-serif" size="2"><input type="radio" name="EducationLevel" value="6">
6</font></td>
<td height="8" width="36%">
<font face="Arial, Helvetica, sans-serif" size="2"><input type="radio" name="EducationLevel" value="7">
7</font></td></tr>
<tr><td height="2" width="16%">
<font face="Arial, Helvetica, sans-serif" size="2"><input type="radio" name="EducationLevel" value="8">
8</font></td>
<td height="2" width="16%">
<font face="Arial, Helvetica, sans-serif" size="2"><input type="radio" name="EducationLevel" value="9">
9</font></td>
<td height="2" width="16%">
<font face="Arial, Helvetica, sans-serif" size="2"><input type="radio" name="EducationLevel" value="10">
10</font></td>
<td height="2" width="16%">
<font face="Arial, Helvetica, sans-serif" size="2"><input type="radio" name="EducationLevel" value="11">
11</font></td>
<td height="2" width="36%">
<font face="Arial, Helvetica, sans-serif" size="2"><input type="radio" name="EducationLevel" value="12">
12</font>
</td></tr></table>
</td></tr></table>
<p><br>
<b><font face="Arial, Helvetica, sans-serif" size="2">Dates / times you are able to meet  <br>
</font></b>
<font face="Arial, Helvetica, sans-serif" size="2">Date</font><font size="3" face="Arial, Helvetica, sans-serif"><input type="text" name="FirstDateToMeet" size="15"></font>      
<font face="Arial, Helvetica, sans-serif" size="2">Time</font><font face="Arial, Helvetica, sans-serif" size="3"><input type="text" name="FirstTimeToMeet" size="15"></font><br>
<font face="Arial, Helvetica, sans-serif" size="2">Date</font><font face="Arial, Helvetica, sans-serif" size="3"><input type="text" name="SecondDateToMeet" size="15"></font>      
<font face="Arial, Helvetica, sans-serif" size="2">Time</font><font face="Arial, Helvetica, sans-serif" size="3">input type="text" name="SecondTimeToMeet" size="15"></font><br>
<font face="Arial, Helvetica, sans-serif" size="2">Date</font><font face="Arial, Helvetica, sans-serif" size="3"><input type="text" name="ThirdDateToMeet" size="15"></font>       
<font face="Arial, Helvetica, sans-serif"size="2">Time</font><font face="Arial, Helvetica, sans-serif" size="3"><input type="text" name="ThirdTimeToMeet" size="15"></font></p>
```

```html
<p>
<font face="Arial, Helvetica, sans-serif" size="2"> <b>We need to meet before...<font size="1">
 </font></b><font face="Arial, Helvetica, sans-serif" size="1"> (eg. Oct. 2nd)</font><br>
<font size="3" face="Arial, Helvetica, sans-serif"><input type="text" name="MeetBefore" size="15">
</font>     <font face="Arial, Helvetica, sans-serif" size="2"><input type="radio"
name="TimeIssue" value="Anytime is fine">Anytime is fine</font></font></p>
<p>
<b><font face="Arial, Helvetica, sans-serif" size="2">How can we help you? </font></b><font face="Arial,
Helvetica, sans-serif" size="1"> (give us as many details as you can)</font><br>
<font face="Arial, Helvetica, sans-serif" size="3"><textarea name="HowCanWeHelp" cols="40" rows="10">
</textarea></font></p>
<p>
<b><font face="Arial, Helvetica, sans-serif" size="2">What library resources have you already used /
checked?  </font></b><font face="Arial, Helvetica, sans-serif" size="1"> (select any/all)</font><br>
<table width="711" border="0" cellspacing="0" cellpadding="0"><tr><td width="181">
<font face="Arial, Helvetica, sans-serif" size="2"><input type="radio" name="OCC" value="Online / card
catalog">Online / Card catalog</font></td>
<td width="215">
<font face="Arial, Helvetica, sans-serif" size="2"><input type="radio" name="RM" value="Reference
materials">Reference materials</font></td>
<td width="315">
<font face="Arial, Helvetica, sans-serif" size="2"><input type="radio" name="B" value="Books">Books</font>
</td></tr>
<tr><td width="181">
<font face="Arial, Helvetica, sans-serif" size="2"><input type="radio" name="MA" value="Magazine
articles">Magazine articles</font></td>
<td width="215">
<font face="Arial, Helvetica, sans-serif" size="2"><input type="radio" name="CD" value="CD-ROMs / Online
databases">CD-ROMs / Online databases</font></td>
<td width="315">
<font face="Arial, Helvetica, sans-serif" size="2"><input type="radio" name="O" value="Other">Other
  <font size="1">(explain)</font>  <input type="text" name="OtherChecked" size="15">
</font></td></tr></table>
<p> </p>
<p><br></p>
<p></p>
<table width="700" border="0" cellspacing="10" cellpadding="1"><tr><td width="242"><div align="right">
<input type="submit" name="send" value="Send Request"></div></td><td width="205"> </td>
<td width="207"><div align="left"><input type="reset" name="clear" value="Clear Form"></div></td>
/tr><tr colspan=3><td colspan=3>
<table width="500" border="1" height="2" align="center" cellpadding="0" cellspacing="0" bgcolor="ffffff">
<tr><td><font size="1" color="#ffffff">.</font></td></tr></table></td></tr><tr><td colspan=3>
<div align="center">
<font face="Arial, Helvetica, sans-serif" size="1"><b>http://</b></font><br> 
<font face="Arial, Helvetica, sans-serif" size="1"><b>&copy; 2002</b></font>
```

```html
<font face="Arial, Helvetica, sans-serif" size="2"><a href="mailto:">
<b><font size="1">Contact Webmaster</font></b></a></font></div></td></tr>
</table></form>
</body>
</html>
```

Meet With a Librarian — Perl Script

```perl
#!/usr/local/bin/perl

# ****************************************************************
# ABOVE is where you MUST specify the path to your
# perl interpreter on your Web server.
# Replace /usr/local/bin/perl with your path.
# ****************************************************************

if ($ENV{'REQUEST_METHOD'}eq"GET"){$buffer = $ENV{'QUERY_STRING'};}
    elsif($ENV{'REQUEST_METHOD'}eq"POST"){
        read(STDIN,$buffer,$ENV{'CONTENT_LENGTH'});
    }
$bufferb = $buffer;
#separate the name of the input from its value.
@forminputs = split(/&/, $bufferb);

foreach $forminput (@forminputs)
{
    #separate the name of the input from its value
    ($name, $value) = split(/=/, $forminput);

    #Un-Webify plus signs and %-encoding
    $value =~ tr/+/ /;
    $value =~ s/%([a-fA-F0-9][a-fA-F0-9])/pack("C", hex($1))/eg;

    #stick them in the in array
    $in{$name} = $value;
}
print "Content-type: text/html\n\n";

################################################
# ABOVE is the required header for a perl script    #
################################################

#####################################################
# (Below) Email received by library containing user-entered information #
#####################################################

# ****************************************************************
# Here's where you MUST specify the path to your
# email program (probably sendmail) ON your Web server.
# Replace /usr/sbin/sendmail with your path.
# ****************************************************************
```

```
open (LMAIL, "|/usr/sbin/sendmail -t");
print LMAIL ("To: $in{LibraryEmail}\n");

print LMAIL ("From: $in{Email}\n");
print LMAIL ("Subject: $in{Form} - patron submission\n");

print LMAIL ("------------------\nPatron information\n\n");

print LMAIL ("Name:\n $in{Name}\n\n");
print LMAIL ("E-mail Address:\n $in{Email}\n\n");
print LMAIL ("Home Address:\n $in{HomeAddr}\n\n");
print LMAIL ("School:\n $in{School}\n\n");
print LMAIL ("Home Phone/Fax:\n $in{HomePhone}\n\n");
print LMAIL ("Teacher's Name:\n $in{Teacher}\n\n");
print LMAIL ("Grade:\n $in{EducationLevel}\n\n");

print LMAIL ("------------------\nSubmitted information \n\n");

print LMAIL ("First date / time to meet:\n $in{FirstDateToMeet}\n $in{FirstTimeToMeet}\n\n");
print LMAIL ("Second date / time to meet:\n $in{SecondDateToMeet}\n $in{SecondDateToMeet}\n\n");
print LMAIL ("Third date / time to meet:\n $in{ThirdDateToMeet}\n $in{ThirdTimeToMeet}\n\n");
print LMAIL ("I need to meet before:\n $in{MeetBefore} $in{TimeIssue}\n\n");
print LMAIL ("How can we help:\n $in{HowCanWeHelp}\n\n");
print LMAIL ("Sources I have already checked:\n ");
print LMAIL ("$in{OCC}, $in{RM}, $in{B}, $in{MA}, $in{CD}, $in{O}, ${OtherChecked}\n\n");

print LMAIL ("\n.\n");

###############################################
# Email received by the user confirming form submission #
###############################################

# ********************************************************
# Here's where you MUST specify the path to your
# email program ON your Web server.
# Replace /usr/sbin/sendmail with your path.
# ********************************************************

open (MAIL, "|/usr/sbin/sendmail -t");

# ********************************************************
# Here's where you MAY customize the email
# response to the user. You may change any wording
# on the form.
# ********************************************************
```

```
print MAIL<<toEnd;
To: $in{Email}
From: $in{LibraryEmail}
Subject: $in{Form}

Thanks for wanting to set up a meeting with one of our librarians.\n\n
A librarian will contact you in the next couple of days to set up an appointment.

toEnd
   print MAIL ("\n.\n");


##########################################
# Screen response to user after submitting the form  #
##########################################

print ("<html><head><title>$in{Form}</title></head>");
print ("<body bgcolor=\"ffffff\">");


# *************************************************************
# Here's where you MAY change the screen response
# the user sees after submitting the form. You may
# change any wording between the quotation marks.
# *************************************************************

print ("Thanks for wanting to set up a meeting with one of our librarians.<p>
A librarian will contact you in the next couple of days to set up an appointment.");


# *************************************************************
# Here's where you MAY change the name of the link
# back to your main page. You may replace Return
# to our main page with your own wording.
# *************************************************************

print ("<p><center><a href=$in{LibraryURL}>Return to our main page.</a></center>");
print ("</body></html>");
```

Find a Class

Do you want to take a class on how to use the library, search the Web, use the library's computers, but don't know when the library offers these classes? Fill out this form and we'll e-mail you a list of fun and interesting classes that are scheduled on (or close to) the days/times you've listed.

Name (first, last)

E-mail address

Home address (+ city)

School you attend

Home phone/fax (+ areacode)

Teacher's name

What grade are you in?
- ○ 3   ○ 4   ○ 5   ○ 6   ○ 7
- ○ 8   ○ 9   ○ 10   ○ 11   ○ 12

What type of class are you looking for?
- ○ How to use the library
- ○ How to locate information
- ○ Internet / Web skills
- ○ How to use the library's computers
- ○ Web searching skills
- ○ How to write a research paper
- ○ Other types of classes (give us as many details as you can)

Dates / times you can attend a class

Date ____ Time ____
Date ____ Time ____
Date ____ Time ____

I need to take a class before... (eg. Oct. 2nd)

○ Anytime is fine

[Send Request]   [Clear Form]

http://
© 2002 Contact Webmaster

Find a Class — HTML Form

```
<html>
<head><title>Find a Class</title></head>
<body bgcolor="#FFFFFF">
<table width="700" border="1" height="85" bgcolor="ffffff">
<tr valign="middle" align="center">
<td>
<p><font halign=center color="#000000" face="Arial, Helvetica, sans-serif" size="+3">
<b><i>Find a Class</i></b></font></p>
</td></tr></table>
<form method="post" action="http://www.yourLibrary.org/cgi-bin/cli2.pl"><p> </p>
<p>
<font face="Arial, Helvetica, sans-serif" size="2"><b>Do you want to take a class on how to use the library,
search the Web, use the library's computers, but <br>don't know when the library offers these classes? Fill out
this form and we'll e-mail you a list of fun <br>and interesting classes that are scheduled on (or close to) the days/
times you've listed.</b></font></p>
<p> </p>
<input type="hidden" name="LibraryEmail" value="you@yourLibrary.org">
<input type="hidden" name="LibraryURL" value="http://www.yourLibrary.org">
<input type="hidden" name="Form" value="Find a Class"><p></p>
<table width="407" border="0" cellspacing="4" cellpadding="1">
<tr><td width="202">
<b><font face="Arial, Helvetica, sans-serif" size="2">Name</font></b><font face="Arial, Helvetica, sans-serif"
size="1">  (first, last)</font><br><font face="Arial, Helvetica, sans-serif" size="2">
<input type="text" name="Name" size="25"></font></td>
<td width="189">
<b><font face="Arial, Helvetica, sans-serif" size="2">E-mail address<br></font></b><font face="Arial, Helvetica,
sans-serif" size="2"><input type="text" name="Email" size="25"></font></td></tr>
<tr><td width="202" height="2">
<b><font face="Arial, Helvetica, sans-serif" size="2">Home address</font> </b><font face="Arial,
Helvetica, sans-serif" size="1"> (+ city)</font><br><font face="Arial, Helvetica, sans-serif" size="2">
<input type="text" name="HomeAddr" size="25"></font></td>
<td width="189" height="2">
<b><font face="Arial, Helvetica, sans-serif" size="2">School you attend<br></font></b><font face="Arial,
Helvetica, sans-serif" size="2"><input type="text" name="School" size="25"></font></td></tr>
<tr><td width="202" height="2">
<b><font face="Arial, Helvetica, sans-serif" size="2">Home phone/fax</font><font face="Arial, Helvetica, sans-
serif" size="1"> </font></b><font face="Arial, Helvetica, sans-serif" size="1"> (+ areacode)</font>
<br><font face="Arial, Helvetica, sans-serif" size="2"><input type="text" name= "HomePhone" size="25">
</font></td>
<td width="189" height="2">
<b><font face="Arial, Helvetica, sans-serif" size="2">Teacher's name<br></font></b><font face="Arial,
Helvetica, sans-serif" size="2"><input type="text" name="Teacher" size="25"></font></td></tr>
<tr><td width="391" colspan="2" height="48">
```

Group 2—Library Instruction Forms/Surveys

```html
<b><font face="Arial, Helvetica, sans-serif" size="2">What grade are you in?</font></b><br>
<table width="87%" border="0" cellspacing="4" cellpadding="0"><tr><td height="8" width="16%">
<font face="Arial, Helvetica, sans-serif" size="2"><input type="radio" name="EducationLevel" value="3">
3</font></td>
<td height="8" width="16%">
<font face="Arial, Helvetica, sans-serif" size="2"><input type="radio" name="EducationLevel" value="4">
4</font></td>
<td height="8" width="16%">
<font face="Arial, Helvetica, sans-serif" size="2"><input type="radio" name="EducationLevel" value="5">
5</font></td>
<td height="8" width="16%">
<font face="Arial, Helvetica, sans-serif" size="2"><input type="radio" name="EducationLevel" value="6">
6</font></td>
<td height="8" width="36%">
<font face="Arial, Helvetica, sans-serif" size="2"><input type="radio" name="EducationLevel" value="7">
7</font></td></tr>
<tr><td height="2" width="16%">
<font face="Arial, Helvetica, sans-serif" size="2"><input type="radio" name="EducationLevel" value="8">
8</font></td>
<td height="2" width="16%">
<font face="Arial, Helvetica, sans-serif" size="2"><input type="radio" name="EducationLevel" value="9">
9</font></td>
<td height="2" width="16%">
<font face="Arial, Helvetica, sans-serif" size="2"><input type="radio" name="EducationLevel" value="10">
10</font></td>
<td height="2" width="16%">
<font face="Arial, Helvetica, sans-serif" size="2"><input type="radio" name="EducationLevel" value="11">
11</font></td>
<td height="2" width="36%">
<font face="Arial, Helvetica, sans-serif" size="2"><input type="radio" name="EducationLevel" value="12">
12</font>
</td></tr></table></td></tr></table>
<p>
<br><b><font face="Arial, Helvetica, sans-serif" size="2">What type of class are you looking for?<br>
</font></b>
<table width="500" border="0" height="152"><tr><td>
<font face="Arial, Helvetica, sans-serif" size="2"><input type="radio" name="Type" value="How to use the library">How to use the library<font size="3"></font></font></td>
<td>
<font face="Arial, Helvetica, sans-serif" size="2"><input type="radio" name="Type" value="How to locate information">How to locate information</font></td></tr>
<tr><td>
<font face="Arial, Helvetica, sans-serif" size="2"><input type="radio" name="Type" value="Internet / Web skills">Internet / Web skills</font></td>
<td>
```

```html
<font face="Arial, Helvetica, sans-serif" size="2"><input type="radio" name="Type" value="How to use the library's computers">How to use the library's computers</font></td></tr>
<tr><td>
<font face="Arial, Helvetica, sans-serif" size="2"><input type="radio" name="Type" value="Web searching skills">Web searching skills</font></td>
<td>
<font face="Arial, Helvetica, sans-serif" size="2"><input type="radio" name="Type" value="How to write a research paper">How to write a research paper</font></td></tr>
<tr><td colspan="2" height="94">
<font face="Arial, Helvetica, sans-serif" size="2"><input type="radio" name="Type" value="Other types of classes">Other types of classes<font face="Arial, Helvetica, sans-serif" size="1"> (give us as many details as you can)</font><br><font size="3"><textarea name="OtherClasses" cols="40" rows="2"></textarea>
</font></font>
</td></tr></table>
<p>
<b><font face="Arial, Helvetica, sans-serif" size="2">Dates / times you can attend a class <br>
</font></b>
<font face="Arial, Helvetica, sans-serif" size="2">Date</font><font size="3"><font face="Arial, Helvetica, sans-serif"><input type="text" name="FirstDayToMeet" size="15">     
</font>
<font face="Arial, Helvetica, sans-serif" size="2">Time</font><font face="Arial, Helvetica, sans-serif" size="3"><input type="text" name="FirstTimeToMeet" size="15"><br><font size="2">Date</font></font>
<font face="Arial, Helvetica, sans-serif" size="3"><input type="text" name="SecondDayToMeet" size="15">    </font><font face="Arial, Helvetica, sans-serif" size="2">Time
</font><font face="Arial, Helvetica, sans-serif" size="3"><input type="text" name="SecondTimeToMeet" size="15"><br>
<font size="2">Date</font></font><font face="Arial, Helvetica, sans-serif" size="3"><input type="text" name="ThirdDayToMeet" size="15">     </font><font face="Arial, Helvetica, sans-serif" size="2">Time</font><font face="Arial, Helvetica, sans-serif" size="3">
<input type="text" name="ThirdTimeToMeet" size="15"></font></font></p>
<p>
<font face="Arial, Helvetica, sans-serif" size="2"><b>I need to take a class before... </b><font face="Arial, Helvetica, sans-serif" size="1"> (eg. Oct. 2nd)</font><br><font size="3"><input type="text" name="NeedBefore" size="15">     </font><input type="radio" name="TimeIssue" value="Time is not an issue"><font face="Arial, Helvetica, sans-serif" size="2"> Anytime is fine</font></font></p>
<p> </p>
<table width="700" border="0" cellspacing="10" cellpadding="1"><tr><td width="244"><div align="right">
<input type="submit" name="send" value="Send Request"></div></td><td width="203"> </td>
<td width="207"><div align="left"><input type="reset" name="clear" value="Clear Form"></div></td></tr>
<tr colspan=3><td colspan=3>
<table width="500" border="1" height="2" align="center" cellpadding="0" cellspacing="0" bgcolor="#ffffff"><tr><td><font size="1" color="#ffffff">.</font></td></tr></table></td></tr>
<tr><td colspan=3><div align="center">
<font face="Arial, Helvetica, sans-serif" size="1"><b>http://</b></font><br><font size="2"> 
```

```html
<font face="Arial, Helvetica, sans-serif" size="1"><b>&copy; 2002</b></font></font>
<font face="Arial, Helvetica, sans-serif" size="2"><a href="mailto:">
<b><font size="1">Contact Webmaster</font></b></a></font></div></td></tr>
</table></form>
</body>
</html>
```

Find a Class — Perl Script

```perl
#!/usr/local/bin/perl

# ****************************************************************
# ABOVE is where you MUST specify the path to your
# perl interpreter on your Web server.
# Replace /usr/local/bin/perl with your path.
# ****************************************************************

if ($ENV{'REQUEST_METHOD'}eq"GET"){$buffer = $ENV{'QUERY_STRING'};}
    elsif($ENV{'REQUEST_METHOD'}eq"POST"){
        read(STDIN,$buffer,$ENV{'CONTENT_LENGTH'});
    }
$bufferb = $buffer;
#separate the name of the input from its value.
@forminputs = split(/&/, $bufferb);

foreach $forminput (@forminputs)
{
    #separate the name of the input from its value
    ($name, $value) = split(/=/, $forminput);

    #Un-Webify plus signs and %-encoding
    $value =~ tr/+/ /;
    $value =~ s/%([a-fA-F0-9][a-fA-F0-9])/pack("C", hex($1))/eg;

    #stick them in the in array
    $in{$name} = $value;
}
print "Content-type: text/html\n\n";

##############################################
# ABOVE is the required header for a perl script     #
##############################################


######################################################
# (Below) Email received by library containing user-entered information #
######################################################


# ****************************************************************
# Here's where you MUST specify the path to your
# email program (probably sendmail) ON your Web server.
# Replace /usr/sbin/sendmail with your path.
# ****************************************************************
#
```

```perl
open (LMAIL, "|/usr/sbin/sendmail -t");
print LMAIL ("To: $in{LibraryEmail}\n");

print LMAIL ("From: $in{Email}\n");
print LMAIL ("Subject: $in{Form} - patron submission\n");

print LMAIL ("------------------\nPatron information\n\n");

print LMAIL ("Name:\n $in{Name}\n\n");
print LMAIL ("E-mail Address:\n $in{Email}\n\n");
print LMAIL ("Home Address:\n $in{HomeAddr}\n\n");
print LMAIL ("School:\n $in{School}\n\n");
print LMAIL ("Home Phone/Fax:\n $in{HomePhone}\n\n");
print LMAIL ("Teacher's Name:\n $in{Teacher}\n\n");
print LMAIL ("Grade:\n $in{EducationLevel}\n\n");

print LMAIL ("------------------\nSubmitted information \n\n");

print LMAIL ("Type of class:\n $in{Type}\n\n");
print LMAIL ("Other types of classes:\n $in{OtherClasses}\n\n");
print LMAIL ("First date / time to attend:\n $in{FirstDayToMeet}\n $in{FirstTimeToMeet}\n\n");
print LMAIL ("Second date / time to attend:\n $in{SecondDayToMeet}\n $in{SecondDateToMeet}\n\n");
print LMAIL ("Third date / time to attend:\n $in{ThirdDayToMeet}\n $in{ThirdTimeToMeet}\n\n");
print LMAIL ("I need to take a class before:\n $in{NeedBefore} $in{TimeIssue}\n\n");

print LMAIL ("\n.\n");

##############################################
# Email received by the user confirming form submission #
##############################################

# ***********************************************************
# Here's where you MUST specify the path to your
# email program ON your Web server.
# Replace /usr/sbin/sendmail with your path.
# ***********************************************************
#

open (MAIL, "|/usr/sbin/sendmail -t");

# ***********************************************************
# Here's where you MAY customize the email
# response to the user. You may change any wording
# on the form.
# ***********************************************************
#
```

```
print MAIL<<toEnd;
To: $in{Email}
From: $in{LibraryEmail}
Subject: $in{Form}

Thanks for completing our Find a Class form.

toEnd
   print MAIL ("\n.\n");


#########################################
# Screen response to user after submitting the form  #
#########################################

print ("<html><head><title>$in{Form}</title></head>");
print ("<body bgcolor=\"ffffff\">");




# ***************************************************************
# Here's where you MAY change the screen response
# the user sees after submitting the form. You may
# change any wording between the quotation marks.
# ***************************************************************

print ("Thanks for completing our Find a Class form.");

# ***************************************************************
# Here's where you MAY change the name of the link
# back to your main page. You may replace Return
# to our main page with your own wording.
# ***************************************************************

print ("<p><center><a href=$in{LibraryURL}>Return to our main page.</a></center>");
print ("</body></html>");
```

Training Interests Survey

Teachers / Librarians / Parents

Please complete this short survey to help us get an idea of how effective our current library training sessions are. We'd also like to find out any new training sessions you'd like us to develop and when you'd like us to offer them. Finally, we'd like to know how you learn about currently offered training sessions as well as how we can notify you of these sessions in the future.

Have you (or your students) attended any training sessions presented by the library? ○ Yes ○ No

    If yes, how many have you / they attended? [   ]

Which session was the most useful / interesting / effective?
[   ]

What new training sessions would you like to see the library offer?
[   ]

What is the most convenient day / time for training sessions?
[   ]

What types of training do you / kids prefer? (select any/all)
○ Instructor-led classes   ○ One-on-one sessions   ○ Printed instructions
○ Web-based tutorials   ○ Audio / Video-based lessons   ○ Other (explain) [   ]

How do you *currently* find out about library programs / training sessions?
○ Newsletter   ○ Bulletin boards   ○ Colleagues   ○ Web site
○ Other (explain) [   ]

How would you like to find out about *future* library programs / training sessions?
○ E-mail   ○ Listserv   ○ Printed articles / Posters   ○ Web site
○ Other (explain) [   ]

Name (first, last)   **E-mail address**
[   ]   [   ]

Name of school   **Grade(s) you teach**
[   ]   [   ]

I am a...

○ Classroom teacher ○ Librarian / Media specialist

○ School staff / Administrator ○ Parent

○ Other (explain) [_____]

[Send Survey]   [Clear Survey]

[_____]

http://

©2002 Contact Webmaster

Group 2—Library Instruction Forms/Surveys

Training Interests Survey — HTML Form

```html
<html>
<head><title>Training Interests Survey</title></head>
<body bgcolor="#FFFFFF">
<table width="700" border="1" height="85" bgcolor="ffffff">
<tr valign="middle" align="center">
<td>
<p>
<font halign=center color="#000000" face="Arial, Helvetica, sans-serif" size="+3">
<b><i>Training Interests Survey</i></b></font></p>
</td></tr></table>
<form method="post" action="http://www.yourLibrary.org/cgi-bin/cli3.pl"><p> </p>
<p>
<font face="Arial, Helvetica, sans-serif" size="2"><b><i>Teachers / Librarians / Parents</i></b></font></p>
<p>
<font face="Arial, Helvetica, sans-serif" size="2"><b>Please complete this short survey to help us get an idea of
how effective our current library training sessions are. <br>We'd also like to find out any new training sessions
you'd like us to develop and when you'd like us to offer them. <br>Finally, we'd like to know how you learn about
currently offered training sessions as well as how we can notify you <br>of these sessions in the future.</b>
</font></p>
<p> </p>
<input type="hidden" name="LibraryEmail" value="you@yourLibrary.org">
<input type="hidden" name="LibraryURL" value="http://www.yourLibrary.org">
<input type="hidden" name="Form" value="Training Interests Survey">
<p>
<font face="Arial, Helvetica, sans-serif" size="2"><b>Have you (or your students) attended any training sessions
presented by the library?</b> 
<input type="radio" name="TrainingAttend" value="Yes">Yes 
<input type="radio" name="TrainingAttend" value="No">No<br>     
</font>
<font face="Arial, Helvetica, sans-serif" size="2"><b>If yes, how many have you / they attended? </b>
<font size="3"><input type="text" name="HowManyTrain" size="5"></font></font></p>
<p>
<b><font face="Arial, Helvetica, sans-serif" size="2">Which session was the most useful / interesting / effective?
  <br></font></b><font face="Arial, Helvetica, sans-serif" size="3"><input type="text"
name="UsefulTrain" size="40"></font></p>
<p>
<b><font face="Arial, Helvetica, sans-serif" size="2">What new training sessions would you like to see the library
offer?<br></font></b><font face="Arial, Helvetica, sans-serif" size="3"><textarea name= "AdditionalTrain"
cols="40" rows="2"></textarea></font></p>
<p>
<b><font face="Arial, Helvetica, sans-serif" size="2">What is the most convenient day / time for training
sessions?  <br></font></b><font face="Arial, Helvetica, sans-serif" size="3"><input type= "text"
name="TrainDayTime" size="40"></font></p>
<p>
```

```html
<font face="Arial, Helvetica, sans-serif" size="2"><b>What types of training do you / kids prefer?</b>
   <font size="1">(select any/all)</font><br></font>
<table width="599" border="0" cellspacing="0" cellpadding="0"><tr><td width="171">
<font face="Arial, Helvetica, sans-serif" size="2"><input type="radio" name="ILC" value="Instructor-led classes">Instructor-led classes</font></td>
<td width="209">
<font face="Arial, Helvetica, sans-serif" size="2"><input type="radio" name="OOOS" value="One-on-one sessions">One-on-one sessions</font></td>
<td width="220">
<font face="Arial, Helvetica, sans-serif" size="2"><input type="radio" name="PHSM" value="Printed instructions">Printed instructions</font></td></tr>
<tr valign="top"><td width="171">
<font face="Arial, Helvetica, sans-serif" size="2"><input type="radio" name="WBT" value="Web-based tutorials">Web-based tutorials</font></td>
<td width="209">
<font face="Arial, Helvetica, sans-serif" size="2"><input type="radio" name="AVBL" value="Audio / video-based lessons">Audio / Video-based lessons</font></td>
<td width="220">
<font face="Arial, Helvetica, sans-serif" size="2"><input type="radio" name="O" value="Other">Other<b>
</b>  <font size="1">(explain)</font>  <font size="2"><input type="text" name="OtherTrainingPrefer" size="10"></font></font><font size="2"><b></b></font>
</td></tr></table>
<p>
<font face="Arial, Helvetica, sans-serif" size="2"><b>How do you <i>currently</i>find out about library programs / training sessions?</b><br>
<input type="radio" name="Currently" value="Newsletter">Newsletter  
<input type="radio" name="Currently" value="Bulletin boards">Bulletin boards   
<input type="radio" name="Currently" value="Colleagues">Colleagues  
<input type="radio" name="Currently" value="Web site">Web site<br>
<input type="radio" name="Currently" value="Other">Other   <font size="1">(explain)</font>
 <font size="2"><input type="text" name="CurrentlyOther" size="10"></font></font></p>
<p>
<font face="Arial, Helvetica, sans-serif" size="2"><b>How would you like to find out about <i>future</i> library programs / training sessions?<br>
<input type="radio" name="Future" value="Email "></b>E-mail  
<input type="radio" name="Future" value="Listserv">Listserv  
<input type="radio" name="Future" value="Printed articles / Posters">Printed articles / Posters   
<input type="radio" name="Future" value="Web site">Web site<br>
<input type="radio" name="Future" value="Other">Other   <font size="1">(explain)
</font> <font size="2"><input type="text" name="FutureOther" size="10"></font></font></p>
<p> </p>
<table width="407" border="0" cellspacing="4" cellpadding="1">
<tr><td width="202">
<b><font face="Arial, Helvetica, sans-serif" size="2">Name</font></b><font face="Arial, Helvetica, sans-serif" size="1">  (first, last)</font><br><font face="Arial, Helvetica, sans-serif" size="2">
<input type="text" name="Name" size="25"></font></td>
```

```html
<td width="189">
<b><font face="Arial, Helvetica, sans-serif" size="2">E-mail address<br></font></b><font face="Arial, Helvetica, sans-serif" size="2"><input type="text" name="Email" size="25"></font></td></tr>
<tr><td width="202" height="2">
<b><font face="Arial, Helvetica, sans-serif" size="2">Name of school<br></font></b><font face="Arial, Helvetica, sans-serif" size="2"><input type="text" name="School" size="25"></font></td>
<td width="189" height="2">
<b><font face="Arial, Helvetica, sans-serif" size="2">Grade(s) you teach<br></font></b><font face="Arial, Helvetica, sans-serif" size="2"><input type="text" name="Grades" size="25"></font></td></tr>
<tr><td width="391" colspan="2" height="20">
<p>
<b><font face="Arial, Helvetica, sans-serif" size="2">I am a...</font></b><br>
<table width="100%" border="0" cellpadding="0" cellspacing="4"><tr><td width="51%">
<font face="Arial, Helvetica, sans-serif" size="2"><input type="radio" name="Iama" value="Classroom teacher">Classroom teacher</font></td>
<td width="49%">
<font face="Arial, Helvetica, sans-serif" size="2"><input type="radio" name="Iama" value="Librarian / Media specialist">Librarian / Media specialist</font></td></tr>
<tr><td width="51%">
<font face="Arial, Helvetica, sans-serif" size="2"><input type="radio" name="Iama" value="School staff / Administrator">School staff / Administrator</font></td>
<td width="49%">
<font face="Arial, Helvetica, sans-serif" size="2"><input type="radio" name="Iama" value="Parent">Parent</font></td></tr>
<tr valign="top"><td colspan="2" height="9">
<font face="Arial, Helvetica, sans-serif" size="2"><input type="radio" name="Iama" value="Other">Other<font face="Arial, Helvetica, sans-serif" size="1">    (explain)</font>
<font face="Arial, Helvetica, sans-serif" size="2"> </font></font><b><font face="Arial, Helvetica, sans-serif" size="1"><font size="2"><input type="text" name="IamaOther" size="15"></font></font></b></font>
</td></tr></table>
</td></tr></table>
<p>  </p>
<table width="700" border="0" cellspacing="10" cellpadding="1"><tr><td width="226"><div align="right">
<input type="submit" name="send" value="Send Survey"></div></td><td width="207"> </td>
<td width="221"><div align="left"><input type="reset" name="clear" value="Clear Survey"></div></td></tr>
<tr colspan=3><td colspan=3>
<table width="500" border="1" height="2" align="center" cellpadding="0" cellspacing="0" bgcolor="ffffff"><tr><td><font size="1" color="#ffffff">.</font></td></tr></table></td></tr><tr>
<td colspan=3><div align="center">
<font face="Arial, Helvetica, sans-serif" size="1"><b>http://</b></font><br> 
<font face="Arial, Helvetica, sans-serif" size="1"><b>&copy;2002</b></font>
<font face="Arial, Helvetica, sans-serif" size="1"><a href="mailto:">
<b>Contact Webmaster</b></a></font></div></td></tr>
</table></form>
</body>
</html>
```

Training Interests Survey — Perl Script

```perl
#!/usr/local/bin/perl

# ***********************************************************
# ABOVE is where you MUST specify the path to your
# perl interpreter on your Web server.
# Replace /usr/local/bin/perl with your path.
# ***********************************************************

if ($ENV{'REQUEST_METHOD'}eq"GET"){$buffer = $ENV{'QUERY_STRING'};}
    elsif($ENV{'REQUEST_METHOD'}eq"POST"){
        read(STDIN,$buffer,$ENV{'CONTENT_LENGTH'});
    }
$bufferb = $buffer;
#separate the name of the input from its value.
@forminputs = split(/&/, $bufferb);

foreach $forminput (@forminputs)
{
    #separate the name of the input from its value
    ($name, $value) = split(/=/, $forminput);

    #Un-Webify plus signs and %-encoding
    $value =~ tr/+/ /;
    $value =~ s/%([a-fA-F0-9][a-fA-F0-9])/pack("C", hex($1))/eg;

    #stick them in the in array
    $in{$name} = $value;
}
print "Content-type: text/html\n\n";

##############################################
# ABOVE is the required header for a perl script  #
##############################################

###################################################
# (Below) Email received by library containing user-entered information #
###################################################

# ***********************************************************
# Here's where you MUST specify the path to your
# email program (probably sendmail) ON your Web server.
# Replace /usr/sbin/sendmail with your path.
# ***********************************************************
```

```perl
open (LMAIL, "|/usr/sbin/sendmail -t");
print LMAIL ("To: $in{LibraryEmail}\n");

print LMAIL ("From: $in{Email}\n");
print LMAIL ("Subject: $in{Form} - patron submission\n");

print LMAIL ("------------------\nPatron information\n\n");

print LMAIL ("Name:\n $in{Name}\n\n");
print LMAIL ("E-mail Address:\n $in{Email}\n\n");
print LMAIL ("School:\n $in{School}\n\n");
print LMAIL ("Gender:\n $in{Gender}\n\n");
print LMAIL ("Grade:\n $in{EducationLevel}\n\n");

print LMAIL ("------------------\nSubmitted information \n\n");
print LMAIL ("------------------\nTraining Sessions \n\n");
print LMAIL ("Have you (or your students) attended any training sessions presented by the library?\n
    $in{TrainingAttend}\n\n");
print LMAIL ("If yes, how many?\n $in{HowManyTrain}\n\n");
print LMAIL ("Which session was the most useful / interesting / effective?\n $in{UsefulTrain}\n\n");
print LMAIL ("What new training sessions would you like to see the library offer?\n $in{AdditionalTrain}\n\n");
print LMAIL ("What is the most convenient day / time for training sessions?\n $in{TrainDayTime}\n\n");
print LMAIL ("What types of training do you / kids prefer?\n $in{ILC}, $in{OOOS}, $in{PHSM}, $in{WBT},
$in{AVBL}, $in{O}\n\n");
print LMAIL ("Other training preferred:\n $in{OtherTraining}\n\n");

print LMAIL ("------------------\nProgram / Training Awareness \n\n");
print LMAIL ("How do you currently find out about library programs / training sessions?\n $in{Currently}\n\n");
print LMAIL ("Other method I find out:\n $in{CurrentlyOther}\n\n");
print LMAIL ("How would you like to find out about future library programs / training sessions?\n $in{Future}\n\n");
print LMAIL ("Other method I would like to find out:\n $in{FutureOther}\n\n");

print LMAIL ("\n.\n");

###########################################
# Email received by the user confirming form submission #
###########################################

# *********************************************
# Here's where you MUST specify the path to your
# email program ON your Web server.
# Replace /usr/sbin/sendmail with your path.
# *********************************************

open (MAIL, "|/usr/sbin/sendmail -t");
```

```
# ***********************************************
# Here's where you MAY customize the email
# response to the user. You may change any wording
# on the form.
# ***********************************************

print MAIL<<toEnd;
To: $in{Email}
From: $in{LibraryEmail}
Subject: $in{Form}

Thanks for taking the time to fill out our Training Interests Survey.\n\n
We will use your input to improve the types of programs and training sessions we offer.


toEnd
    print MAIL ("\n.\n");


###########################################
# Screen response to user after submitting the form  #
###########################################

print ("<html><head><title>$in{Form}</title></head>");
print ("<body bgcolor=\"ffffff\">");


# ***********************************************
# Here's where you MAY change the screen response
# the user sees after submitting the form. You may
# change any wording between the quotation marks.
# ***********************************************

print ("Thanks for taking the time to fill out our Training Interests Survey.<p>
We will use your input to improve the types of programs and training sessions we offer.");


# ***********************************************
# Here's where you MAY change the name of the link
# back to your main page. You may replace Return
# to our main page with your own wording.
# ***********************************************

print ("<p><center><a href=$in{LibraryURL}>Return to our main page.</a></center>");
print ("</body></html>");
```

"What Do You Want To Learn" Survey

Please fill out this short survey to let us know the things you'd like to learn about school assignments, computers, and the library.

School (select any/all)
- ○ How to find homework help on-line
- ○ How to create a bibliography
- ○ How to write a research paper
- ○ What is plagiarism? (and how to avoid it)

The Library (select any/all)
- ○ How to *really* use the library
- ○ Searching the library's catalog
- ○ Library database basics
- ○ Citing books, magazine / newspaper articles

Computers (select any/all)
- ○ PC / Windows basics
- ○ How to search the Web
- ○ Chat
- ○ Staying safe on-line
- ○ Macintosh basics
- ○ How to create a Web site
- ○ FTP / Computer viruses
- ○ Citing Web-based resources

Name (first, last)

E-mail address

School you attend

Gender
○ Female ○ Male

What grade are you in?
○ 3   ○ 4   ○ 5   ○ 6   ○ 7
○ 8   ○ 9   ○ 10 ○ 11 ○ 12

[Send Survey]   [Clear Survey]

http://
© 2002 Contact Webmaster

"What Do You Want to Learn" Survey — HTML Form

```
<html>
<head><title>"What Do You Want To Learn" Survey</title></head>
<body bgcolor="#FFFFFF">
<table width="700" border="1" bordercolor="000000" height="85" bgcolor="#ffffff">
<tr valign="middle" align="center">
<td>
<p>
<font halign=center color="#000000" face="Arial, Helvetica, sans-serif" size="+3">
<b><i>&quot;What Do You Want To Learn&quot; Survey</i></b></font></p>
</td></tr></table>
<form method="post" action="http://www.yourLibrary.org/cgi-bin/cli4.pl" name="">
<p> </p><p>
<font face="Arial, Helvetica, sans-serif" size="2"><b>Please fill out this short survey to let us know the things you'd like to learn about school assignments, <br>computers, and the library</b></font><font face="Arial, Helvetica, sans-serif" size="2"><b>.</b></font><br></p>
<p>
<input type="hidden" name="LibraryEmail" value="you@yourLibrary.org">
<input type="hidden" name="LibraryURL" value="http://www.yourLibrary.org">
<input type="hidden" name="Form" value="&quot;What Do You Want To Learn&quot; Survey"></p>
<p> </p>
<p></p><p>
<b><font face="Arial, Helvetica, sans-serif" size="2">School</font></b>  <font face="Arial, Helvetica, sans-serif" size="1">(select any/all)</font><br>
<table width="560" border="0" cellspacing="0" cellpadding="0"><tr><td width="255">
<font face="Arial, Helvetica, sans-serif" size="2"><input type="radio" name="S1" value="How to find homework help on-line">How to find homework help on-line</font></td>
<td width="305">
<font face="Arial, Helvetica, sans-serif" size="2"><input type="radio" name="S2" value="How to write a research paper">How to write a research paper</font></td></tr>
<tr><td width="255">
<font face="Arial, Helvetica, sans-serif" size="2"><input type="radio" name="S3" value="How to create a bibliography">How to create a bibliography</font></td>
<td width="305">
<font face="Arial, Helvetica, sans-serif" size="2"><input type="radio" name="S4" value="What is plagiarism? (and how to avoid it)">What is plagiarism? (and how to avoid it)</font></td></tr></table>
<p>
<b><font face="Arial, Helvetica, sans-serif" size="2">The Library</font></b>  <font face="Arial, Helvetica, sans-serif" size="1">(select any/all)</font><br>
<table width="684" border="0" cellspacing="0" cellpadding="0"><tr><td width="255">
<font face="Arial, Helvetica, sans-serif" size="2"><input type="radio" name="L1" value="How to really use the library">How to <i>really</i> use the library</font></td>
<td width="429">
<font face="Arial, Helvetica, sans-serif" size="2"><input type="radio" name="L2" value="Library database
```

```html
basics">Library database basics</font></td></tr>
<tr valign="top"><td width="255">
<input type="radio" name="L3" value="Searching the library's catalog">Searching the library's catalog</font>
</td>
<td width="429">
<font face="Arial, Helvetica, sans-serif" size="2"><input type="radio" name="L4" value="Citing books, magazine / newspaper articles">Citing books, magazine / newspaper articles</font></td></tr></table>
<p>
<b><font face="Arial, Helvetica, sans-serif" size="2">Computers</font></b>  <font face="Arial, Helvetica, sans-serif" size="1">(select any/all)</font><br>
<table width="576" border="0" cellspacing="0" cellpadding="0"><tr><td width="254">
<font face="Arial, Helvetica, sans-serif" size="2"><input type="radio" name="C1" value="PC / Windows basics">PC / Windows basics</font></td>
<td width="322">
<font face="Arial, Helvetica, sans-serif" size="2"><input type="radio" name="C2" value="Macintosh basics">Macintosh basics</font></td></tr>
<tr><td width="254">
<font face="Arial, Helvetica, sans-serif" size="2"><input type="radio" name="C3" value="How to search the Web">How to search the Web</font></td>
<td width="322">
<font face="Arial, Helvetica, sans-serif" size="2"><input type="radio" name="C4" value="How to create a Web site">How to create a Web site</font></td></tr>
<tr><td width="254">
<font face="Arial, Helvetica, sans-serif" size="2"><input type="radio" name="C5" value="Chat ">
Chat </font></td>
<td width="322">
<font face="Arial, Helvetica, sans-serif" size="2"><input type="radio" name="C6" value="FTP / Computer viruses">FTP / Computer viruses</font></td></tr>
<tr><td width="254">
<font face="Arial, Helvetica, sans-serif" size="2"><input type="radio" name="C7" value="Staying safe on-line">Staying safe on-line</font></td>
<td width="322">
<font face="Arial, Helvetica, sans-serif" size="2"><input type="radio" name="C8" value="Citing Web-based resources">Citing Web-based resources</font></td></tr></table>
<p><br><br>
<table width="407" border="0" cellspacing="4" cellpadding="1">
<tr><td width="202">
<b><font face="Arial, Helvetica, sans-serif" size="2">Name</font></b><font face="Arial, Helvetica, sans-serif" size="1">  (first, last)</font><br><font face="Arial, Helvetica, sans-serif" size="2">
<input type="text" name="Name" size="25"></font></td>
<td width="189">
<b><font face="Arial, Helvetica, sans-serif" size="2">E-mail address<br></font></b><font face="Arial, Helvetica, sans-serif" size="2"><input type="text" name="Email" size="25"></font></td></tr>
<tr><td width="202" height="2">
<b><font face="Arial, Helvetica, sans-serif" size="2">School you attend<br></font></b><font face="Arial,
```

```html
Helvetica, sans-serif" size="2"><input type="text" name="School" size="25"></font></td>
<td width="189" height="2">
<b><font face="Arial, Helvetica, sans-serif" size="2">Gender<br></font></b>
<input type="radio" name="Gender" value="Female"><font face="Arial, Helvetica, sans-serif" size="2">Female
</font>
<input type="radio" name="Gender" value="Male"><font face="Arial, Helvetica, sans-serif" size="2">Male
</font></td></tr>
<tr><td width="391" colspan="2" height="48">
<b><font face="Arial, Helvetica, sans-serif" size="2">What grade are you in?</font></b><br><font face="Arial, Helvetica, sans-serif" size="2"></font>
<table width="87%" border="0" cellspacing="4" cellpadding="0"><tr><td height="8" width="16%">
<font face="Arial, Helvetica, sans-serif" size="2"><input type="radio" name="EducationLevel" value="3">
3</font></td>
<td height="8" width="16%">
<font face="Arial, Helvetica, sans-serif" size="2"><input type="radio" name="EducationLevel" value="4">
4</font></td>
<td height="8" width="16%">
<font face="Arial, Helvetica, sans-serif" size="2"><input type="radio" name="EducationLevel" value="5">
5</font></td>
<td height="8" width="16%">
<font face="Arial, Helvetica, sans-serif" size="2"><input type="radio" name="EducationLevel" value="6">
6</font></td>
<td height="8" width="36%">
<font face="Arial, Helvetica, sans-serif" size="2"><input type="radio" name="EducationLevel" value="7">
7</font></td></tr>
<tr><td height="2" width="16%">
<font face="Arial, Helvetica, sans-serif" size="2"><input type="radio" name="EducationLevel" value="8">
8</font></td>
<td height="2" width="16%">
<font face="Arial, Helvetica, sans-serif" size="2"><input type="radio" name="EducationLevel" value="9">
9</font></td>
<td height="2" width="16%">
<font face="Arial, Helvetica, sans-serif" size="2"><input type="radio" name="EducationLevel" value="10">
10</font></td>
<td height="2" width="16%">
<font face="Arial, Helvetica, sans-serif" size="2"><input type="radio" name="EducationLevel" value="11">
11</font></td>
<td height="2" width="36%">
<font face="Arial, Helvetica, sans-serif" size="2"><input type="radio" name="EducationLevel" value="12">
12</font>
</td></tr></table>
</td></tr></table>
<p> </p>
<table width="700" border="0" cellspacing="10" cellpadding="1"><tr><td width="226"><div align="right">
<input type="submit" name="send" value="Send Survey"></div></td><td width="207"> </td>
<td width="221"><div align="left"><input type="reset" name="clear" value="Clear Survey"></div></td></tr>
```

```
<tr colspan=3><td colspan=3>
<table width="500" border="1" bordercolor="#000000" height="2" align="center" cellpadding="0"
cellspacing="0" bgcolor="#ffffff"><tr><td><font size="1" color="#ffffff">.</font></td></tr></table></td></tr>
<tr><td colspan=3><div align="center">
<font face="Arial, Helvetica, sans-serif" size="1"><b>http://</b></font><br> 
<font face="Arial, Helvetica, sans-serif" size="1"><b>&copy; 2002</b></font>
<font face="Arial, Helvetica, sans-serif" size="2"><a href="mailto:">
<b><font size="1">Contact Webmaster</font></b></a></font></div></td></tr>
</table></form>
</body>
</html>
```

"What Do You Want to Learn" Survey — Perl Script

```perl
#!/usr/local/bin/perl

# ***************************************************************
# ABOVE is where you MUST specify the path to your
# perl interpreter on your Web server.
# Replace /usr/local/bin/perl with your path.
# ***************************************************************

if ($ENV{'REQUEST_METHOD'}eq"GET"){$buffer = $ENV{'QUERY_STRING'};}
    elsif($ENV{'REQUEST_METHOD'}eq"POST"){
        read(STDIN,$buffer,$ENV{'CONTENT_LENGTH'});
    }
$bufferb = $buffer;
#separate the name of the input from its value.
@forminputs = split(/&/, $bufferb);

foreach $forminput (@forminputs)
{
    #separate the name of the input from its value
    ($name, $value) = split(/=/, $forminput);

    #Un-Webify plus signs and %-encoding
    $value =~ tr/+/ /;
    $value =~ s/%([a-fA-F0-9][a-fA-F0-9])/pack("C", hex($1))/eg;

    #stick them in the in array
    $in{$name} = $value;
}
print "Content-type: text/html\n\n";

################################################
# ABOVE is the required header for a perl script       #
################################################

########################################################
# (Below) Email received by library containing user-entered information #
########################################################

# ***************************************************************
# Here's where you MUST specify the path to your
# email program (probably sendmail) ON your Web server.
# Replace /usr/sbin/sendmail with your path.
# ***************************************************************
```

```
open (LMAIL, "|/usr/sbin/sendmail -t");
print LMAIL ("To: $in{LibraryEmail}\n");
print LMAIL ("From: $in{Email}\n");
print LMAIL ("Subject: $in{Form} - patron submission\n");

print LMAIL ("------------------\nPatron information\n\n");


print LMAIL ("Name:\n $in{Name}\n\n");
print LMAIL ("E-mail Address:\n $in{Email}\n\n");
print LMAIL ("School:\n $in{School}\n\n");
print LMAIL ("Gender:\n $in{Gender}\n\n");
print LMAIL ("Grade:\n $in{EducationLevel}\n\n");

print LMAIL ("------------------\nSubmitted information \n\n");

print LMAIL ("------------------\nWhat Do You Want To Learn? \n\n");

print LMAIL ("School:\n $in{S1}, $in{S2}, $in{S3}, $in{S4}\n\n");

print LMAIL ("Library / Reading:\n $in{L1}, $in{L2}, $in{L3}, $in{L4}\n\n");

print LMAIL ("Computers:\n $in{C1}, $in{C2},$in{C3}, $in{C4}, $in{C5}, $in{C6}, $in{C7}, $in{C8}\n\n");

print LMAIL ("\n.\n");

############################################
# Email received by the user confirming form submission #
############################################

# *********************************************************
# Here's where you MUST specify the path to your
# email program ON your Web server.
# Replace /usr/sbin/sendmail with your path.
# *********************************************************

open (MAIL, "|/usr/sbin/sendmail -t");

# *********************************************************
# Here's where you MAY customize the email
# response to the user. You may change any wording
# of the message.
# *********************************************************

print MAIL<<toEnd;
```

```
To: $in{Email}
From: $in{LibraryEmail}
Subject: $in{Form}

Thanks for completing our What Do You Want To Learn Survey.\n\n

toEnd
   print MAIL ("\n.\n");

##########################################
# Screen response to user after submitting the form  #
##########################################

print ("<html><head><title>$in{Form}</title></head>");
print ("<body bgcolor=\"ffffff\">");



# *************************************************************
# Here's where you MAY change the screen response
# the user sees after submitting the form. You may
# change any wording between the quotation marks.
# *************************************************************

print ("Thanks for completing our What Do You Want To Learn Survey.");

# *************************************************************
# Here's where you MAY change the name of the link
# back to your main page. You may replace Return
# to our main page with your own wording.
# *************************************************************

print ("<p><center><a href=$in{LibraryURL}>Return to our main page.</a></center>");
print ("</body></html>");
```

Instant Web Forms & Surveys

Group 3 — Library Computer Forms / Surveys

In this section you'll find a Web-based form that will enable students to reserve one of your library's computers on a day and at a time convenient to them. Here you'll also find two surveys that will enable both library-based and home-based students to give your staff input on their level of computer knowledge, information about how they use the Internet, and how they feel about your library's Web site.

Reserve a Library Computer
Do students hate to wait in line to use one of your library's computers? Provide them with this form so that they can ask to reserve a computer on a specific date and at a specific time. Put a link to this form on any of your Web site's Web search or technology pages.

Library Cybersurfer Survey
If you have students who use your library's computers to access the Internet and you'd like to know more about them so that you can help them better use your computers, the Internet, and your library's Web site, make sure you place a link to this survey periodically on your library's home page.

Home Cybersurfer Survey
If students use an Internet-connected computer at home, have them complete this brief survey so that you can learn how they use the Internet and your library's Web site when they're not in your library. Put a link to this survey periodically on your library's home page.

Reserve a Library Computer

Do you hate to wait in line to use one of the library's computers? Fill out this form to reserve a computer on a specific date and at a specific time. All reservations must be made at least 24 hours in advance. Dates/times are assigned on a first-come-first-serve basis. We'll e-mail you to let you know when a computer is reserved for you.

Name (first, last)

E-mail address

Home address (+ city)

School you attend

Home phone/fax (+ areacode)

Teacher's name

What grade are you in?
- ○ 3   ○ 4   ○ 5   ○ 6   ○ 7
- ○ 8   ○ 9   ○ 10   ○ 11   ○ 12

Date / time you would like to reserve a library computer (list two times that will work)

Date _____   Time _____
Date _____   Time _____

[Send Reservation]   [Clear Form]

http://

© 2002 Contact Webmaster

Group 3—Library Computer Forms/Surveys

Reserve a Library Computer — HTML Form

```html
<html>
<head><title>Reserve a Library Computer</title></head>
<body bgcolor="#FFFFFF">
<table width="700" border="1" height="85" bgcolor="ffffff">
<tr valign="middle" align="center"><td>
<p>
<font halign=center color="#000000" face="Arial, Helvetica, sans-serif" size="+3">
<b><i>Reserve a Library Computer</i></b></font></p>
</td></tr></table>
<form method="post" action="http://www.yourLibrary.org/cgi-bin/clc1.pl"><p> </p>
<p>
<font face="Arial, Helvetica, sans-serif" size="2"><b>Do you hate to wait in line to use one of the library's computers? Fill out this form to reserve a computer <br>on a specific date and at a specific time. All reservations must be made at least 24 hours in advance. <br>Dates/times are assigned on a first-come-first-serve basis. We'll e-mail you to let you know when a <br>computer is reserved for you.</b></font>
</p><p> </p>
<input type="hidden" name="LibraryEmail" value="you@yourLibrary.org">
<input type="hidden" name="LibraryURL" value="http://www.yourLibrary.org">
<input type="hidden" name="Form" value="Reserve a Library Computer">
<p></p>
<table width="407" border="0" cellspacing="4" cellpadding="1">
<tr><td width="202">
<b><font face="Arial, Helvetica, sans-serif" size="2">Name</font></b><font face="Arial, Helvetica, sans-serif" size="1">  (first, last)</font><br><font face="Arial, Helvetica, sans-serif" size="2"><input type="text" name="Name" size="25"></font></td>
<td width="189">
<b><font face="Arial, Helvetica, sans-serif" size="2">E-mail address<br></font></b><font face="Arial, Helvetica, sans-serif" size="2"><input type="text" name="Email" size="25">
</font></td></tr>
<tr><td width="202" height="2">
<b><font face="Arial, Helvetica, sans-serif" size="2">Home address</font><font face="Arial, Helvetica, sans-serif" size="1"> </font></b><font face="Arial, Helvetica, sans-serif" size="1"> (+ city)</font>
<br><font face="Arial, Helvetica, sans-serif" size="2"><input type= "text" name= "HomeAddr" size="25">
</font></td>
<td width="189" height="2">
<b><font face="Arial, Helvetica, sans-serif" size="2">School you attend<br></font></b><font face="Arial, Helvetica, sans-serif" size="2"><input type="text" name="School" size="25"></font></td></tr>
<tr><td width="202" height="2">
<b><font face="Arial, Helvetica, sans-serif" size="2">Home phone/fax</font>  </b><font face="Arial, Helvetica, sans-serif" size="1">(+ areacode)</font><br><font face="Arial, Helvetica, sans-serif" size="2">
<input type="text" name="HomePhone" size="25"></font></td>
<td width="189" height="2">
<b><font face="Arial, Helvetica, sans-serif" size="2">Teacher's name<br></font></b><font face="Arial,
```

```html
Helvetica, sans-serif" size="2"><input type="text" name="Teacher" size="25"></font></td></tr>
<tr><td width="391" colspan="2" height="48">
<b><font face="Arial, Helvetica, sans-serif" size="2">What grade are you in?</font></b><br>
<table width="87%" border="0" cellspacing="4" cellpadding="0"><tr><td height="8" width="16%">
<font face="Arial, Helvetica, sans-serif" size="2"><input type="radio" name="EducationLevel" value="3">
3</font></td>
<td height="8" width="16%">
<font face="Arial, Helvetica, sans-serif" size="2"><input type="radio" name="EducationLevel" value="4">
4</font></td>
<td height="8" width="16%">
<font face="Arial, Helvetica, sans-serif" size="2"><input type="radio" name="EducationLevel" value="5">
5</font></td>
<td height="8" width="16%">
<font face="Arial, Helvetica, sans-serif" size="2"><input type="radio" name="EducationLevel" value="6">
6</font></td>
<td height="8" width="36%">
<font face="Arial, Helvetica, sans-serif" size="2"><input type="radio" name="EducationLevel" value="7">
7</font></td></tr>
<tr><td height="2" width="16%">
<font face="Arial, Helvetica, sans-serif" size="2"><input type="radio" name="EducationLevel" value="8">
8</font></td>
<td height="2" width="16%">
<font face="Arial, Helvetica, sans-serif" size="2"><input type="radio" name="EducationLevel" value="9">
9</font></td>
<td height="2" width="16%">
<font face="Arial, Helvetica, sans-serif" size="2"><input type="radio" name="EducationLevel" value="10">
10</font></td>
<td height="2" width="16%">
<font face="Arial, Helvetica, sans-serif" size="2"><input type="radio" name="EducationLevel" value="11">
11</font></td>
<td height="2" width="36%">
<font face="Arial, Helvetica, sans-serif" size="2"><input type="radio" name="EducationLevel" value="12">
12</font>
</td></tr></table>
</td></tr></table>
<p><br>
<b><font face="Arial, Helvetica, sans-serif" size="2">Date / time you would like to reserve a library computer
</font></b>  <font face="Arial, Helvetica, sans-serif" size="1">(list two times that will work)</font><br>
<font face="Arial, Helvetica, sans-serif" size="2">Date</font><font face="Arial, Helvetica, sans-serif">
<input type="text" name="DateToReserve" size="15"></font>      
<font face="Arial, Helvetica, sans-serif" size="2">Time </font><font face="Arial, Helvetica, sans-serif">
<input type="text" name="TimeToReserve" size="15"></font><br>
<font face="Arial, Helvetica, sans-serif" size="2">Date</font><font face="Arial, Helvetica, sans-serif">
<input type="text" name="DateToReserve2" size="15"></font>      
<font face="Arial, Helvetica, sans-serif" size="2">Time</font><font face="Arial, Helvetica, sans-serif">
```

```html
<input type="text" name="TimeToReserve2" size="15"></font></p>
<p> </p>
<table width="700" border="0" cellspacing="10" cellpadding="1"><tr><td width="262"><div align="right">
<input type="submit" name="send" value="Send Reservation"></div></td><td width="185"> </td>
<td width="207"><div align="left"><input type="reset" name="clear" value="Clear Form"></div></td></tr>
<tr colspan=3><td colspan=3>
<table width="500" border="1" height="2" align="center" cellpadding="0" cellspacing="0"
bgcolor="ffffff"><tr><td><font size="1" color="#ffffff">.</font></td></tr></table></td></tr><tr>
<td colspan=3><div align="center">
<font face="Arial, Helvetica, sans-serif" size="1"><b>http://</b></font><br> 
<font face="Arial, Helvetica, sans-serif" size="1"><b>&copy; 2002</b></font>
<font face="Arial, Helvetica, sans-serif" size="2"><a href="mailto:">
<b><font size="1">Contact Webmaster</font></b></a></font></div></td></tr>
</table></form>
</body>
</html>
```

Reserve a Library Computer — Perl Script

```perl
#!/usr/local/bin/perl

# ***************************************************
# ABOVE is where you MUST specify the path to your
# perl interpreter on your Web server.
# Replace /usr/local/bin/perl with your path.
# ***************************************************

if ($ENV{'REQUEST_METHOD'}eq"GET"){$buffer = $ENV{'QUERY_STRING'};}
    elsif($ENV{'REQUEST_METHOD'}eq"POST"){
        read(STDIN,$buffer,$ENV{'CONTENT_LENGTH'});
    }
$bufferb = $buffer;
#separate the name of the input from its value.
@forminputs = split(/&/, $bufferb);

foreach $forminput (@forminputs)
{
    #separate the name of the input from its value
    ($name, $value) = split(/=/, $forminput);

    #Un-Webify plus signs and %-encoding
    $value =~ tr/+/ /;
    $value =~ s/%([a-fA-F0-9][a-fA-F0-9])/pack("C", hex($1))/eg;

    #stick them in the in array
    $in{$name} = $value;
}
print "Content-type: text/html\n\n";

###############################################
# ABOVE is the required header for a perl script       #
###############################################


############################################################
# (Below) Email received by library containing user-entered information #
############################################################


# ***************************************************
# Here's where you MUST specify the path to your
# email program (probably sendmail) ON your Web server.
# Replace /usr/sbin/sendmail with your path.
# ***************************************************
```

Group 3—Library Computer Forms/Surveys

```
open (LMAIL, "|/usr/sbin/sendmail -t");
print LMAIL ("To: $in{LibraryEmail}\n");

print LMAIL ("From: $in{Email}\n");
print LMAIL ("Subject: $in{Form} - patron submission\n");

print LMAIL ("------------------\nPatron information\n\n");

print LMAIL ("Name:\n $in{Name}\n\n");
print LMAIL ("E-mail Address:\n $in{Email}\n\n");
print LMAIL ("Home Address:\n $in{HomeAddr}\n\n");
print LMAIL ("School:\n $in{School}\n\n");
print LMAIL ("Home Phone/Fax:\n $in{HomePhone}\n\n");
print LMAIL ("Teacher's Name:\n $in{Teacher}\n\n");
print LMAIL ("Grade:\n $in{EducationLevel}\n\n");

print LMAIL ("------------------\nSubmitted information \n\n");
print LMAIL ("First date / time:\n $in{DateToReserve}\n $in{TimeToReserve}\n\n");
print LMAIL ("Second date / time:\n $in{DateToReserve2}\n $in{TimeToReserve2}\n\n");

print LMAIL ("\n.\n");

##############################################
# Email received by the user confirming form submission #
##############################################

# ***********************************************************
# Here's where you MUST specify the path to your
# email program ON your Web server.
# Replace /usr/sbin/sendmail with your path.
# ***********************************************************

open (MAIL, "|/usr/sbin/sendmail -t");

# ***********************************************************
# Here's where you MAY customize the email
# response to the user. You may change any wording
# on the form.
# ***********************************************************

print MAIL<<toEnd;
To: $in{Email}
From: $in{LibraryEmail}
Subject: $in{Form}
```

Thanks for sending us a library computer reservation.\n\n
A librarian will contact you in the next couple of days to let you know if a computer is available on the day and at the time you requested.

```
toEnd
    print MAIL ("\n.\n");


##########################################
# Screen response to user after submitting the form  #
##########################################

print ("<html><head><title>$in{Form}</title></head>");
print ("<body bgcolor=\"ffffff\">");


# *************************************************************
# Here's where you MAY change the screen response
# the user sees after submitting the form. You may
# change any wording between the quotation marks.
# *************************************************************
print ("Thanks for sending us a library computer reservation.<p>
A librarian will contact you in the next couple of days to let you know if a computer is available on the day and at the time you requested.");


# *************************************************************
# Here's where you MAY change the name of the link
# back to your main page. You may replace Return
# to our main page with your own wording.
# *************************************************************

print ("<p><center><a href=$in{LibraryURL}>Return to our main page.</a></center>");
print ("</body></html>");
```

Library Cybersurfer Survey

If you use the library's computers to connect to the Internet, we'd like you to fill out this short survey to let us know how you use the Internet and our library's Web site while in the library.

Your Computer Experience

What is your level of computer knowledge?
○ Beginner   ○ Intermediate   ○ Expert

Where do you have access to a computer outside of the library? (select any/all)
○ Home   ○ School   ○ Community organization   ○ Other   ○ No access

Can you connect to the Internet using that computer?   ○ Yes   ○ No

Library Computers

How often do you use the library's computers?
○ More than once a day   ○ Once a day   ○ Every other day
○ 2+ times a week   ○ Once a week   ○ 2+ times a month

How do you use the library's computers? (select any/all)
○ Online catalog   ○ Library databases   ○ Web browsing   ○ Searching   ○ E-mail   ○ Other uses

How many pages do you print each time you use a library computer?
○ None   ○ 1-4 pages   ○ 5-10 pages   ○ 11-15 pages   ○ 16-20 pages   ○ Over 20 pages

Your Internet Use

How did you find out that the library has Internet access?
○ Friends   ○ Library posters, etc   ○ Librarians
○ Local news   ○ Teachers   ○ Other

How often do you use the Internet at the library?
○ More than once a day   ○ Once a day   ○ Every other day
○ 2+ times a week   ○ Once a week   ○ 2+ times a month

When do you use the Internet at the library? (select any/all)
○ Morning   ○ Early afternoon   ○ Late afternoon   ○ Evening

What would make using the Internet at the library easier?

[text box]

The Library's Web Site

How many times have you visited the library's Web site? [ ]

How often do you visit the library's Web site?
- ○ More than once a day
- ○ Once a day
- ○ Every other day
- ○ 2+ times a week
- ○ Once a week
- ○ 2+ times a month

How long have you used the library's Web site?
- ○ Less than a month
- ○ One month to six months
- ○ More than six months
- ○ Less than a year
- ○ One to two years
- ○ More than two years

How did you find out about the library's Web site?
- ○ Friends
- ○ Library posters, etc.
- ○ Librarians
- ○ Link from another Web site
- ○ Teachers
- ○ Other

Which sections / pages of the library's Web site do you view most often?

[text area]

Name (first, last)
[ ]

E-mail address
[ ]

School you attend
[ ]

Gender
- ○ Female ○ Male

What grade are you in?
- ○ 3   ○ 4   ○ 5   ○ 6   ○ 7
- ○ 8   ○ 9   ○ 10 ○ 11 ○ 12

[Send Survey]   [Clear Survey]

http://
© 2002 Contact Webmaster

Library Cybersurfer Survey — HTML Form

```html
<html>
<head><title>Library Cybersurfer Survey</title></head>
<body bgcolor="#FFFFFF">
<table width="700" border="1" bordercolor="000000" height="85" bgcolor="#ffffff">
<tr valign="middle" align="center">
<td>
<p>
<font halign=center color="#000000" face="Arial, Helvetica, sans-serif" size="+3">
<b><i>Library Cybersurfer Survey</i></b></font></p>
</td></tr></table>
<form method="post" action="http://www.yourLibrary.org/cgi-bin/clc2.pl"><p> </p>
<p>
<font face="Arial, Helvetica, sans-serif" size="2"><b>If you use the library's computers to connect to the Internet, we'd like you to fill out this short <br>survey to let us know how you use the Internet and our library's Web site while in the library.</b></font><br></p>
<p>
<input type="hidden" name="LibraryEmail" value="you@yourLibrary.org">
<input type="hidden" name="LibraryURL" value="http://www.yourLibrary.org">
<input type="hidden" name="Form" value="Library Cybersurfer Survey">
</p>
<p> </p>
<b><font face="Arial, Helvetica, sans-serif" size="3">Your Computer Experience</font></b>
<p></p><p>
<font face="Arial, Helvetica, sans-serif" size="2"><b>What is your level of computer knowledge?</b><br>
<input type="radio" name="Expertise" value="Beginner">Beginner   
<input type="radio" name="Expertise" value="Intermediate">Intermediate   
<input type="radio" name="Expertise" value="Expert">Expert<br></font></p>
<p>
<b><font face="Arial, Helvetica, sans-serif" size="2">Where do you have access to a computer outside of the library?  </font></b><font face="Arial, Helvetica, sans-serif" size="1">(select any/all)
</font><font face="Arial, Helvetica, sans-serif" size="2"><br>
<input type="radio" name="H" value="Home">Home   
<input type="radio" name="S" value="School">School   
<input type="radio" name="CO" value="Community organization">Community organization   
<input type="radio" name="OT" value="Other">Other   
<input type="radio" name="NA" value="No access">No access</font></p>
<p>
<b><font face="Arial, Helvetica, sans-serif" size="2">Can you connect to the Internet using that computer? </font></b><font face="Arial, Helvetica, sans-serif" size="2">
<input type="radio" name="Internet" value="Yes">Yes 
<input type="radio" name="Internet" value="No">No  </font></p>
<p><br>
```

```html
<b><font face="Arial, Helvetica, sans-serif" size="3">Library Computers</font></b></p>
<p>
<b><font face="Arial, Helvetica, sans-serif" size="2">How often do you use the library's computers?<br>
</font></b>
<table width="500" border="0" cellspacing="0" cellpadding="0"><tr><td width="182">
<input type="radio" name="OftenUse" value="More than once a day"><font face="Arial, Helvetica, sans-serif" size="2">More than once a day</font></td>
<td width="126">
<font face="Arial, Helvetica, sans-serif" size="2"><input type="radio" name="OftenUse" value="Once a day">Once a day</font></td>
<td width="192">
<font face="Arial, Helvetica, sans-serif" size="2"><input type="radio" name="OftenUse" value="Every other day">Every other day</font></td></tr>
<tr><td width="182">
<font face="Arial, Helvetica, sans-serif" size="2"><input type="radio" name="OftenUse" value="2+ times a week">2+ times a week</font></td>
<td width="126">
<font face="Arial, Helvetica, sans-serif" size="2"><input type="radio" name="OftenUse" value="Once a week">Once a week</font></td>
<td width="192">
<font face="Arial, Helvetica, sans-serif" size="2"><input type="radio" name="OftenUse" value="2+ times a month">2+ times a month</font></td></tr></table>
<p>
<font face="Arial, Helvetica, sans-serif" size="2"><b>How do you use the library's computers?</b>
</font>  <font face="Arial, Helvetica, sans-serif" size="1">(select any/all)</font><br>
<input type="radio" name="OC" value="Online catalog"><font face="Arial, Helvetica, sans-serif" size="2">Online catalog   
<input type="radio" name="LD" value="Library databases">Library databases   
<input type="radio" name="WB" value="Web browsing">Web browsing   
<input type="radio" name="R" value="Searching">Searching   
<input type="radio" name="E" value="Email">E-mail   
<input type="radio" name="OU" value="Other uses">Other uses<br></font></p>
<p>
<font face="Arial, Helvetica, sans-serif" size="2"><b>How many pages do you print each time you use a library computer?</b><br>
<input type="radio" name="Pages" value="None"><font face="Arial, Helvetica, sans-serif" size="2">None   
<input type="radio" name="Pages" value="1-4 pages">1-4 pages   
<input type="radio" name="Pages" value="5-10 pages">5-10 pages   
<input type="radio" name="Pages" value="11-15 pages">11-15 pages   
<input type="radio" name="Pages" value="16-20 pages">16-20 pages   
<input type="radio" name="Pages" value="Over 20 pages">Over 20 pages</font></font></p>
<p><br>
<b><font face="Arial, Helvetica, sans-serif" size="3">Your Internet Use</font></b></p>
<p>
```

```html
<font face="Arial, Helvetica, sans-serif" size="2"><b>How did you find out that the library has Internet access?<br></b></font>
<table width="450" border="0" cellspacing="0" cellpadding="0"><tr><td width="127">
<font face="Arial, Helvetica, sans-serif" size="2"><input type="radio" name="Access" value="Friends">
Friends</font></td>
<td width="161">
<font face="Arial, Helvetica, sans-serif" size="2"><input type="radio" name="Access" value="Library posters, etc.">Library posters, etc.</font></td>
<td width="112">
<font face="Arial, Helvetica, sans-serif" size="2"><input type="radio" name="Access" value="Librarians">
Librarians</font></td></tr>
<tr><td width="127">
<font face="Arial, Helvetica, sans-serif" size="2"><input type="radio" name="Access" value="Local news">
Local news</font></td>
<td width="161">
<font face="Arial, Helvetica, sans-serif" size="2"><input type="radio" name="Access" value="Teachers">
Teachers</font></td>
<td width="112">
<font face="Arial, Helvetica, sans-serif" size="2"><input type="radio" name="Access" value="Other">
Other</font>
</td></tr></table>
<p>
<font face="Arial, Helvetica, sans-serif" size="2"><b>How often do you use the Internet at the library?</b><br>
</font>
<table width="500" border="0" cellspacing="0" cellpadding="0"><tr><td width="200">
<font face="Arial, Helvetica, sans-serif" size="2"><input type="radio" name="InternetUse" value="More than once a day">More than once a day</font></td>
<td width="132">
<font face="Arial, Helvetica, sans-serif" size="2"><input type="radio" name="InternetUse" value="Once a day">Once a day</font></td>
<td width="168">
<font face="Arial, Helvetica, sans-serif" size="2"><input type="radio" name="InternetUse" value="Every other day">Every other day</font></td></tr>
<tr><td width="200">
<font face="Arial, Helvetica, sans-serif" size="2"><input type="radio" name="InternetUse" value="2+ times a week">2+ times a week</font></td>
<td width="132">
<font face="Arial, Helvetica, sans-serif" size="2"><input type="radio" name="InternetUse" value="Once a week">Once a week</font></td>
<td width="168">
<font face="Arial, Helvetica, sans-serif" size="2"><input type="radio" name="InternetUse" value="2+ times a month">2+ times a month</font>
</td></tr></table>
<p>
<font face="Arial, Helvetica, sans-serif" size="2"><b>When do you use the Internet at the library?</b>
```

```html
</font>  <font face="Arial, Helvetica, sans-serif" size="1">(select any/all)</font><br>
<input type="radio" name="M" value="Morning">Morning  
<input type="radio" name="EA" value="Early afternoon">Early afternoon  
<input type="radio" name="LA" value="Late aftenoon">Late afternoon  
<input type="radio" name="EE" value="Evening">Evening</font></p>
<p>
<font face="Arial, Helvetica, sans-serif" size="2"><b>What would make using the Internet at the library easier?<br></b><font size="3"><textarea name="Easier" cols="40" rows="2"></textarea></font></font>
</p><p><br>
<b><font face="Arial, Helvetica, sans-serif" size="3">The Library's Web Site</font></b></p>
<p>
<font face="Arial, Helvetica, sans-serif" size="2"><b>How many times have you visited the library's Web site? </b><font size="3"><input type="text" name="Times" size="5"></font><br></font></p>
<p>
<font face="Arial, Helvetica, sans-serif" size="2"><b>How often do you visit the library's Web site?</b><br>
</font>
<table width="500" border="0" cellspacing="0" cellpadding="0"><tr><td width="177">
<font face="Arial, Helvetica, sans-serif" size="2"><input type="radio" name="OftenVisit" value="More than once a day">More than once a day</font></td>
<td width="122">
<font face="Arial, Helvetica, sans-serif" size="2"><input type="radio" name="OftenVisit" value="Once a day">Once a day</font></td>
<td width="201">
<font face="Arial, Helvetica, sans-serif" size="2"><input type="radio" name="OftenVisit" value="Every other day">Every other day</font></td></tr>
<tr><td width="177">
<font face="Arial, Helvetica, sans-serif" size="2"><input type="radio" name="OftenVisit" value="2+ times a week">2+ times a week</font></td>
<td width="122">
<font face="Arial, Helvetica, sans-serif" size="2"><input type="radio" name="OftenVisit" value="Once a week">Once a week</font></td>
<td width="201">
<font face="Arial, Helvetica, sans-serif" size="2"><input type="radio" name="OftenVisit" value="2+ times a month">2+ times a month</font></td></tr></table>
<p>
<font face="Arial, Helvetica, sans-serif" size="2"><b>How long have you used the library's Web site?</b></font>
<table width="500" border="0" cellspacing="0" cellpadding="0"><tr><td width="155">
<font face="Arial, Helvetica, sans-serif" size="2"><input type="radio" name="LongUsed" value="Less than a month">Less than a month</font></td>
<td width="185">
<font face="Arial, Helvetica, sans-serif" size="2"><input type="radio" name="LongUsed" value="One month to six months">One month to six months</font></td>
<td width="160">
<font face="Arial, Helvetica, sans-serif" size="2"><input type="radio" name="LongUsed" value="More than six months">More than six months</font></td></tr>
```

```
<tr><td width="155">
<font face="Arial, Helvetica, sans-serif" size="2"><input type="radio" name="LongUsed" value="Less than a year">Less than a year</font></td>
<td width="185">
<font face="Arial, Helvetica, sans-serif" size="2"><input type="radio" name="LongUsed" value="One to two years">One to two years</font></td>
<td width="160">
<font face="Arial, Helvetica, sans-serif" size="2"><input type="radio" name="LongUsed" value="More than two years">More than two years</font></td></tr></table>
<p>
<font face="Arial, Helvetica, sans-serif" size="2"><b>How did you find out about the library's Web site?<br>
</b></font>
<table width="500" border="0" cellspacing="0" cellpadding="0"><tr><td width="196">
<font face="Arial, Helvetica, sans-serif" size="2"><input type="radio" name="Hear" value="Friends">
Friends</font></td>
<td width="164">
<font face="Arial, Helvetica, sans-serif" size="2"><input type="radio" name="Hear" value="Library posters, etc.">Library posters, etc.</font></td>
<td width="140">
<font face="Arial, Helvetica, sans-serif" size="2"><input type="radio" name="Hear" value="Librarians">
Librarians</font></td></tr>
<tr><td width="196">
<font face="Arial, Helvetica, sans-serif" size="2"><input type="radio" name="Hear" value="Link from another Web site">Link from another Web site</font></td>
<td width="164">
<font face="Arial, Helvetica, sans-serif" size="2"><input type="radio" name="Hear" value="Teachers">
Teachers</font></td>
<td width="140">
<font face="Arial, Helvetica, sans-serif" size="2"><input type="radio" name="Hear" value="Other">
Other</font>
</td></tr></table>
<p>
<font face="Arial, Helvetica, sans-serif" size="2"><b>Which sections / pages of the library's Web site do you view most often?<br></b><font face="Arial, Helvetica, sans-serif" size="3"><textarea name= "Features" cols="40" rows="2"></textarea></font></font></p>
<p> </p>
<table width="407" border="0" cellspacing="4" cellpadding="1"><tr><td width="202">
<b><font face="Arial, Helvetica, sans-serif" size="2">Name</font></b><font face="Arial, Helvetica, sans-serif" size="1">  (first, last)</font><br><font face="Arial, Helvetica, sans-serif" size="2">
<input type="text" name="Name" size="25"></font></td>
<td width="189">
<b><font face="Arial, Helvetica, sans-serif" size="2">E-mail address<br></font></b><font face="Arial, Helvetica, sans-serif" size="2"><input type="text" name="Email" size="25"></font></td></tr>
<tr><td width="202" height="2">
<b><font face="Arial, Helvetica, sans-serif" size="2">School you attend<br></font></b><font face="Arial,
```

```html
Helvetica, sans-serif" size="2"><input type="text" name="School" size="25"></font></td>
<td width="189" height="2">
<b><font face="Arial, Helvetica, sans-serif" size="2">Gender<br></font></b>
<input type="radio" name="Gender" value="Female"><font face="Arial, Helvetica, sans-serif" size="2">
Female</font>
<input type="radio" name="Gender" value="Male"><font face="Arial, Helvetica, sans-serif" size="2">
Male</font></td></tr>
<tr><td width="391" colspan="2" height="48">
<b><font face="Arial, Helvetica, sans-serif" size="2">What grade are you in?</font></b><br>
<table width="87%" border="0" cellspacing="4" cellpadding="0"><tr><td height="8" width="16%">
<font face="Arial, Helvetica, sans-serif" size="2"><input type="radio" name="EducationLevel" value="3">
3</font></td>
<td height="8" width="16%">
<font face="Arial, Helvetica, sans-serif" size="2"><input type="radio" name="EducationLevel" value="4">
4</font></td>
<td height="8" width="16%">
<font face="Arial, Helvetica, sans-serif" size="2"><input type="radio" name="EducationLevel" value="5">
5</font></td>
<td height="8" width="16%">
<font face="Arial, Helvetica, sans-serif" size="2"><input type="radio" name="EducationLevel" value="6">
6</font></td>
<td height="8" width="36%">
<font face="Arial, Helvetica, sans-serif" size="2"><input type="radio" name="EducationLevel" value="7">
7</font></td></tr>
<tr><td height="2" width="16%">
<font face="Arial, Helvetica, sans-serif" size="2"><input type="radio" name="EducationLevel" value="8">
8</font></td>
<td height="2" width="16%">
<font face="Arial, Helvetica, sans-serif" size="2"><input type="radio" name="EducationLevel" value="9">
9</font></td>
<td height="2" width="16%">
<font face="Arial, Helvetica, sans-serif" size="2"><input type="radio" name="EducationLevel" value="10">
10</font></td>
<td height="2" width="16%">
<font face="Arial, Helvetica, sans-serif" size="2"><input type="radio" name="EducationLevel" value="11">
11</font></td>
<td height="2" width="36%">
<font face="Arial, Helvetica, sans-serif" size="2"><input type="radio" name="EducationLevel" value="12">
12</font>
</td></tr></table>
</td></tr></table>
<p>  </p>
<table width="700" border="0" cellspacing="10" cellpadding="1"><tr><td width="226"><div align="right">
<input type="submit" name="send" value="Send Survey"></div></td><td width="207"> </td>
<td width="221"><div align="left"><input type="reset" name="clear" value="Clear Survey">/div></td></tr>
```

```html
<tr colspan=3><td colspan=3>
<table width="500" border="1" bordercolor="#000000" height="2" align="center" cellpadding="0" cellspacing="0" bgcolor="#ffffff"><tr><td><font size="1" color="#ffffff">.</font></td></tr></table></td></tr>
<tr><td colspan=3><div align="center">
<font face="Arial, Helvetica, sans-serif" size="1"><b>http://</b></font><br> 
<font face="Arial, Helvetica, sans-serif" size="1"><b>&copy; 2002</b></font>
<font face="Arial, Helvetica, sans-serif" size="2"><a href="mailto:">
<b><font size="1">Contact Webmaster</font></b></a></font></div></td></tr>
</table></form>
</body>
</html>
```

Library Cybersurfer Survey — Perl Script

```perl
#!/usr/local/bin/perl

# ****************************************************
# ABOVE is where you MUST specify the path to your
# perl interpreter on your Web server.
# Replace /usr/local/bin/perl with your path.
# ****************************************************

if ($ENV{'REQUEST_METHOD'}eq"GET"){$buffer = $ENV{'QUERY_STRING'};}
    elsif($ENV{'REQUEST_METHOD'}eq"POST"){
        read(STDIN,$buffer,$ENV{'CONTENT_LENGTH'});
    }
$bufferb = $buffer;
#separate the name of the input from its value.
@forminputs = split(/&/, $bufferb);

foreach $forminput (@forminputs)
{
    #separate the name of the input from its value
    ($name, $value) = split(/=/, $forminput);

    #Un-Webify plus signs and %-encoding
    $value =~ tr/+/ /;
    $value =~ s/%([a-fA-F0-9][a-fA-F0-9])/pack("C", hex($1))/eg;

    #stick them in the in array
    $in{$name} = $value;
}
print "Content-type: text/html\n\n";

###############################################
# ABOVE is the required header for a perl script    #
###############################################

#################################################
# (Below) Email received by library containing user-entered information #
#################################################

# ****************************************************
# Here's where you MUST specify the path to your
# email program (probably sendmail) ON your Web server.
# Replace /usr/sbin/sendmail with your path.
# ****************************************************
```

Group 3—Library Computer Forms/Surveys 131

```perl
open (LMAIL, "|/usr/sbin/sendmail -t");
print LMAIL ("To: $in{LibraryEmail}\n");

print LMAIL ("From: $in{Email}\n");
print LMAIL ("Subject: $in{Form} - patron submission\n");

print LMAIL ("-------------------\nPatron information\n\n");

print LMAIL ("Name:\n $in{Name}\n\n");
print LMAIL ("E-mail Address:\n $in{Email}\n\n");
print LMAIL ("School:\n $in{School}\n\n");
print LMAIL ("Gender:\n $in{Gender}\n\n");
print LMAIL ("Grade:\n $in{EducationLevel}\n\n");

print LMAIL ("-------------------\nSubmitted information \n\n");
print LMAIL ("-------------------\nYour Computer Experience\n\n");
print LMAIL ("What is your level of computer knowledge?\n $in{Expertise}\n\n");
print LMAIL ("Where do you have access to a computer outside of the library?\n $in{H}, $in{S}, $in{CO}, $in{OT}, $in{NA}\n\n");
print LMAIL ("Is there Internet access on the computer(s)?\n $in{Internet}\n\n");
print LMAIL ("-------------------\nLibrary Computers \n\n");
print LMAIL ("How often do you use the library's computers?\n $in{OftenUse}\n\n");
print LMAIL ("How do you use the library's computers?\n $in{OC} $in{LD}, $in{WB}, $in{R}, $in{E}, $in{OU}\n\n");
print LMAIL ("How many pages do you print each time you use the Internet?\n $in{Pages}\n\n");
print LMAIL ("-------------------\nYour Internet Use \n\n");
print LMAIL ("How did you find out that the library has Internet access?\n $in{Access}\n\n");
print LMAIL ("How often do you use the Internet at the library?\n{InternetUse}\n\n");
print LMAIL ("When do you use the Internet at the library?\n $in{M}, $in{EA}, $in{LA}, $in{EE}\n\n");
print LMAIL ("What would make using the Internet at the library easier?\n $in{Easier}\n\n");
print LMAIL ("-------------------\nThe Library's Web site\n\n");
print LMAIL ("How many times have you visited the library's Web site?\n $in{Times}\n\n");
print LMAIL ("How often do you visit the library's Web site?\n $in{OftenVisit}\n\n");
print LMAIL ("How long have you used the library's Web site?\n $in{LongUsed}\n\n");
print LMAIL ("How did you find out / hear about the library's Web site?\n $in{Hear}\n\n");
print LMAIL ("Which sections / pages of the library's Web site do you view most often?\n $in{Features}\n\n");

print LMAIL ("\n.\n");

##############################################
# Email received by the user confirming form submission #
##############################################

# ***********************************************************
# Here's where you MUST specify the path to your
```

```
# email program ON your Web server.
# Replace /usr/sbin/sendmail with your path.
# ***********************************************************

open (MAIL, "|/usr/sbin/sendmail -t");


# ***********************************************************
# Here's where you MAY customize the email
# response to the user. You may change any wording
# on the form.
# ***********************************************************

print MAIL<<toEnd;
To: $in{Email}
From: $in{LibraryEmail}
Subject: $in{Form}


Thanks for taking the time to fill out our Library Cybersurfer Survey.\n\n
We will use your input to help us improve our Web site.

toEnd
    print MAIL ("\n.\n");


##########################################
# Screen response to user after submitting the form  #
##########################################

print ("<html><head><title>$in{Form}</title></head>");
print ("<body bgcolor=\"ffffff\">");


# ***********************************************************
# Here's where you MAY change the screen response
# the user sees after submitting the form. You may
# change any wording between the quotation marks.
# ***********************************************************

print ("Thanks for taking the time to fill out our Library Cybersurfer Survey.<p>
We will use your input to help us improve our Web site.");


# ***********************************************************
# Here's where you MAY change the name of the link
# back to your main page. You may replace Return
# to our main page with your own wording.
```

***
print ("<p> <a href=$in{LibraryURL}>Return to our main page.</a> ");
print ("</body></html>");

Home Cybersurfer Survey

Please fill out this short survey to let us know how you use the Internet and our library's Web site when you are on-line at home.

Your Computer

What is your level of computer knowledge?
○ Beginner   ○ Intermediate   ○ Expert

How do you use your home computer? (select any/all)
○ Word processing   ○ E-mail   ○ Web browsing   ○ Games   ○ Graphics   ○ Other programs

What kind of computer do you use at home?
○ Windows (PC)   ○ Macintosh   ○ Don't know

How often do you use the library's computers?
○ Lots   ○ Sometimes   ○ Once in awhile   ○ Never

The Internet and Your Computer

How fast is your home Internet connection?
○ Less than 56K   ○ 56K   ○ Cable modem   ○ DSL   ○ T1/T3   ○ Don't know

Which Web browser(s) do you use at home? (select any/all)
○ Internet Explorer   ○ Netscape   ○ AOL   ○ Other   ○ Don't know

Your Internet Use at Home

How often do you use the Internet at home?
○ More than once a day   ○ Once a day   ○ Every other day
○ 2+ times a week   ○ Once a week   ○ 2+ times a month

How long have you used the Internet?
○ Less than a month   ○ One month to six months   ○ More than six months
○ Less than a year   ○ One to two years   ○ More than two years

When do you use the Internet? (select any/all)
○ Morning   ○ Early afternoon   ○ Late afternoon   ○ Early evening   ○ Night   ○ Late night

The Library's Web Site

How many times have you visited the library's Web site from your home computer? [____]

How often do you visit the library's Web site from home?
- ○ More than once a day
- ○ Once a day
- ○ Every other day
- ○ 2+ times a week
- ○ Once a week
- ○ 2+ times a month

How long have you used the library's Web site?
- ○ Less than a month
- ○ One month to six months
- ○ More than six months
- ○ Less than a year
- ○ One to two years
- ○ More than two years

How did you find out about the library's Web site?
- ○ Friends
- ○ Library posters, etc.
- ○ Librarians
- ○ Link from another Web site
- ○ Teachers
- ○ Other

Which sections / pages of the library's Web site do you use most often?
[text area]

Name (first, last)
[____]

E-mail address
[____]

School you attend
[____]

Gender
- ○ Female ○ Male

What grade are you in?
- ○ 3 ○ 4 ○ 5 ○ 6 ○ 7
- ○ 8 ○ 9 ○ 10 ○ 11 ○ 12

[Send Survey] [Clear Survey]

http://
© 2002 Contact Webmaster

Home Cybersurfer Survey — HTML Form

```html
<html>
<head><title>Home Cybersurfer Survey</title></head>
<body bgcolor="#FFFFFF">
<table width="700" border="1" height="85" bordercolor="#000000" bgcolor="#ffffff">
<tr valign="middle" align="center">
<td>
<p>
<font halign=center color="#000000" face="Arial, Helvetica, sans-serif" size="+3">
<b><i>Home Cybersurfer Survey</i></b></font></p>
</td></tr></table>
<form method="post" action="http://www.yourLibrary.org/cgi-bin/clc3.pl"><p> </p>
<p>
<b><font size="2" face="Arial, Helvetica, sans-serif">Please fill out this short survey to let us know how you use the Internet and our library's Web site when<br> you are on-line at home.</font></b></p>
<p>
<input type="hidden" name="LibraryEmail" value="you@yourLibrary.org">
<input type="hidden" name="LibraryURL" value="http://www.yourLibrary.org">
<input type="hidden" name="Form" value="Home Cybersurfer Survey">
</p>
<p> </p>
<b><font face="Arial, Helvetica, sans-serif" size="3">Your Computer</font></b>
<p></p><p>
<font face="Arial, Helvetica, sans-serif" size="2"><b>What is your level of computer knowledge?</b><br>
<input type="radio" name="Expertise" value="Beginner">Beginner   
<input type="radio" name="Expertise" value="Intermediate">Intermediate   
<input type="radio" name="Expertise" value="Expert">Expert<br></font></p>
<p>
<b><font face="Arial, Helvetica, sans-serif" size="2">How do you use your home computer?  
</font></b><font face="Arial, Helvetica, sans-serif" size="1">(select any/all)</font>
<font face="Arial, Helvetica, sans-serif" size="2"><br>
<input type="radio" name="WP" value="Word processing">Word processing   
<input type="radio" name="E" value="E-mail">E-mail   
<input type="radio" name="WB" value="Web browsing">Web browsing   
<input type="radio" name="G" value="Games">Games   
<input type="radio" name="GR" value="Graphics">Graphics   
<input type="radio" name="OP" value="Other programs">Other programs</font></p>
<p>
<b><font face="Arial, Helvetica, sans-serif" size="2">What kind of computer do you use at home?<br>
</font></b><font face="Arial, Helvetica, sans-serif" size="2">
<input type="radio" name="Computer" value="Windows (PC)">Windows (PC) 
<input type="radio" name="Computer" value="Macintosh">Macintosh  
<input type="radio" name="Computer" value="Don't know">Don't know</font></p>
<p>
```

Group 3—Library Computer Forms/Surveys

```html
<b><font face="Arial, Helvetica, sans-serif" size="2">How often do you use the library's computers?<br>
</font></b><font face="Arial, Helvetica, sans-serif" size="2">
<input type="radio" name="LibraryComputers" value="Lots">Lots 
<input type="radio" name="LibraryComputers" value="Sometimes">Sometimes  
<input type="radio" name="LibraryComputers" value="Once in awhile">Once in awhile    
<input type="radio" name="LibraryComputers" value="Never">Never</font></p>
<p><br>
<b><font face="Arial, Helvetica, sans-serif" size="3">The Internet and Your Computer</font></b></p>
<p>
<b><font face="Arial, Helvetica, sans-serif" size="2">How fast is your home Internet connection?</font>
</b><font face="Arial, Helvetica, sans-serif" size="2"><br>
<input type="radio" name="Fast" value="Less than 56K">Less than 56K   
<input type="radio" name="Fast" value="56K">56K   
<input type="radio" name="Fast" value="Cable modem">Cable modem   
<input type="radio" name="Fast" value="DSL">DSL   
<input type="radio" name="Fast" value="T1/T3">T1/T3   
<input type="radio" name="Fast" value="Don't know">Don't know</font><br></p>
<p>
<b><font face="Arial, Helvetica, sans-serif" size="2">Which Web browser(s) do you use at home?
  </font></b><font face="Arial, Helvetica, sans-serif" size="1">(select any/all)</font>
<font face="Arial, Helvetica, sans-serif" size="2"><br>
<input type="radio" name="IE" value="Internet explorer">Internet Explorer   
<input type="radio" name="NET" value="Netscape">Netscape   
<input type="radio" name="AOL" value="AOL">AOL   
<input type="radio" name="O" value="Other">Other  
<input type="radio" name="DK" value="Don't know">Don't know</font></p>
<p><br>
<b><font face="Arial, Helvetica, sans-serif" size="3">Your Internet Use at Home</font></b></p>
<p>
<font face="Arial, Helvetica, sans-serif" size="2"><b>How often do you use the Internet at home?<br>
</b></font>
<table width="500" border="0" cellspacing="0" cellpadding="0"><tr><td width="182">
<font face="Arial, Helvetica, sans-serif" size="2"><input type="radio" name="OftenUse" value="More than once a day">More than once a day</font></td>
<td width="126">
<font face="Arial, Helvetica, sans-serif" size="2"><input type="radio" name="OftenUse" value="Once a day">Once a day</font></td>
<td width="192">
<font face="Arial, Helvetica, sans-serif" size="2"><input type="radio" name="OftenUse" value="Every other day">Every other day</font></td></tr>
<tr><td width="182">
<font face="Arial, Helvetica, sans-serif" size="2"><input type="radio" name="OftenUse" value="2+ times a week">2+ times a week</font></td>
<td width="126">
<font face="Arial, Helvetica, sans-serif" size="2"><input type="radio" name="OftenUse" value="Once a
```

```html
week">Once a week</font></td>
<td width="192">
<font face="Arial, Helvetica, sans-serif" size="2"><input type="radio" name="OftenUse" value="2+ times a month">2+ times a month</font>
</td></tr></table>
<p>
<font face="Arial, Helvetica, sans-serif" size="2"><b>How long have you used the Internet?</b></font>
<br>
<table width="500" border="0" cellspacing="0" cellpadding="0"><tr><td width="155">
<font face="Arial, Helvetica, sans-serif" size="2"><input type="radio" name="LongUsed" value="Less than a month">Less than a month</font></td>
<td width="185">
<font face="Arial, Helvetica, sans-serif" size="2"><input type="radio" name="LongUsed" value="One month to six months">One month to six months</font></td>
<td width="160">
<font face="Arial, Helvetica, sans-serif" size="2"><input type="radio" name="LongUsed" value="More than six months">More than six months</font></td></tr>
<tr><td width="155">
<font face="Arial, Helvetica, sans-serif" size="2"><input type="radio" name="LongUsed" value="Less than a year">Less than a year</font></td>
<td width="185">
<font face="Arial, Helvetica, sans-serif" size="2"><input type="radio" name="LongUsed" value="One to two years">One to two years</font></td>
<td width="160">
<font face="Arial, Helvetica, sans-serif" size="2"><input type="radio" name="LongUsed" value="More than two years">More than two years</font></td></tr></table>
<p>
<font face="Arial, Helvetica, sans-serif" size="2"><b>When do you use the Internet?</b>  
</font><font face="Arial, Helvetica, sans-serif" size="1">(select any/all)</font><br><font face="Arial, Helvetica, sans-serif" size="2">
<input type="radio" name="M" value="Morning">Morning  
<input type="radio" name="EA" value="Early afternoon">Early afternoon  
<input type="radio" name="LA" value="Late afternoon">Late afternoon  
<input type="radio" name="EE" value="Early evening">Early evening  
<input type="radio" name="N" value="Night">Night  
<input type="radio" name="LN" value="Late night">Late night</font></p>
<p><br>
<b><font face="Arial, Helvetica, sans-serif" size="3">The Library's Web Site</font></b></p>
<p>
<font face="Arial, Helvetica, sans-serif" size="2"><b>How many times have you visited the library's Web site from your home computer? </b><font size="3"><input type="text" name="Visits" size="5"></font><br>
</font></p>
<p>
<font face="Arial, Helvetica, sans-serif" size="2"><b>How often do you visit the library's Web site from home?
</b></font><br></font>
```

```html
<table width="500" border="0" cellspacing="0" cellpadding="0"><tr><td width="182">
<font face="Arial, Helvetica, sans-serif" size="2"><input type="radio" name="OftenVisit" value="More than once a day">More than once a day</font></td>
<td width="126">
<font face="Arial, Helvetica, sans-serif" size="2"><input type="radio" name="OftenVisit" value="Once a day">Once a day</font></td>
<td width="192">
<font face="Arial, Helvetica, sans-serif" size="2"><input type="radio" name="OftenVisit" value="Every other day">Every other day</font></td></tr>
<tr><td width="182">
<font face="Arial, Helvetica, sans-serif" size="2"><input type="radio" name="OftenVisit" value="2+ times a week">2+ times a week</font></td>
<td width="126">
<font face="Arial, Helvetica, sans-serif" size="2"><input type="radio" name="OftenVisit" value="Once a week">Once a week</font></td>
<td width="192">
<font face="Arial, Helvetica, sans-serif" size="2"><input type="radio" name="OftenVisit" value="2+ times a month">2+ times a month</font>
</td></tr></table>
<p></p><p>
<font face="Arial, Helvetica, sans-serif" size="2"><b>How long have you used the library's Web site?</b><br>
</font></font>
<table width="500" border="0" cellspacing="0" cellpadding="0"><tr><td width="155">
<font face="Arial, Helvetica, sans-serif" size="2"><input type="radio" name="LongUsedW" value="Less than a month">Less than a month</font></td>
<td width="185">
<font face="Arial, Helvetica, sans-serif" size="2"><input type="radio" name="LongUsedW" value="One month to six months">One month to six months</font></td>
<td width="160">
<font face="Arial, Helvetica, sans-serif" size="2"><input type="radio" name="LongUsedW" value="More than six months">More than six months</font></td></tr>
<tr><td width="155">
<font face="Arial, Helvetica, sans-serif" size="2"><input type="radio" name="LongUsedW" value="Less than a year">Less than a year</font></td>
<td width="185">
<font face="Arial, Helvetica, sans-serif" size="2"><input type="radio" name="LongUsedW" value="One to two years">One to two years</font></td>
<td width="160">
<font face="Arial, Helvetica, sans-serif" size="2"><input type="radio" name="LongUsedW" value="More than two years">More than two years</font></td></tr></table>
<p>
<font face="Arial, Helvetica, sans-serif" size="2"><b>How did you find out about the library's Web site?</b>
</font><br>
<table width="500" border="0" cellspacing="0" cellpadding="0"><tr><td width="196">
<font face="Arial, Helvetica, sans-serif" size="2"><input type="radio" name="Hear" value="Friends">
```

```html
Friends</font></font></td>
<td width="164">
<font face="Arial, Helvetica, sans-serif" size="2"><input type="radio" name="Hear" value="Library posters, etc.">Library posters, etc.</font></td>
<td width="140">
<font face="Arial, Helvetica, sans-serif" size="2"><input type="radio" name="Hear" value="Librarians"> Librarians</font></td></tr>
<tr><td width="196">
<font face="Arial, Helvetica, sans-serif" size="2"><input type="radio" name="Hear" value="Link from another Web site">Link from another Web site</font></td>
<td width="164">
<font face="Arial, Helvetica, sans-serif" size="2"><input type="radio" name="Hear" value="Teachers"> Teachers</font></td>
<td width="140">
<font face="Arial, Helvetica, sans-serif" size="2"><input type="radio" name="Hear" value="Other"> Other</font></td></tr></table>
<p>
<font face="Arial, Helvetica, sans-serif" size="2"><b>Which sections / pages of the library's Web site do you use most often?</b><br><font face="Arial, Helvetica, sans-serif" size="3"><textarea name= "Features" cols="40" rows="2"></textarea></font></font></p>
<p> </p>
<table width="407" border="0" cellspacing="4" cellpadding="1"><tr><td width="202">
<b><font face="Arial, Helvetica, sans-serif" size="2">Name</font></b><font face="Arial, Helvetica, sans-serif" size="1">  (first, last)</font><br><font face="Arial, Helvetica, sans-serif" size="2">
<input type="text" name="Name" size="25"></font></td>
<td width="189">
<b><font face="Arial, Helvetica, sans-serif" size="2">E-mail address<br></font></b><font face="Arial, Helvetica, sans-serif" size="2"><input type="text" name="Email" size="25"></font></td></tr>
<tr><td width="202" height="2">
<b><font face="Arial, Helvetica, sans-serif" size="2">School you attend<br></font></b><font face="Arial, Helvetica, sans-serif" size="2"><input type="text" name="School" size="25"></font></td>
<td width="189" height="2">
<b><font face="Arial, Helvetica, sans-serif" size="2">Gender<br></font></b>
<input type="radio" name="Gender" value="Female"><font face="Arial, Helvetica, sans-serif" size="2">Female </font>
<input type="radio" name="Gender" value="Male"><font face="Arial, Helvetica, sans-serif" size="2">Male </font></td></tr>
<tr><td width="391" colspan="2" height="48">
<b><font face="Arial, Helvetica, sans-serif" size="2">What grade are you in?</font></b><br>
<font face="Arial, Helvetica, sans-serif" size="2"></font>
<table width="87%" border="0" cellspacing="4" cellpadding="0"><tr><td height="8" width="16%">
<font face="Arial, Helvetica, sans-serif" size="2"><input type="radio" name="EducationLevel" value="3"> 3</font></td>
<td height="8" width="16%">
<font face="Arial, Helvetica, sans-serif" size="2"><input type="radio" name="EducationLevel" value="4">
```

```html
4</font></td>
<td height="8" width="16%">
<font face="Arial, Helvetica, sans-serif" size="2"><input type="radio" name="EducationLevel" value="5">
5</font></td>
<td height="8" width="16%">
<font face="Arial, Helvetica, sans-serif" size="2"><input type="radio" name="EducationLevel" value="6">
6</font></td>
<td height="8" width="36%">
<font face="Arial, Helvetica, sans-serif" size="2"><input type="radio" name="EducationLevel" value="7">
7</font></td></tr>
<tr><td height="2" width="16%">
<font face="Arial, Helvetica, sans-serif" size="2"><input type="radio" name="EducationLevel" value="8">
8</font></td>
<td height="2" width="16%">
<font face="Arial, Helvetica, sans-serif" size="2"><input type="radio" name="EducationLevel" value="9">
9</font></td>
<td height="2" width="16%">
<font face="Arial, Helvetica, sans-serif" size="2"><input type="radio" name="EducationLevel" value="10">
10</font></td>
<td height="2" width="16%">
<font face="Arial, Helvetica, sans-serif" size="2"><input type="radio" name="EducationLevel" value="11">
11</font></td>
<td height="2" width="36%">
<font face="Arial, Helvetica, sans-serif" size="2"><input type="radio" name="EducationLevel" value="12">
12</font>
</td></tr></table>
</td></tr></table>
<p> </p>
<table width="700" border="0" cellspacing="10" cellpadding="1"><tr><td width="226"><div align="right">
<input type="submit" name="send" value="Send Survey"></div></td><td width="207"> </td>
<td width="221"><div align="left"><input type="reset" name="clear" value="Clear Survey"></div></td></tr>
<tr colspan=3><td colspan=3>
<table width="500" border="1" bordercolor="#000000" height="2" align="center" cellpadding="0"
cellspacing="0" bgcolor="#ffffff"><tr><td><font size="1" color="#ffffff">.</font></td></tr></table>
</td></tr><tr><td colspan=3><div align="center">
<font face="Arial, Helvetica, sans-serif" size="1"><b>http://</b></font><br><font size="2"> 
<font face="Arial, Helvetica, sans-serif" size="1"><b>&copy; 2002</b></font></font>
<font face="Arial, Helvetica, sans-serif" size="2"><a href="mailto:">
<b><font size="1">Contact Webmaster</font></b></a></font></div></td></tr>
</table></form>
</body>
</html>
```

Home Cybersurfer Survey — Perl Script

```perl
#!/usr/local/bin/perl

# ***************************************************************
# ABOVE is where you MUST specify the path to your
# perl interpreter on your Web server.
# Replace /usr/local/bin/perl with your path.
# ***************************************************************

if ($ENV{'REQUEST_METHOD'}eq"GET"){$buffer = $ENV{'QUERY_STRING'};}
    elsif($ENV{'REQUEST_METHOD'}eq"POST"){
        read(STDIN,$buffer,$ENV{'CONTENT_LENGTH'});
    }
$bufferb = $buffer;
#separate the name of the input from its value.
@forminputs = split(/&/, $bufferb);

foreach $forminput (@forminputs)
{
    #separate the name of the input from its value
    ($name, $value) = split(/=/, $forminput);

    #Un-Webify plus signs and %-encoding
    $value =~ tr/+/ /;
    $value =~ s/%([a-fA-F0-9][a-fA-F0-9])/pack("C", hex($1))/eg;

    #stick them in the in array
    $in{$name} = $value;
}
print "Content-type: text/html\n\n";

#################################################
# ABOVE is the required header for a perl script      #
#################################################

###########################################################
# (Below) Email received by library containing user-entered information #
###########################################################

# ***************************************************************
# Here's where you MUST specify the path to your
# email program (probably sendmail) ON your Web server.
# Replace /usr/sbin/sendmail with your path.
# ***************************************************************
```

Group 3—Library Computer Forms/Surveys

```
open (LMAIL, "|/usr/sbin/sendmail -t");
print LMAIL ("To: $in{LibraryEmail}\n");

print LMAIL ("From: $in{Email}\n");
print LMAIL ("Subject: $in{Form} - patron submission\n");

print LMAIL ("-------------------\nPatron information\n\n");

print LMAIL ("Name:\n $in{Name}\n\n");
print LMAIL ("E-mail Address:\n $in{Email}\n\n");
print LMAIL ("School:\n $in{School}\n\n");
print LMAIL ("Gender:\n $in{Gender}\n\n");
print LMAIL ("Grade:\n $in{EducationLevel}\n\n");

print LMAIL ("-------------------\nSubmitted information \n\n");
print LMAIL ("-------------------\nYour Computer\n\n");
print LMAIL ("What is your level of computer knowledge?\n $in{Expertise}\n\n");
print LMAIL ("How do you use your home computer?\n $in{WP}, $in{E}, $in{WB}, $in{G}, $in{GR}, $in{OP}\n\n");
print LMAIL ("What kind of computer do you use at home?\n $in{Computer}\n\n");
print LMAIL ("How often do you use the library's computers?\n $in{LibraryComputers}\n\n");

print LMAIL ("-------------------\nThe Internet and Your Computer\n\n");
print LMAIL ("How fast is your home Internet connection?\n $in{Fast}\n\n");
print LMAIL ("Which Web browser(s) do you use at home?\n  $in{IE}, $in{NET}, $in{AOL}, $in{O}, $in{DK}\n\n");

print LMAIL ("-------------------\nYour Internet Use at Home\n\n");
print LMAIL ("How often do you use the Internet at home?\n $in{InternetUse}\n\n");
print LMAIL ("How long have you used the Internet?\n $in{LongUsedInternet}\n\n");
print LMAIL ("When do you use the Internet?\n $in{M}, $in{EA}, $in{LA}, $in{EE}, $in{N}, $in{LN}\n\n");

print LMAIL ("-------------------\nThe Library's Web site\n\n");
print LMAIL ("How many times have you visited the library's Web site from your home computer?\n $in{Visits}\n\n");
print LMAIL ("How often do you visit the library's Web site from home?\n $in{OftenVisitSite}\n\n");
print LMAIL ("How long have you used the library's Web site?\n $in{LongUsedSite}\n\n");
print LMAIL ("How did you find out / hear about the library's Web site?\n $in{FindOut}\n\n");
print LMAIL ("Which sections / pages of the library's Web site do you view most often?\n $in{Features}\n\n");

print LMAIL ("\n.\n");

##############################################
# Email received by the user confirming form submission #
##############################################
```

```
# ***********************************************
# Here's where you MUST specify the path to your
# email program ON your Web server.
# Replace /usr/sbin/sendmail with your path.
# ***********************************************

open (MAIL, "|/usr/sbin/sendmail -t");

# ***************************************************
# Here's where you MAY customize the email
# response to the user. You may change any wording
# on the form.
# ***************************************************

print MAIL<<toEnd;
To: $in{Email}
From: $in{LibraryEmail}
Subject: $in{Form}

Thanks for taking the time to fill out our Home Cybersurfer Survey.\n\n
We will use your input to help us improve our Web site and its content.

toEnd
    print MAIL ("\n.\n");

##########################################
# Screen response to user after submitting the form  #
##########################################

print ("<html><head><title>$in{Form}</title></head>");
print ("<body bgcolor=\"ffffff\">");

# ***************************************************
# Here's where you MAY change the screen response
# the user sees after submitting the form. You may
# change any wording between the quotation marks.
# ***************************************************

print ("Thanks for taking the time to fill out our Home Cybersurfer Survey.<p>
We will use your input to help us improve our Web site and its content.");

# ***********************************************
# Here's where you MAY change the name of the link
# back to your main page. You may replace Return
```

```
# to our main page with your own wording.
# *************************************************************
print ("<p><center><a href=$in{LibraryURL}>Return to our main page.</a></center>");
print ("</body></html>");
```

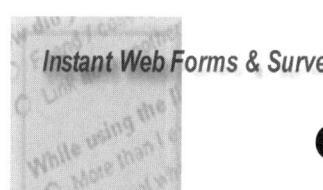

Instant Web Forms & Surveys

Group 4 — Library Web Site Forms / Surveys

In this section you'll find two Web-based forms that will let students suggest a new link, report a broken link. If you want to make your Web site more user-friendly, consider providing visiting students with an online guest book form so that they can send you their greetings, opinions, and thoughts about your library and Web site! Here you'll also find a survey that will let students give your staff their opinions about the content and arrangement of information on your Web site.

Suggest a New Web Link
Encourage students to take a few minutes to recommend a new Web link they've found. Students can provide you with the site's URL, why they think you should add it your Web site, and even where on your site they think it should be located. Place a link to this form on any/all of your Web site's pages.

Report a Broken Link or Problem
It's a time-consuming job keeping all of your Web site links current. Students can help by reporting any changed or broken links they run into while using your Web site, any graphics/images that don't load properly, or any plug-ins that you need to acquire and/or update. Students can also let you know if they notice any typos, grammatical errors, or any other problems with your site. Put a link to this form on any/all of your Web site's pages.

Sign Our Guest Book
Whether students are visiting your Web site from a distant country or from just down the street, encourage them to take a few minutes to add their name and comments to your virtual guest book. Post the most appropriate messages on your Web site so that your students and staff can see what other kids and teens think about your Web site. Put a link to the guest book on your library's home page.

Library Web Site Survey
If you'd like to know what your students, as well as long-distance student visitors, think of your library's Web site, have them complete this brief survey. Place a link to this survey periodically on your library's home page.

How to Evaluate a Web Site
Teaching students how to evaluate a Web site can be a daunting task. Use this form to help kids not only evaluate the Web sites they visit, but also learn some of the key questions they need to ask themselves about what they see and read on-line. Put a link to this form on your homework help and home pages.

Suggest a New Web Link

Take a few minutes to recommend a great Web link you've found. Fill out the form below and tell us why you think we should add it to our Web site, and where on our site you think it should be located.

Name (first, last)

E-mail address

Home address (+ city)

School you attend

Home phone/fax (+ areacode)

Teacher's name

What grade are you in?
- ○ 3
- ○ 4
- ○ 5
- ○ 6
- ○ 7
- ○ 8
- ○ 9
- ○ 10
- ○ 11
- ○ 12

The new Web site URL

http://

Describe the new Web site

Reason(s) for suggesting this site

Where on *our* Web site would you place the link to this site?

[Send Suggestion]   [Clear Form]

http://

© 2002 Contact Webmaster

Group 4—Library Web Site Forms/Surveys

Suggest a New Web Link — HTML Form

```
<html>
<head><title>Suggest a New Web Link</title></head>
<body bgcolor="#FFFFFF">
<table width="700" border="1" bordercolor="#000000" height="85" bgcolor="#ffffff">
<tr valign="middle" align="center">
<td>
<p>
<font halign=center color="#000000" face="Arial, Helvetica, sans-serif" size="+3">
<b><i>Suggest a New Web Link</i></b></font></p>
</td></tr></table>
<form method="post" action="http://www.yourLibrary.org/cgi-bin/clw1.pl"><p> </p>
<p>
<font face="Arial, Helvetica, sans-serif" size="2"><b>Take a few minutes to recommend a great Web link you've found. Fill out the form below and tell us <br>why you think we should add it to our Web site, and where on our site you think it should be located.</b></font></p>
<p> </p>
<input type="hidden" name="LibraryEmail" value="you@yourLibrary.org">
<input type="hidden" name="LibraryURL" value="http://www.yourLibrary.org">
<input type="hidden" name="Form" value="Suggest a New Web Link">
<p></p>
<table width="407" border="0" cellspacing="4" cellpadding="1">
<tr><td width="202">
<b><font face="Arial, Helvetica, sans-serif" size="2">Name</font></b><font face="Arial, Helvetica, sans-serif" size="1">  (first, last)</font><br><font face="Arial, Helvetica, sans-serif" size="2">
<input type="text" name="Name" size="25"></font></td>
<td width="189">
<b><font face="Arial, Helvetica, sans-serif" size="2">E-mail address<br></font></b><font face="Arial, Helvetica, sans-serif" size="2"><input type="text" name="Email" size="25"></font></td></tr>
<tr><td width="202" height="2">
<b><font face="Arial, Helvetica, sans-serif" size="2">Home address</font>  </b><font face="Arial, Helvetica, sans-serif" size="1">(+ city)</font><br><font face="Arial, Helvetica, sans-serif" size="2"><input type="text" name="HomeAddr" size="25"></font></td>
<td width="189" height="2">
<b><font face="Arial, Helvetica, sans-serif" size="2">School you attend<br></font></b><font face="Arial, Helvetica, sans-serif" size="2"><input type="text" name="School" size="25"></font></td></tr>
<tr><td width="202" height="2">
<b><font face="Arial, Helvetica, sans-serif" size="2">Home phone/fax</font><font face="Arial, Helvetica, sans-serif" size="1"> </font></b><font face="Arial, Helvetica, sans-serif" size="1"> (+ areacode)</font><br><font face="Arial, Helvetica, sans-serif" size="2"><input type="text" name="HomePhone" size="25"></font></td>
<td width="189" height="2">
<b><font face="Arial, Helvetica, sans-serif" size="2">Teacher's name<br></font></b><font face="Arial, Helvetica, sans-serif" size="2"><input type="text" name="Teacher" size="25"></font></td></tr>
```

```html
<tr><td width="391" colspan="2" height="48">
<b><font face="Arial, Helvetica, sans-serif" size="2">What grade are you in?</font></b><br><font face="Arial, Helvetica, sans-serif" size="2"></font>
<table width="87%" border="0" cellspacing="4" cellpadding="0"><tr><td height="8" width="16%">
<font face="Arial, Helvetica, sans-serif" size="2"><input type="radio" name="EducationLevel" value="3">
3</font></td>
<td height="8" width="16%">
<font face="Arial, Helvetica, sans-serif" size="2"><input type="radio" name="EducationLevel" value="4">
4</font></td>
<td height="8" width="16%">
<font face="Arial, Helvetica, sans-serif" size="2"><input type="radio" name="EducationLevel" value="5">
5</font></td>
<td height="8" width="16%">
<font face="Arial, Helvetica, sans-serif" size="2"><input type="radio" name="EducationLevel" value="6">
6</font></td>
<td height="8" width="36%">
<font face="Arial, Helvetica, sans-serif" size="2"><input type="radio" name="EducationLevel" value="7">
7</font></td></tr>
<tr><td height="2" width="16%">
<font face="Arial, Helvetica, sans-serif" size="2"><input type="radio" name="EducationLevel" value="8">
8</font></td>
<td height="2" width="16%">
<font face="Arial, Helvetica, sans-serif" size="2"><input type="radio" name="EducationLevel" value="9">
9</font></td>
<td height="2" width="16%">
<font face="Arial, Helvetica, sans-serif" size="2"><input type="radio" name="EducationLevel" value="10">
10</font></td>
<td height="2" width="16%">
<font face="Arial, Helvetica, sans-serif" size="2"><input type="radio" name="EducationLevel" value="11">
11</font></td>
<td height="2" width="36%">
<font face="Arial, Helvetica, sans-serif" size="2"><input type="radio" name="EducationLevel" value="12">
12</font>
</td></tr></table>
</td></tr></table>
<p><br>
<b><font face="Arial, Helvetica, sans-serif" size="2">The new Web site URL</font></b><br>
<font face="Arial, Helvetica, sans-serif" size="3"><input type="text" name="URL" size="40" value= "http://">
</font></p>
<p>
<b><font face="Arial, Helvetica, sans-serif" size="2">Describe the new Web site</font></b><br>
<font face="Arial, Helvetica, sans-serif" size="3"><textarea name="Description" cols="40" rows="2">
</textarea></font></p>
<p>
<b><font face="Arial, Helvetica, sans-serif" size="2">Reason(s) for suggesting this site</font></b>
```

Group 4—Library Web Site Forms/Surveys

```
<br><font face="Arial, Helvetica, sans-serif" size="3"><textarea name="Reason" cols="40" rows="2">
</textarea></font></p>
<p>
<b><font face="Arial, Helvetica, sans-serif" size="2">Where on <i>our</i>Web site would you place the link to
this site?</font></b><br><font face="Arial, Helvetica, sans-serif" size="3"><textarea name= "Placement"
cols="40" rows="2"></textarea></font></p>
<p> </p>
<table width="700" border="0" cellspacing="10" cellpadding="1"><tr> <td width="270"><div align="right">
<input type="submit" name="send" value="Send Suggestion"></div></td><td width="177"> </td>
<td width="207"><div align="left"><input type="reset" name="clear" value="Clear Form"></div></td></tr>
<tr colspan=3><td colspan=3>
<table width="500" border="1" bordercolor="#000000" height="2" align="center" cellpadding="0"
cellspacing="0" bgcolor="#ffffff"><tr><td><font size="1" color="#ffffff">.</font></td></tr></table>
</td></tr><tr><td colspan=3><div align="center">
<font face="Arial, Helvetica, sans-serif" size="1"><b>http://</b></font><br> 
<font face="Arial, Helvetica, sans-serif" size="1"><b>&copy; 2002</b></font>
<font face="Arial, Helvetica, sans-serif" size="2"><a href="mailto:">
<b><font size="1">Contact Webmaster</font></b></a></font></div></td></tr>
</table></form>
</body>
</html>
```

Suggest a New Web Link — Perl Script

```perl
#!/usr/local/bin/perl

# ***************************************************************
# ABOVE is where you MUST specify the path to your
# perl interpreter on your Web server.
# Replace /usr/local/bin/perl with your path.
# ***************************************************************

if ($ENV{'REQUEST_METHOD'}eq"GET"){$buffer = $ENV{'QUERY_STRING'};}
    elsif($ENV{'REQUEST_METHOD'}eq"POST"){
        read(STDIN,$buffer,$ENV{'CONTENT_LENGTH'});
    }
$bufferb = $buffer;
#separate the name of the input from its value.
@forminputs = split(/&/, $bufferb);

foreach $forminput (@forminputs)
{
    #separate the name of the input from its value
    ($name, $value) = split(/=/, $forminput);

    #Un-Webify plus signs and %-encoding
    $value =~ tr/+/ /;
    $value =~ s/%([a-fA-F0-9][a-fA-F0-9])/pack("C", hex($1))/eg;

    #stick them in the in array
    $in{$name} = $value;
}
print "Content-type: text/html\n\n";

##############################################
# ABOVE is the required header for a perl script    #
##############################################

##############################################################
# (Below) Email received by library containing user-entered information #
##############################################################

# ***************************************************************
# Here's where you MUST specify the path to your
# email program (probably sendmail) ON your Web server.
# Replace /usr/sbin/sendmail with your path.
# ***************************************************************
```

```
open (LMAIL, "I/usr/sbin/sendmail -t");
print LMAIL ("To: $in{LibraryEmail}\n");

print LMAIL ("From: $in{Email}\n");
print LMAIL ("Subject: $in{Form} - patron submission\n");

print LMAIL ("-------------------\nPatron information\n\n");

print LMAIL ("Name:\n $in{Name}\n\n");
print LMAIL ("E-mail Address:\n $in{Email}\n\n");
print LMAIL ("Home Address:\n $in{HomeAddr}\n\n");
print LMAIL ("School:\n $in{School}\n\n");
print LMAIL ("Home Phone/Fax:\n $in{HomePhone}\n\n");
print LMAIL ("Teacher's Name:\n $in{Teacher}\n\n");
print LMAIL ("Grade:\n $in{EducationLevel}\n\n");

print LMAIL ("------------------\nSubmitted information \n\n");

print LMAIL ("Web site URL:\n $in{URL}\n\n");
print LMAIL ("Description of the Web site:\n $in{Description}\n\n");
print LMAIL ("Reason for suggesting this site:\n $in{Reason}\n\n");
print LMAIL ("Where on the library Web site I would place the link:\n $in{Placement}\n\n");

print LMAIL ("\n.\n");

###############################################
# Email received by the user confirming form submission #
###############################################

# **********************************************************
# Here's where you MUST specify the path to your
# email program ON your Web server.
# Replace /usr/sbin/sendmail with your path.
# **********************************************************

open (MAIL, "I/usr/sbin/sendmail -t");

# **********************************************************
# Here's where you MAY customize the email
# response to the user. You may change any wording
# on the form.
# **********************************************************

print MAIL<<toEnd;
To: $in{Email}
```

From: $in{LibraryEmail}
Subject: $in{Form}

Thanks for sending us your suggestion for a new Web link.\n\n
We are always looking for new online resources to enrich our Web site.

toEnd
   print MAIL ("\n.\n");

###
Screen response to user after submitting the form
###

print ("<html><head><title>$in{Form}</title></head>");
print ("<body bgcolor=\"ffffff\">");

**
Here's where you MAY change the screen response
the user sees after submitting the form. You may
change any wording between the quotation marks.
**

print ("Thanks for sending us your suggestion for a new Web link.<p>
We are always looking for new online resources to enrich our Web site.");

**
Here's where you MAY change the name of the link
back to your main page. You may replace Return
to our main page with your own wording.
**

print ("<p><center><a href=$in{LibraryURL}>Return to our main page.</a></center>");
print ("</body></html>");

Report a Broken Link or Problem

Please report any changed or broken links you find while using our Web site or any graphics that don't load properly. Also, let us know if you notice any typos, grammar errors, or other problems with our site. We'll send you an e-mail message informing you when we've fixed the problem(s).

Name (first, last)

E-mail address

Home address (+ city)

School you attend

Home phone/fax (+ areacode)

Teacher's name

What grade are you in?
- ○ 3   ○ 4   ○ 5   ○ 6   ○ 7
- ○ 8   ○ 9   ○ 10   ○ 11   ○ 12

Name of the Web page where the problem is found (eg., Online Reference, Kids Page)

Type of problem
○ Link doesn't work   ○ Typo / Grammar error   ○ Image doesn't load   ○ Other

Describe the problem (give us as many details as you can)

If a broken link, what is the *current* URL?
http://

If a changed link, what is the *new* URL?
http://

[Send Report]   [Clear Form]

http://
© 2002 Contact Webmaster

Report a Broken Link or Problem — HTML Form

```html
<html>
<head><title>Report a Broken Link or Problem</title></head>
<body bgcolor="#FFFFFF">
<table width="700" border="1" height="85" bgcolor="ffffff">
<tr valign="middle" align="center"><td><p>
<font halign=center color="#000000" face="Arial, Helvetica, sans-serif" size="+3">
<b><i>Report a Broken Link or Problem</i></b></font></p>
</td></tr></table>
<form method="post" action="http://www.yourLibrary.org/cgi-bin/clw2.pl"><p> </p>
<p>
<font face="Arial, Helvetica, sans-serif" size="2"><b>Please report any changed or broken links you find while using our Web site or any graphics that <br>don't load properly. Also, let us know if you notice any typos, grammar errors, or other problems <br>with our site. We'll send you an e-mail message informing you when we've fixed the problem(s).</b></font></p>
<p> </p>
<input type="hidden" name="LibraryEmail" value="you@yourLibrary.org">
<input type="hidden" name="LibraryURL" value="http://www.yourLibrary.org">
<input type="hidden" name="Form" value="Report a Broken Link or Problem"><p></p>
<table width="407" border="0" cellspacing="4" cellpadding="1">
<tr><td width="202">
<b><font face="Arial, Helvetica, sans-serif" size="2">Name</font></b><font face="Arial, Helvetica, sans-serif" size="1">  (first, last)</font><br><font face="Arial, Helvetica, sans-serif" size="2">
<input type="text" name="Name" size="25"></font></td>
<td width="189">
<b><font face="Arial, Helvetica, sans-serif" size="2">E-mail address<br></font></b><font face="Arial, Helvetica, sans-serif" size="2"><input type="text" name="Email" size="25"></font></td></tr>
<tr><td width="202" height="2">
<b><font face="Arial, Helvetica, sans-serif" size="2">Home address</font><font face="Arial, Helvetica, sans-serif" size="1">  </font></b><font face="Arial, Helvetica, sans-serif" size="1">(+ city)
</font><br><font face="Arial, Helvetica, sans-serif" size="2"><input type="text" name="HomeAddr" size="25">
</font></td>
<td width="189" height="2">
<b><font face="Arial, Helvetica, sans-serif" size="2">School you attend<br></font></b><font face="Arial, Helvetica, sans-serif" size="2"><input type="text" name="School" size="25"></font></td></tr>
<tr><td width="202" height="2">
<b><font face="Arial, Helvetica, sans-serif" size="2">Home phone/fax</font><font face="Arial, Helvetica, sans-serif" size="1"> </font></b><font face="Arial, Helvetica, sans-serif" size="1"> 
(+ areacode)</font><font face="Arial, Helvetica, sans-serif" size="2"></font><br><font face="Arial, Helvetica, sans-serif" size="2"><input type="text" name="HomePhone" size="25"></font></td>
<td width="189" height="2">
<b><font face="Arial, Helvetica, sans-serif" size="2">Teacher's name<br></font></b><font face="Arial, Helvetica, sans-serif" size="2"><input type="text" name="Teacher" size="25"></font></td></tr>
<tr><td width="391" colspan="2" height="60">
```

```html
<b><font face="Arial, Helvetica, sans-serif" size="2">What grade are you in?</font></b><br>
<table width="87%" border="0" cellspacing="4" cellpadding="0"><tr><td height="8" width="16%">
<font face="Arial, Helvetica, sans-serif" size="2"><input type="radio" name="EducationLevel" value="3">
3</font></td>
<td height="8" width="16%">
<font face="Arial, Helvetica, sans-serif" size="2"><input type="radio" name="EducationLevel" value="4">
4</font></td>
<td height="8" width="16%">
<font face="Arial, Helvetica, sans-serif" size="2"><input type="radio" name="EducationLevel" value="5">
5</font></td>
<td height="8" width="16%">
<font face="Arial, Helvetica, sans-serif" size="2"><input type="radio" name="EducationLevel" value="6">
6</font></td>
<td height="8" width="36%">
<font face="Arial, Helvetica, sans-serif" size="2"><input type="radio" name="EducationLevel" value="7">
7</font></td></tr>
<tr><td height="2" width="16%">
<font face="Arial, Helvetica, sans-serif" size="2"><input type="radio" name="EducationLevel" value="8">
8</font></td>
<td height="2" width="16%">
<font face="Arial, Helvetica, sans-serif" size="2"><input type="radio" name="EducationLevel" value="9">
9</font></td>
<td height="2" width="16%">
<font face="Arial, Helvetica, sans-serif" size="2"><input type="radio" name="EducationLevel" value="10">
10</font></td>
<td height="2" width="16%">
<font face="Arial, Helvetica, sans-serif" size="2"><input type="radio" name="EducationLevel" value="11">
11</font></td>
<td height="2" width="36%">
<font face="Arial, Helvetica, sans-serif" size="2"><input type="radio" name="EducationLevel" value="12">
12</font>
</td></tr></table>
</td></tr></table>
<p><br>
<b><font face="Arial, Helvetica, sans-serif" size="2">Name of the Web page where the problem is found
</font></b><font face="Arial, Helvetica, sans-serif" size="1">   (eg., Online Reference, Kids Page)  </font><br><font face="Arial, Helvetica, sans-serif" size="3">
<input type="text" name="SpecificPage" size="40"></font></p>
<p>
<b><font face="Arial, Helvetica, sans-serif" size="2">Type of problem<br></font></b><font face="Arial, Helvetica, sans-serif" size="2">
<input type="radio" name="TypeOfProblem" value="Link doesn't work">Link doesn't work    
<input type="radio" name="TypeOfProblem" value="Typo / Grammar error">Typo / Grammar error    
<input type="radio" name="TypeOfProblem" value="Image doesn't load">Image doesn't load 
```

```html
  
<input type="radio" name="TypeOfProblem" value="Other">Other</font></p>
<p>
<b><font face="Arial, Helvetica, sans-serif" size="2">Describe the problem<font size="1"> 
</font></font></b><font face="Arial, Helvetica, sans-serif" size="1"> (give us as many details as you
can) </font><br><font face="Arial, Helvetica, sans-serif" size="3"><textarea name= "Description"
cols="40" rows="2"></textarea></font></p>
<p>
<b><font face="Arial, Helvetica, sans-serif" size="2">If a broken link, what is the <i>current</i> URL?</font>
</b><br><font face="Arial, Helvetica, sans-serif" size="3"><input type="text" name= "BrokenURL" size="40"
value="http://"></font></p>
<p>
<b><font face="Arial, Helvetica, sans-serif" size="2">If a changed link, what is the <i>new</i> URL?</font>
</b><br><font face="Arial, Helvetica, sans-serif" size="3"><input type="text" name= "NewURL" size="40"
value="http://"></font></p>
<p>  </p>
<table width="700" border="0" cellspacing="10" cellpadding="1"><tr><td width="234"><div align="right">
<input type="submit" name="send" value="Send Report"></div></td><td width="213"> </td>
<td width="207"><div align="left"><input type="reset" name="clear" value="Clear Form"></div></td>
</tr><tr colspan=3><td colspan=3>
<table width="500" border="1" height="2" align="center" cellpadding="0" cellspacing="0"
bgcolor="ffffff"><tr><td><font size="1" color="#ffffff">.</font></td></tr></table></td></tr><tr>
<td colspan=3><div align="center">
<font face="Arial, Helvetica, sans-serif" size="1"><b>http://</b></font><br><font size="2"> 
<font face="Arial, Helvetica, sans-serif" size="1"><b>&copy; 2002</b></font></font>
<font face="Arial, Helvetica, sans-serif" size="2"><a href="mailto:">
<b><font size="1">Contact Webmaster</font></b></a></font></div></td></tr>
</table></form>
</body>
</html>
```

Group 4—Library Web Site Forms/Surveys 159

Report a Broken Link or Problem — Perl Script

```perl
#!/usr/local/bin/perl

# ***************************************************************
# ABOVE is where you MUST specify the path to your
# perl interpreter on your Web server.
# Replace /usr/local/bin/perl with your path.
# ***************************************************************

if ($ENV{'REQUEST_METHOD'}eq"GET"){$buffer = $ENV{'QUERY_STRING'};}
    elsif($ENV{'REQUEST_METHOD'}eq"POST"){
        read(STDIN,$buffer,$ENV{'CONTENT_LENGTH'});
    }
$bufferb = $buffer;
#separate the name of the input from its value.
@forminputs = split(/&/, $bufferb);

foreach $forminput (@forminputs)
{
    #separate the name of the input from its value
    ($name, $value) = split(/=/, $forminput);

    #Un-Webify plus signs and %-encoding
    $value =~ tr/+/ /;
    $value =~ s/%([a-fA-F0-9][a-fA-F0-9])/pack("C", hex($1))/eg;

    #stick them in the in array
    $in{$name} = $value;
}
print "Content-type: text/html\n\n";

##############################################
# ABOVE is the required header for a perl script    #
##############################################

#####################################################
# (Below) Email received by library containing user-entered information #
#####################################################

# ***************************************************************
# Here's where you MUST specify the path to your
# email program (probably sendmail) ON your Web server.
# Replace /usr/sbin/sendmail with your path.
# ***************************************************************
```

```perl
open (LMAIL, "|/usr/sbin/sendmail -t");
print LMAIL ("To: $in{LibraryEmail}\n");

print LMAIL ("From: $in{Email}\n");
print LMAIL ("Subject: $in{Form} - patron submission\n");

print LMAIL ("------------------\nPatron information\n\n");

print LMAIL ("Name:\n $in{Name}\n\n");
print LMAIL ("E-mail Address:\n $in{Email}\n\n");
print LMAIL ("Home Address:\n $in{HomeAddr}\n\n");
print LMAIL ("School:\n $in{School}\n\n");
print LMAIL ("Home Phone/Fax:\n $in{HomePhone}\n\n");
print LMAIL ("Teacher's Name:\n $in{Teacher}\n\n");
print LMAIL ("Grade:\n $in{EducationLevel}\n\n");

print LMAIL ("------------------\nSubmitted information \n\n");

print LMAIL ("Specific Web page where the problem exists:\n $in{SpecificPage}\n\n");
print LMAIL ("Type of problem:\n $in{TypeOfProblem}\n\n");
print LMAIL ("Description of the problem:\n $in{Description}\n\n");
print LMAIL ("Current broken URL:\n $in{BrokenURL}\n\n");
print LMAIL ("Correct URL:\n $in{NewURL}\n\n");

print LMAIL ("\n.\n");

############################################
# Email received by the user confirming form submission #
############################################

# **********************************************************
# Here's where you MUST specify the path to your
# email program ON your Web server.
# Replace /usr/sbin/sendmail with your path.
# **********************************************************

open (MAIL, "|/usr/sbin/sendmail -t");

# **********************************************************
# Here's where you MAY customize the email
# response to the user. You may change any wording
# on the form.
# **********************************************************
```

```
print MAIL<<toEnd;
To: $in{Email}
From: $in{LibraryEmail}
Subject: $in{Form}

Thanks for letting us know about a broken link or other problem with our Web site.\n\n
We will get it fixed as soon as we can.

toEnd
   print MAIL ("\n.\n");


##########################################
# Screen response to user after submitting the form  #
##########################################

print ("<html><head><title>$in{Form}</title></head>");
print ("<body bgcolor=\"ffffff\">");




# ***************************************************************
# Here's where you MAY change the screen response
# the user sees after submitting the form. You may
# change any wording between the quotation marks.
# ***************************************************************

print ("Thanks for letting us know about a broken link or other problem with our Web site.<p>
We will get it fixed as soon as we can.");

# ***************************************************************
# Here's where you MAY change the name of the link
# back to your main page. You may replace Return
# to our main page with your own wording.
# ***************************************************************

print ("<p><center><a href=$in{LibraryURL}>Return to our main page.</a></center>");
print ("</body></html>");
```

Sign Our Guest Book

Whether you're a student visiting our Web site from a distant country or from just down the street, please take a few minutes to add your name and comments to our on-line guest book.

Name (first, last)

E-mail address

Home address (+ city)

School you attend

Home phone/fax (+ areacode)

Teacher's name

What grade are you in?

- ○ 3 ○ 4 ○ 5 ○ 6 ○ 7
- ○ 8 ○ 9 ○ 10 ○ 11 ○ 12

Your comments

[Send to Guest Book]   [Clear Form]

http://

© 2002 Contact Webmaster

Sign Our Guest Book — HTML Form

```html
<html>
<head><title>Sign Our Guest Book</title></head>
<body bgcolor="#FFFFFF">
<table width="700" border="1" height="85" bgcolor="ffffff">
<tr valign="middle" align="center"><td>
<p><font halign=center color="#000000" face="Arial, Helvetica, sans-serif" size="+3">
<b><i>Sign Our Guest Book</i></b></font></p>
</td></tr></table>
<form method="post" action="http://www.yourLibrary.org/cgi-bin/clw3.pl"><p> </p>
<p>
<b><font size="2" face="Arial, Helvetica, sans-serif">Whether you're a student visiting our Web site from a distant country or from just down the street, <br>please take a few minutes to add your name and comments to our on-line guest book.</font></b></p>
<p> </p>
<input type="hidden" name="LibraryEmail" value="you@yourLibrary.org">
<input type="hidden" name="LibraryURL" value="http://www.yourLibrary.org">
<input type="hidden" name="Form" value="Sign Our Guest Book">
<p></p>
<table width="407" border="0" cellspacing="4" cellpadding="1">
<tr><td width="202">
<b><font face="Arial, Helvetica, sans-serif" size="2">Name</font></b><font face="Arial, Helvetica, sans-serif" size="1">  (first, last)</font><br><font face="Arial, Helvetica, sans-serif" size="2">
<input type="text" name="Name" size="25"></font></td>
<td width="189">
<b><font face="Arial, Helvetica, sans-serif" size="2">E-mail address<br></font></b><font face="Arial, Helvetica, sans-serif" size="2"><input type="text" name="Email" size="25"></font></td></tr>
<tr><td width="202" height="2">
<b><font face="Arial, Helvetica, sans-serif" size="2">Home address</font><font face="Arial, Helvetica, sans-serif" size="1"> </font></b><font face="Arial, Helvetica, sans-serif" size="1"> (+ city)
</font><br><font face="Arial, Helvetica, sans-serif" size="2"><input type="text" name="HomeAddr" size="25">
</font></td>
<td width="189" height="2">
<b><font face="Arial, Helvetica, sans-serif" size="2">School you attend<br></font></b><font face="Arial, Helvetica, sans-serif" size="2"><input type="text" name="School" size="25"></font></td></tr>
<tr><td width="202" height="2">
<b><font face="Arial, Helvetica, sans-serif" size="2">Home phone/fax</font><font face="Arial, Helvetica, sans-serif" size="1"> </font></b><font face="Arial, Helvetica, sans-serif" size="1"> (+areacode)
</font><br><font face="Arial, Helvetica, sans-serif" size="2"><input type="text" name= "HomePhone" size="25"></font></td>
<td width="189" height="2">
<b><font face="Arial, Helvetica, sans-serif" size="2">Teacher's name<br></font></b><font face="Arial, Helvetica, sans-serif" size="2"><input type="text" name="Teacher" size="25"></font></td></tr>
<tr><td width="391" colspan="2" height="48">
```

```html
<b><font face="Arial, Helvetica, sans-serif" size="2">What grade are you in?</font></b><br>
<font face="Arial, Helvetica, sans-serif" size="2"></font>
<table width="87%" border="0" cellspacing="4" cellpadding="0"><tr><td height="8" width="16%">
<font face="Arial, Helvetica, sans-serif" size="2"><input type="radio" name="EducationLevel" value="3">
3</font></td>
<td height="8" width="16%">
<font face="Arial, Helvetica, sans-serif" size="2"><input type="radio" name="EducationLevel" value="4">
4</font></td>
<td height="8" width="16%">
<font face="Arial, Helvetica, sans-serif" size="2"><input type="radio" name="EducationLevel" value="5">
5</font></td>
<td height="8" width="16%">
<font face="Arial, Helvetica, sans-serif" size="2"><input type="radio" name="EducationLevel" value="6">
6</font></td>
<td height="8" width="36%">
<font face="Arial, Helvetica, sans-serif" size="2"><input type="radio" name="EducationLevel" value="7">
7</font></td></tr>
<tr><td height="2" width="16%">
<font face="Arial, Helvetica, sans-serif" size="2"><input type="radio" name="EducationLevel" value="8">
8</font></td>
<td height="2" width="16%">
<font face="Arial, Helvetica, sans-serif" size="2"><input type="radio" name="EducationLevel" value="9">
9</font></td>
<td height="2" width="16%">
<font face="Arial, Helvetica, sans-serif" size="2"><input type="radio" name="EducationLevel" value="10">
10</font></td>
<td height="2" width="16%">
<font face="Arial, Helvetica, sans-serif" size="2"><input type="radio" name="EducationLevel" value="11">
11</font></td>
<td height="2" width="36%">
<font face="Arial, Helvetica, sans-serif" size="2"><input type="radio" name="EducationLevel" value="12">
12</font>
</td></tr></table>
</td></tr></table>
<p><br>
<b><font face="Arial, Helvetica, sans-serif" size="2">Your comments</font></b><br><font face= "Arial, Helvetica, sans-serif" size="3"><textarea name="Comments" cols="40" rows="10"></textarea></font></p>
<p> </p>
<table width="700" border="0" cellspacing="10" cellpadding="1"><tr><td width="281"><div align="right">
<input type="submit" name="send" value="Send to Guest Book"></div></td><td width="166"> </td>
<td width="207"><div align="left"><input type="reset" name="clear" value="Clear Form"></div></td>
</tr><tr colspan=3><td colspan=3>
<table width="500" border="1" height="2" align="center" cellpadding="0" cellspacing="0" bgcolor="ffffff"><tr>
<td><font size="1" color="#ffffff">.</font></td></tr></table></td></tr><tr><td colspan=3><div align="center">
<font face="Arial, Helvetica, sans-serif" size="1"><b>http://</b></font><br> 
```

```html
<font face="Arial, Helvetica, sans-serif" size="1"><b>&copy; 2002</b></font>
<font face="Arial, Helvetica, sans-serif" size="2"><a href="mailto:">
<b><font size="1">Contact Webmaster</font></b></a></font></div></td></tr>
</table></form>
</body>
</html>
```

Sign Our Guest Book — Perl Script

```perl
#!/usr/local/bin/perl

# ************************************************************
# ABOVE is where you MUST specify the path to your
# perl interpreter on your Web server.
# Replace /usr/local/bin/perl with your path.
# ************************************************************

if ($ENV{'REQUEST_METHOD'}eq"GET"){$buffer = $ENV{'QUERY_STRING'};}
    elsif($ENV{'REQUEST_METHOD'}eq"POST"){
        read(STDIN,$buffer,$ENV{'CONTENT_LENGTH'});
    }
$bufferb = $buffer;
#separate the name of the input from its value.
@forminputs = split(/&/, $bufferb);

foreach $forminput (@forminputs)
{
    #separate the name of the input from its value
    ($name, $value) = split(/=/, $forminput);

    #Un-Webify plus signs and %-encoding
    $value =~ tr/+/ /;
    $value =~ s/%([a-fA-F0-9][a-fA-F0-9])/pack("C", hex($1))/eg;

    #stick them in the in array
    $in{$name} = $value;
}
print "Content-type: text/html\n\n";

##############################################
# ABOVE is the required header for a perl script    #
##############################################


#################################################
# (Below) Email received by library containing user-entered information #
#################################################


# ************************************************************
# Here's where you MUST specify the path to your
# email program (probably sendmail) ON your Web server.
# Replace /usr/sbin/sendmail with your path.
# ************************************************************
```

```
open (LMAIL, "l/usr/sbin/sendmail -t");
print LMAIL ("To: $in{LibraryEmail}\n");

print LMAIL ("From: $in{Email}\n");
print LMAIL ("Subject: $in{Form} - patron submission\n");

print LMAIL ("------------------\nPatron information\n\n");

print LMAIL ("Name:\n $in{Name}\n\n");
print LMAIL ("E-mail Address:\n $in{Email}\n\n");
print LMAIL ("Home Address:\n $in{HomeAddr}\n\n");
print LMAIL ("School:\n $in{School}\n\n");
print LMAIL ("Home Phone/Fax:\n $in{HomePhone}\n\n");
print LMAIL ("Teacher's Name:\n $in{Teacher}\n\n");
print LMAIL ("Grade:\n $in{EducationLevel}\n\n");

print LMAIL ("------------------\nSubmitted information \n\n");

print LMAIL ("Comments:\n $in{Comments}\n\n");

print LMAIL ("\n.\n");

################################################
# Email received by the user confirming form submission #
################################################

# ***********************************************************
# Here's where you MUST specify the path to your
# email program ON your Web server.
# Replace /usr/sbin/sendmail with your path.
# ***********************************************************
#

open (MAIL, "l/usr/sbin/sendmail -t");

# ***********************************************************
# Here's where you MAY customize the email
# response to the user. You may change any wording
# on the form.
# ***********************************************************
#

print MAIL<<toEnd;
To: $in{Email}
From: $in{LibraryEmail}
Subject: $in{Form}
```

Thanks for signing our guest book.\n\n
Please visit us again soon.

```
toEnd
    print MAIL ("\n.\n");
```

```
###########################################
# Screen response to user after submitting the form  #
###########################################

print ("<html><head><title>$in{Form}</title></head>");
print ("<body bgcolor=\"ffffff\">");

# ***************************************************************
# Here's where you MAY change the screen response
# the user sees after submitting the form. You may
# change any wording between the quotation marks.
# ***************************************************************

print ("Thanks for signing our guest book.<p>
Please visit us again soon.");

# ***************************************************************
# Here's where you MAY change the name of the link
# back to your main page. You may replace Return
# to our main page with your own wording.
# ***************************************************************

print ("<p><center><a href=$in{LibraryURL}>Return to our main page.</a></center>");
print ("</body></html>");
```

Library Web Site Survey

We'd like to know what you think of our Web site. Please fill out this short survey in order to help us create the best possible Web site.

You and Our Web Site

How many times have you visited our Web site? [　　　]

How did you find out about our Web site?
- ○ Friends
- ○ Library posters, etc
- ○ Librarians
- ○ Link from another Web site
- ○ Teachers
- ○ Other

While using the Web site I found...
- ○ More than I needed
- ○ Exactly what I needed
- ○ Some of what I needed
- ○ Little of value
- ○ Nothing of value

When you need help using our Web site what do you do?
- ○ Ask a librarian
- ○ Ask a friend
- ○ Read printed "help" docs
- ○ Use online help screens
- ○ Quit using the Web site
- ○ Don't ask for help

Web Site Content

Which sections / pages of our Web site do you use most often?

[　　　]

What do you like *most* about our Web site?

[　　　]

What do you like *least* about our Web site?

[　　　]

What makes our Web site hard to use?

[　　　]

What new Web sites would you like us to add to our Web site?

Grade Our Web Site

(1-poor 2-fair 3-good 4-very good 5-great)

	1	2	3	4	5
Well organized information	○	○	○	○	○
Easy to read	○	○	○	○	○
Easy to locate links	○	○	○	○	○
Contains important information / Web links	○	○	○	○	○
Contains up-to-date information / Web links	○	○	○	○	○
Nice to look at	○	○	○	○	○
Web pages load quickly	○	○	○	○	○
Good instructions / help	○	○	○	○	○
Easy to give comments / feedback	○	○	○	○	○
Overall rating	○	○	○	○	○

Name (first, last)

E-mail address

School you attend

Gender
○ Female   ○ Male

What grade are you in?
○ 3   ○ 4   ○ 5   ○ 6   ○ 7
○ 8   ○ 9   ○ 10   ○ 11   ○ 12

[Send Survey]   [Clear Survey]

http://
© 2002 Contact Webmaster

Library Web Site Survey — HTML Form

```html
<html>
<head><title>Library Web Site Survey</title></head>
<body bgcolor="#FFFFFF">
<table width="700" border="1" height="85" bgcolor="ffffff">
<tr valign="middle" align="center"><td>
<p>
<font halign=center color="#000000" face="Arial, Helvetica, sans-serif" size="5">
<b><i><font size="+3"> Library Web Site Survey</font></i></b></font></p>
</td></tr></table>
<form method="post" action="http://www.yourLibrary.org/cgi-bin/clw4.pl"><p> </p>
<p><font face="Arial, Helvetica, sans-serif" size="2"><b>We'd like to know what you think of our Web site. Please fill out this short survey in order to help us <br>create the best possible Web site.</b></font>
</p><p> </p>
<input type="hidden" name="LibraryEmail" value="you@yourLibrary.org">
<input type="hidden" name="LibraryURL" value="http://www.yourLibrary.org">
<input type="hidden" name="Form" value="Library Web Site Survey">
<p></p><p>
<b><font face="Arial, Helvetica, sans-serif" size="3">You and Our Web Site</font></b></p>
<p>
<font face="Arial, Helvetica, sans-serif" size="2"><b>How many times have you visited our Web site?</b>
<font size="3"> <input type="text" name="TimesVisited" size="5"></font></font></p>
<p>
<font face="Arial, Helvetica, sans-serif" size="2"><b>How did you find out about our Web site?<br>
</b></font>
<table width="552" border="0" cellspacing="0" cellpadding="0"><tr><td width="212">
<font face="Arial, Helvetica, sans-serif" size="2"><input type="radio" name="Access" value="Friends">
Friends</font></td>
<td width="164">
<font face="Arial, Helvetica, sans-serif" size="2"><input type="radio" name="Access" value="Library posters, etc.">Library posters, etc.</font></td>
<td width="176">
<font face="Arial, Helvetica, sans-serif" size="2"><input type="radio" name="Access" value="Librarians">
Librarians</font></td></tr>
<tr><td width="212">
<font face="Arial, Helvetica, sans-serif" size="2"><input type="radio" name="Access" value="Link from another Web site">Link from another Web site</font></td>
<td width="164">
<font face="Arial, Helvetica, sans-serif" size="2"><input type="radio" name="Access" value="Teachers">Teachers</font></td>
<td width="176">
<font face="Arial, Helvetica, sans-serif" size="2"><input type="radio" name="Access" value="Other">
Other</font></td></tr></table>
<p>
```

```
<font face="Arial, Helvetica, sans-serif" size="2"><b>While using the Web site I found...</b></font><br>
<table width="524" border="0" cellspacing="0" cellpadding="0"><tr><td width="162">
<font face="Arial, Helvetica, sans-serif" size="2"><input type="radio" name="IFound" value="More than I needed">More than I needed</font></td>
<td width="173">
<font face="Arial, Helvetica, sans-serif" size="2"><input type="radio" name="IFound" value="Exactly what I needed">Exactly what I needed</font></td>
<td width="189">
<font face="Arial, Helvetica, sans-serif" size="2"><input type="radio" name="IFound" value="Some of what I needed">Some of what I needed</font></td></tr>
<tr><td width="162">
<font face="Arial, Helvetica, sans-serif" size="2"><input type="radio" name="IFound" value="Little of value">Little of value</font></td>
<td width="173">
<font face="Arial, Helvetica, sans-serif" size="2"><input type="radio" name="IFound" value="Nothing of value">Nothing of value </font></td>
<td width="189"> </td></tr></table>
<p>
<font face="Arial, Helvetica, sans-serif" size="2">
<p>
<font face="Arial, Helvetica, sans-serif" size="2"><b>When you need help using our Web site what do you do?<br></b></font></font>
<table width="582" border="0" cellspacing="0" cellpadding="0"><tr><td width="193">
<font face="Arial, Helvetica, sans-serif" size="2"><b><input type="radio" name="HelpDo" value="Ask a librarian"></b><font face="Arial, Helvetica, sans-serif" size="2">Ask a librarian</font></font></td>
<td width="189">
<font face="Arial, Helvetica, sans-serif" size="2"><input type="radio" name="HelpDo" value="Ask a friend">
Ask a friend</font></td>
<td width="239">
<font face="Arial, Helvetica, sans-serif" size="2"><input type="radio" name="HelpDo" value="Read printed &quot;help&quot; docs">Read printed &quot;help&quot; docs</font></td></tr>
<tr><td width="193">
<font face="Arial, Helvetica, sans-serif" size="2"><input type="radio" name="HelpDo" value="Use online help screens">Use online help screens</font></td>
<td width="189">
<font face="Arial, Helvetica, sans-serif" size="2"><input type="radio" name="HelpDo" value="Quit using the Web site">Quit using the Web site</font></td>
<td width="239>
<font face="Arial, Helvetica, sans-serif" size="2"><input type="radio" name="HelpDo" value="Don't ask for help">Don't ask for help</font></td></tr></table>
<p><br>
<b><font face="Arial, Helvetica, sans-serif" size="3">Web Site Content</font></b></p>
<p>
<font face="Arial, Helvetica, sans-serif" size="2"><b>Which sections / pages of our Web site do you use most often?</b><br><font face="Arial, Helvetica, sans-serif" size="3"><textarea name= "Features" cols="40"
```

```
rows="2"></textarea></font><br></font></p>
<p>
<font face="Arial, Helvetica, sans-serif" size="2"><b>What do you like <i>most</i> about our Web site?<br>
</b><font face="Arial, Helvetica, sans-serif" size="3"><textarea name= "Most" cols="40" rows="2">
</textarea></font></font></p>
<p>
<font face="Arial, Helvetica, sans-serif" size="2"><b>What do you like <i>least</i> about our Web site?<br>
</b><font face="Arial, Helvetica, sans-serif" size="3"><textarea name= "Least" cols="40" rows="2">
</textarea></font></font></p>
<p>
<font face="Arial, Helvetica, sans-serif" size="2"><b>What makes our Web site hard to use?<br>
</b><font face="Arial, Helvetica, sans-serif" size="3"><textarea name="Difficult" cols="40" rows="2">
</textarea></font></font></p>
<p>
<font face="Arial, Helvetica, sans-serif" size="2"><b>What new Web sites would you like us to add to our Web
site?<br></b><font face="Arial, Helvetica, sans-serif" size="3"><textarea name="Added" cols="40" rows="2">
</textarea></font></font></p>
<p><br>
<b><font face="Arial, Helvetica, sans-serif" size="3">Grade Our Web Site</font><br>
<br>
</b><font face="Arial, Helvetica, sans-serif" size="1">(1-poor   2-fair    
3-good   4-very good   5-great)</font>
<table width="480" border="0"><tr align="center">
<td> </td>
<td><font face="Arial, Helvetica, sans-serif" size="1"><b>1</b></font></td>
<td><font face="Arial, Helvetica, sans-serif" size="1"><b>2</b></font></td>
<td><font face="Arial, Helvetica, sans-serif" size="1"><b>3</b></font></td>
<td><font face="Arial, Helvetica, sans-serif" size="1"><b>4</b></font></td>
<td><font face="Arial, Helvetica, sans-serif" size="1"><b>5</b></font></td></tr>
<tr>
<td><font face="Arial, Helvetica, sans-serif" size="2">Well organized information</font></td>
<td><input type="radio" name="Organized" value="poor"></td>
<td><input type="radio" name="Organized" value="fair"></td>
<td><input type="radio" name="Organized" value="good"></td>
<td><input type="radio" name="Organized" value="very good"></td>
<td><input type="radio" name="Organized" value="excellent"></td></tr>
<tr>
<td><font face="Arial, Helvetica, sans-serif" size="2">Easy to read</font></td>
<td><input type="radio" name="Writing" value="poor"></td>
<td><input type="radio" name="Writing" value="fair"></td>
<td><input type="radio" name="Writing" value="good"></td>
<td><input type="radio" name="Writing" value="very good"></td>
<td><input type="radio" name="Writing" value="excellent"></td></tr>
<tr>
<td><font face="Arial, Helvetica, sans-serif" size="2">Easy to locate links</font></td>
```

```html
<td><input type="radio" name="Moving" value="poor"></td>
<td><input type="radio" name="Moving" value="fair"></td>
<td><input type="radio" name="Moving" value="good"></td>
<td><input type="radio" name="Moving" value="very good"></td>
<td><input type="radio" name="Moving" value="excellent"></td></tr>
<tr>
<td><font face="Arial, Helvetica, sans-serif" size="2">Contains important information / Web links</font></td>
<td><input type="radio" name="Important" value="poor"></td>
<td><input type="radio" name="Important" value="fair"></td>
<td><input type="radio" name="Important" value="good"></td>
<td><input type="radio" name="Important" value="very good"></td>
<td><input type="radio" name="Important" value="excellent"></td></tr>
<tr>
<td><font face="Arial, Helvetica, sans-serif" size="2">Contains up-to-date information / Web links</font></td>
<td><input type="radio" name="UpToDate" value="poor"></td>
<td><input type="radio" name="UpToDate" value="fair"></td>
<td><input type="radio" name="UpToDate" value="good"></td>
<td><input type="radio" name="UpToDate" value="very good"></td>
<td><input type="radio" name="UpToDate" value="excellent"></td></tr>
<tr>
<td><font face="Arial, Helvetica, sans-serif" size="2">Nice to look at</font></td>
<td><input type="radio" name="Visual" value="poor"></td>
<td><input type="radio" name="Visual" value="fair"></td>
<td><input type="radio" name="Visual" value="good"></td>
<td><input type="radio" name="Visual" value="very good"></td>
<td><input type="radio" name="Visual" value="excellent"></td></tr>
<tr>
<td><font face="Arial, Helvetica, sans-serif" size="2">Web pages load quickly</font></td>
<td><input type="radio" name="Web" value="poor"></td>
<td><input type="radio" name="Web" value="fair"></td>
<td><input type="radio" name="Web" value="good"></td>
<td><input type="radio" name="Web" value="very good"></td>
<td><input type="radio" name="Web" value="excellent"></td></tr>
<tr>
<td><font face="Arial, Helvetica, sans-serif" size="2">Good instructions / help</font></td>
<td><input type="radio" name="Help" value="poor"></td>
<td><input type="radio" name="Help" value="fair"></td>
<td><input type="radio" name="Help" value="good"></td>
<td><input type="radio" name="Help" value="very good"></td>
<td><input type="radio" name="Help" value="excellent"></td></tr>
<tr>
<td><font face="Arial, Helvetica, sans-serif" size="2">Easy to give comments / feedback</font></td>
<td><input type="radio" name="Feedback" value="poor"></td>
<td><input type="radio" name="Feedback" value="fair"></td>
<td><input type="radio" name="Feedback" value="good"></td>
```

Group 4—Library Web Site Forms/Surveys

```html
<td><input type="radio" name="Feedback" value="very good"></td>
<td><input type="radio" name="Feedback" value="excellent"></td></tr>
<tr>
<td><font face="Arial, Helvetica, sans-serif" size="2"><b>Overall rating</b></font></td>
<td><input type="radio" name="Overall" value="poor"></td>
<td><input type="radio" name="Overall" value="fair"></td>
<td><input type="radio" name="Overall" value="good"></td>
<td><input type="radio" name="Overall" value="very good"></td>
<td><input type="radio" name="Overall" value="excellent"></td></tr></table>
<p>
<font face="Arial, Helvetica, sans-serif" size="2"><br></font> </p>
<table width="407" border="0" cellspacing="4" cellpadding="1">
<tr><td width="202">
<b><font face="Arial, Helvetica, sans-serif" size="2">Name</font></b><font face="Arial, Helvetica, sans-serif" size="1">  (first, last)</font><br><font face="Arial, Helvetica, sans-serif" size="2">
<input type="text" name="Name" size="25"></font></td>
<td width="189">
<b><font face="Arial, Helvetica, sans-serif" size="2">E-mail address<br></font></b><font face="Arial, Helvetica, sans-serif" size="2"><input type="text" name="Email" size="25"></font></td></tr>
<tr><td width="202" height="2">
<b><font face="Arial, Helvetica, sans-serif" size="2">School you attend<br></font></b><font face="Arial, Helvetica, sans-serif" size="2"><input type="text" name="School" size="25"></font></td>
<td width="189" height="2">
<b><font face="Arial, Helvetica, sans-serif" size="2">Gender<br></font></b>
<input type="radio" name="Gender" value="Female"><font face="Arial, Helvetica, sans-serif" size="2">
Female</font>
<input type="radio" name="Gender" value="Male"><font face="Arial, Helvetica, sans-serif" size="2">
Male</font></td></tr>
<tr><td width="391" colspan="2" height="48">
<b><font face="Arial, Helvetica, sans-serif" size="2">What grade are you in?</font></b><br>
<font face="Arial, Helvetica, sans-serif" size="2"></font>
<table width="87%" border="0" cellspacing="4" cellpadding="0"><tr><td height="8" width="16%">
<font face="Arial, Helvetica, sans-serif" size="2"><input type="radio" name="EducationLevel" value="3">
3</font></td>
<td height="8" width="16%">
<font face="Arial, Helvetica, sans-serif" size="2"><input type="radio" name="EducationLevel" value="4">
4</font></td>
<td height="8" width="16%">
<font face="Arial, Helvetica, sans-serif" size="2"><input type="radio" name="EducationLevel" value="5">
5</font></td>
<td height="8" width="16%">
<font face="Arial, Helvetica, sans-serif" size="2"><input type="radio" name="EducationLevel" value="6">
6</font></td>
<td height="8" width="36%">
<font face="Arial, Helvetica, sans-serif" size="2"><input type="radio" name="EducationLevel" value="7">
```

```html
7</font></td></tr>
<tr><td height="2" width="16%">
<font face="Arial, Helvetica, sans-serif" size="2"><input type="radio" name="EducationLevel" value="8">
8</font></td>
<td height="2" width="16%">
<font face="Arial, Helvetica, sans-serif" size="2"><input type="radio" name="EducationLevel" value="9">
9</font></td>
<td height="2" width="16%">
<font face="Arial, Helvetica, sans-serif" size="2"><input type="radio" name="EducationLevel" value="10">
10</font></td>
<td height="2" width="16%">
<font face="Arial, Helvetica, sans-serif" size="2"><input type="radio" name="EducationLevel" value="11">
11</font></td>
<td height="2" width="36%">
<font face="Arial, Helvetica, sans-serif" size="2"><input type="radio" name="EducationLevel" value="12">
12</font>
</td></tr></table>
</td></tr></table>
<p>  </p>
<table width="700" border="0" cellspacing="10" cellpadding="1"><tr><td width="226"><div align="right">
<input type="submit" name="send" value="Send Survey"></div></td><td width="207"> </td>
<td width="221"><div align="left"><input type="reset" name="clear" value="Clear Survey"></div></td></tr>
<tr colspan=3><td colspan=3>
<table width="500" border="1" height="2" align="center" cellpadding="0" cellspacing="0" bgcolor="ffffff">
<tr><td><font size="1" color="#ffffff">.</font></td></tr></table></td></tr><tr><td colspan=3>
<div align="center">
<font face="Arial, Helvetica, sans-serif" size="1"><b>http://</b></font><br><font size="2"> 
<font face="Arial, Helvetica, sans-serif" size="1"><b>&copy; 2002</b></font></font>
<font face="Arial, Helvetica, sans-serif" size="2"><a href="mailto:">
<b><font size="1">Contact Webmaster</font></b></a></font></div></td></tr>
</table></form>
</body>
</html>
```

Group 4—Library Web Site Forms/Surveys

Library Web Site Survey — Perl Script

```perl
#!/usr/local/bin/perl

# *****************************************************************
# ABOVE is where you MUST specify the path to your
# perl interpreter on your Web server.
# Replace /usr/local/bin/perl with your path.
# *****************************************************************

if ($ENV{'REQUEST_METHOD'}eq"GET"){$buffer = $ENV{'QUERY_STRING'};}
    elsif($ENV{'REQUEST_METHOD'}eq"POST"){
        read(STDIN,$buffer,$ENV{'CONTENT_LENGTH'});
    }
$bufferb = $buffer;
#separate the name of the input from its value.
@forminputs = split(/&/, $bufferb);

foreach $forminput (@forminputs)
{
    #separate the name of the input from its value
    ($name, $value) = split(/=/, $forminput);

    #Un-Webify plus signs and %-encoding
    $value =~ tr/+/ /;
    $value =~ s/%([a-fA-F0-9][a-fA-F0-9])/pack("C", hex($1))/eg;

    #stick them in the in array
    $in{$name} = $value;
}
print "Content-type: text/html\n\n";

##############################################
# ABOVE is the required header for a perl script     #
##############################################


####################################################
# (Below) Email received by library containing user-entered information #
####################################################


# *****************************************************************
# Here's where you MUST specify the path to your
# email program (probably sendmail) ON your Web server.
# Replace /usr/sbin/sendmail with your path.
# *****************************************************************
#
```

```
open (LMAIL, "|/usr/sbin/sendmail -t");
print LMAIL ("To: $in{LibraryEmail}\n");
print LMAIL ("From: $in{Email}\n");
print LMAIL ("Subject: $in{Form} - patron submission\n");

print LMAIL ("------------------\nPatron information\n\n");


print LMAIL ("Name:\n $in{Name}\n\n");
print LMAIL ("E-mail Address:\n $in{Email}\n\n");
print LMAIL ("School:\n $in{School}\n\n");
print LMAIL ("Gender:\n $in{Gender}\n\n");
print LMAIL ("Grade:\n $in{EducationLevel}\n\n");

print LMAIL ("------------------\nSubmitted information \n\n");
print LMAIL ("------------------\nYou and Our Web Site \n\n");

print LMAIL ("How many times have you visited our Web site?\n $in{TimesVisited}\n\n");
print LMAIL ("How did you find out about our Web site?\n $in{FindOut}\n\n");
print LMAIL ("While using the Web site I found...\n $in{IFound}\n\n");
print LMAIL ("When you need help using our Web site what do you do?\n $in{HelpDo}\n\n");
print LMAIL ("------------------\nWeb Site Content\n\n");

print LMAIL ("Sections / pages I view most often:\n $in{Features}\n\n");
print LMAIL ("What I like most about the library's Web site:\n $in{Most}\n\n");
print LMAIL ("What I like least about the library's Web site:\n $in{Least}\n\n");
print LMAIL ("What I find difficult to use on the Web site:\n $in{Difficult}\n\n");
print LMAIL ("What I would like to see added to the Web site:\n $in{Added}\n\n");
print LMAIL ("------------------\nGrade Our Web Site\n\n");
print LMAIL ("Library Web site grades\n\n");
print LMAIL ("Well organized information:\t $in{Organized}\n");
print LMAIL ("Easy to read:\t $in{Writing}\n");
print LMAIL ("Easy to locate links:\t $in{Moving}\n");
print LMAIL ("Contains important information / Web links:\t $in{Important}\n");
print LMAIL ("Contains up-to-date information / Web links:\t $in{UpToDate}\n");
print LMAIL ("Nice to look at:\t $in{Visual}\n");
print LMAIL ("Web page loads quickly:\t $in{Web}\n");
print LMAIL ("Good instructions / help:\t $in{Help}\n");
print LMAIL ("Easy to give comments / feedback:\t $in{Feedback}\n");
print LMAIL ("OVERALL RATING:\t $in{Overall}\n");

print LMAIL ("\n.\n");

##############################################
# Email received by the user confirming form submission #
```

Group 4—Library Web Site Forms/Surveys

```
###########################################

# ***********************************************
# Here's where you MUST specify the path to your
# email program ON your Web server.
# Replace /usr/sbin/sendmail with your path.
# ***********************************************

open (MAIL, "|/usr/sbin/sendmail -t");

# ***********************************************
# Here's where you MAY customize the email
# response to the user. You may change any wording
# on the form.
# ***********************************************

print MAIL<<toEnd;
To: $in{Email}
From: $in{LibraryEmail}
Subject: $in{Form}

Thanks for taking the time to fill out our Web Site Survey.\n\n
We will use your input to help us improve our Web site and its content.

toEnd
    print MAIL ("\n.\n");

#########################################
# Screen response to user after submitting the form  #
#########################################

print ("<html><head><title>Library Web Site Survey Submitted</title></head>");
print ("<body bgcolor=\"ffffff\">");

# ***********************************************
# Here's where you MAY change the screen response
# the user sees after submitting the form. You may
# change any wording between the quotation marks.
# ***********************************************

print ("Thanks for taking the time to fill out our Web Site Survey.<p>
We will use your input to help us improve our Web site and its content.");

# ***********************************************
# Here's where you MAY change the name of the link
```

```
# back to your main page. You may replace Return
# to our main page with your own wording.
# ************************************************************

print ("<p><center><a href=$in{LibraryURL}>Return to our main page.</a></center>");
print ("</body></html>");
```

How to Evaluate a Web Site

When evaluating a Web site you need to ask yourself a number of key questions about what you see and read. Fill out this form to learn which questions to ask yourself when viewing a Web site.

Name (first, last)

E-mail address

Home address (+ city)

School you attend

Home phone/fax (+ areacode)

Teacher's name

What grade are you in?

○ 3   ○ 4   ○ 5   ○ 6   ○ 7
○ 8   ○ 9   ○ 10   ○ 11   ○ 12

Authority

Who created the content of the Web site?

Does the Web site offer a group / organization point-of-view?   ○ Yes   ○ No

Is there a link to the author or group?   ○ Yes   ○ No

Are information sources cited?   ○ Yes   ○ No

Currency

When was the Web site last updated?

Are Web pages dated?   ○ Yes   ○ No

What is the copyright date?

Are there dead links on pages?   ○ Yes   ○ No

Organization

Can kids / teens easily find the information on this site?   ○ Yes   ○ No

Audience

Is the subject appropriate for kids / teens?	○ Yes	○ No
Will kids / teens find the text easy to read?	○ Yes	○ No
Are the graphics appropriate for kids / teens?	○ Yes	○ No

Scope

What topics are covered? [_____]

Are there links to other similar sites? ○ Yes   ○ No

Uniqueness

Is information unique to the Web? ○ Yes   ○ No

If no, where else can you find it? [_____]

Functionality

Is the Web site easy to connect to?	○ Yes	○ No
Do Web pages load quickly?	○ Yes	○ No
Do graphics load quickly and completely?	○ Yes	○ No

Help

Are help instructions easy to find?	○ Yes	○ No
Are help instructions written for kids / teens?	○ Yes	○ No

[Send Evaluation]   [Clear Form]

[_____]

http://

© 2002 Contact Webmaster

How to Evaluate a Web Site — HTML Form

```
<html>
<head><title>How to Evaluate a Web Site</title></head>
<body bgcolor="#FFFFFF">
<table width="700" border="1" bordercolor="#000000" height="85" bgcolor="#ffffff">
<tr valign="middle" align="center"><td>
<p>
<font halign=center color="#000000" face="Arial, Helvetica, sans-serif" size="+3">
<b><i>How to Evaluate a Web Site</i></b></font></p>
</td></tr></table>
<form method="post" action="http://www.yourLibrary.org/cgi-bin/clw1.pl" name=""><p> </p>
<p>
<font face="Arial, Helvetica, sans-serif" size="2"><b>When evaluating a Web site you need to ask yourself a number of key questions about what you <br>see and read. Fill out this form to learn which questions to ask yourself when viewing a Web site.</b></font></p>
<p> </p>
<input type="hidden" name="LibraryEmail" value="you@yourLibrary.org">
<input type="hidden" name="LibraryURL" value="http://www.yourLibrary.org">
<input type="hidden" name="Form" value="How to Evaluate a Web Site">
<p></p>
<table width="407" border="0" cellspacing="4" cellpadding="1">
<tr><td width="202">
<b><font face="Arial, Helvetica, sans-serif" size="2">Name</font></b><font face="Arial, Helvetica, sans-serif" size="1">  (first, last)</font><br><font face="Arial, Helvetica, sans-serif" size="2">
<input type="text" name="Name" size="25"></font></td>
<td width="189">
<b><font face="Arial, Helvetica, sans-serif" size="2">E-mail address<br></font></b><font face="Arial, Helvetica, sans-serif" size="2"><input type="text" name="Email" size="25"></font></td></tr>
<tr><td width="202" height="2">
<b><font face="Arial, Helvetica, sans-serif" size="2">Home address</font>  </b><font face="Arial, Helvetica, sans-serif" size="1">(+ city)</font><br><font face="Arial, Helvetica, sans-serif" size="2">
<input type="text" name="HomeAddr" size="25"></font></td>
<td width="189" height="2">
<b><font face="Arial, Helvetica, sans-serif" size="2">School you attend<br></font></b><font face="Arial, Helvetica, sans-serif" size="2"><input type="text" name="School" size="25"></font></td></tr>
<tr><td width="202" height="2">
<b><font face="Arial, Helvetica, sans-serif" size="2">Home phone/fax</font>  </b><font face="Arial, Helvetica, sans-serif" size="1">(+ areacode)</font><br><font face="Arial, Helvetica, sans-serif" size="2"><input type="text" name="HomePhone" size="25"></font></td>
<td width="189" height="2">
<b><font face="Arial, Helvetica, sans-serif" size="2">Teacher's name<br></font></b><font face="Arial, Helvetica, sans-serif" size="2"><input type="text" name="Teacher" size=25></font></td></tr>
<tr><td width="391" colspan="2" height="48">
<b><font face="Arial, Helvetica, sans-serif" size="2">What grade are you in?</font></b><br>
```

```html
<font face="Arial, Helvetica, sans-serif" size="2"></font>
<table width="87%" border="0" cellspacing="4" cellpadding="0"><tr><td height="8" width="16%">
<font face="Arial, Helvetica, sans-serif" size="2"><input type="radio" name="EducationLevel" value="3">
3</font></td>
<td height="8" width="16%">
<font face="Arial, Helvetica, sans-serif" size="2"><input type="radio" name="EducationLevel" value="4">
4</font></td>
<td height="8" width="16%">
<font face="Arial, Helvetica, sans-serif" size="2"><input type="radio" name="EducationLevel" value="5">
5</font></td>
<td height="8" width="16%">
<font face="Arial, Helvetica, sans-serif" size="2"><input type="radio" name="EducationLevel" value="6">
6</font></td>
<td height="8" width="36%">
<font face="Arial, Helvetica, sans-serif" size="2"><input type="radio" name="EducationLevel" value="7">
7</font></td></tr>
<tr><td height="2" width="16%">
<font face="Arial, Helvetica, sans-serif" size="2"><input type="radio" name="EducationLevel" value="8">
8</font></td>
<td height="2" width="16%">
<font face="Arial, Helvetica, sans-serif" size="2"><input type="radio" name="EducationLevel" value="9">
9</font></td>
<td height="2" width="16%">
<font face="Arial, Helvetica, sans-serif" size="2"><input type="radio" name="EducationLevel" value="10">
10</font></td>
<td height="2" width="16%">
<font face="Arial, Helvetica, sans-serif" size="2"><input type="radio" name="EducationLevel" value="11">
11</font></td>
<td height="2" width="36%">
<font face="Arial, Helvetica, sans-serif" size="2"><input type="radio" name="EducationLevel" value="12">
12</font>
</td></tr></table>
</td></tr></table>
<p><br></p>
<p><b><font face="Arial, Helvetica, sans-serif" size="3">Authority</font></b></p>
<p>
<b><font face="Arial, Helvetica, sans-serif" size="2">Who created the content of the Web site?</font>
</b> <font face="Arial, Helvetica, sans-serif" size="3"><input type="text" name="Created" size= "20">
</font></p>
<table width="577" border="0" cellpadding="0" cellspacing="0">
<tr><td width="402" height="15">
<b><font face="Arial, Helvetica, sans-serif" size="2">Does the Web site offer a group / organization point-of-view?</font></b></td>
<td width="149" height="15"><font size="2"><font face="Arial, Helvetica, sans-serif">
<input type="radio" name="PointOfView" value="Yes">Yes  
```

Group 4—Library Web Site Forms/Surveys

```
<input type="radio" name="PointOfView" value="No">No</font></font></td></tr>
<tr><td width="402" height="37">
<b><font face="Arial, Helvetica, sans-serif" size="2">Is there a link to the author or group?</font></b></td>
<td width="149" height="37"><font size="2"><font face="Arial, Helvetica, sans-serif">
<input type="radio" name="Link" value="Yes">Yes  
<input type="radio" name="Link" value="No">No</font></font></td></tr>
<tr><td width="402">
<font size="2" face="Arial, Helvetica, sans-serif"><b>Are information sources cited?</b></font></td>
<td width="149"><font size="2"><font face="Arial, Helvetica, sans-serif">
<input type="radio" name="SourcesCIted" value="Yes">Yes  
<input type="radio" name="SourcesCIted" value="No">No</font></font></td></tr></table>
<p>
<b><font face="Arial, Helvetica, sans-serif" size="3"><br>Currency</font></b></p>
<p>
<b><font face="Arial, Helvetica, sans-serif" size="2">When was the Web site last updated?</font></b>
<font face="Arial, Helvetica, sans-serif" size="3"> <input type="text" name="Updated" size="10">
</font></p>
<p>
<b><font face="Arial, Helvetica, sans-serif" size="2">Are Web pages dated?</font></b>  
<font size="2"><font face="Arial, Helvetica, sans-serif">
<input type="radio" name="DatedPages" value="Yes">Yes  
<input type="radio" name="DatedPages" value="No">No</font></font></p>
<p>
<b><font face="Arial, Helvetica, sans-serif" size="2">What is the copyright date?</font></b><font face="Arial, Helvetica, sans-serif" size="3"> <font face="Arial, Helvetica, sans-serif" size="3">
</font><input type="text" name="Copyright" size="10"></font></p>
<p>
<b><font face="Arial, Helvetica, sans-serif" size="2">Are there dead links on pages?</font></b>
  <font size="2"><font face="Arial, Helvetica, sans-serif">
<input type="radio" name="Dead" value="Yes">Yes  
<input type="radio" name="Dead" value="No">No</font></font></p>
<p>
<b><font face="Arial, Helvetica, sans-serif" size="3"><br>Organization</font></b></p>
<p>
<b><font face="Arial, Helvetica, sans-serif" size="2">Can kids / teens easily find the information on this site?
</font></b>  <font size="2"><font face="Arial, Helvetica, sans-serif">
<input type="radio" name="Organization" value="Yes">Yes  
<input type="radio" name="Organization" value="No">No</font></font></p>
<p><br>
<b><font face="Arial, Helvetica, sans-serif" size="3">Audience</font></b></p>
<table width="506" border="0" cellspacing="0" cellpadding="0">
<tr><td width="304">
<b><font face="Arial, Helvetica, sans-serif" size="2">Is the subject appropriate for kids / teens?</font></b>
</td><td width="202"><font size="2"><font face="Arial, Helvetica, sans-serif">
<input type="radio" name="Subject" value="Yes">Yes  
```

```html
<input type="radio" name="Subject" value="No">No</font></font></td></tr>
<tr><td width="304" height="35">
<b><font face="Arial, Helvetica, sans-serif" size="2">Will kids / teens find the text easy to read?</font></b>
</td><td width="202" height="35"><font size="2"><font face="Arial, Helvetica, sans-serif">
<input type="radio" name="Read" value="Yes">Yes  
<input type="radio" name="Read" value="No">No</font></font></td></tr>
<tr><td width="304">
<b><font face="Arial, Helvetica, sans-serif" size="2">Are the graphics appropriate for kids / teens?</font></b>
</td><td width="202"><font size="2"><font face="Arial, Helvetica, sans-serif">
<input type="radio" name="Graphics" value="Yes">Yes  
<input type="radio" name="Graphics" value="No">No</font></font></td></tr></table>
<p>
<br><b><font face="Arial, Helvetica, sans-serif" size="3">Scope</font></b></p>
<p>
<b><font face="Arial, Helvetica, sans-serif" size="2">What topics are covered?</font></b> 
<font face="Arial, Helvetica, sans-serif" size="3"><input type="text" name="Topics" size="20"></font></p>
<p>
<b><font face="Arial, Helvetica, sans-serif" size="2">Are there links to other similar sites?</font></b>
  <font size="2"><font face="Arial, Helvetica, sans-serif">
<input type="radio" name= "OtherSitesL" value="Yes">Yes  
<input type="radio" name="OtherSitesL" value="No">No</font></font></p>
<p><br>
<b><font face="Arial, Helvetica, sans-serif" size="3">Uniqueness</font></b></p>
<p>
<b><font face="Arial, Helvetica, sans-serif" size="2">Is information unique to the Web?</font></b>
  <font size="2"><font face="Arial, Helvetica, sans-serif">
<input type="radio" name="Unique" value="Yes">Yes  
<input type="radio" name="Unique" value="No">No</font></font></p>
<p>
<b><font face="Arial, Helvetica, sans-serif" size="2">If no, where else can you find it?</font></b>  
<font face="Arial, Helvetica, sans-serif" size="3"><input type="text" name="WhereElse" size="20">
</font></p>
<p><br>
<b><font face="Arial, Helvetica, sans-serif" size="3">Functionality</font></b></p>
<table width="500" border="0" cellspacing="0" cellpadding="0">
<tr><td>
<b><font face="Arial, Helvetica, sans-serif" size="2">Is the Web site easy to connect to?</font></b></td>
<td><font size="2"><font face="Arial, Helvetica, sans-serif">
<input type="radio" name="Connect" value="Yes">Yes  
<input type="radio" name="Connect" value="No">No</font></font></td></tr>
<tr><td height="35">
<b><font face="Arial, Helvetica, sans-serif" size="2">Do Web pages load quickly?</font></b></td>
<td height="35"><font size="2"><font face="Arial, Helvetica, sans-serif">
<input type="radio" name="Quickly" value="Yes">Yes  
<input type="radio" name="Quickly" value="No">No</font></font></td></tr>
```

```html
<tr><td>
<b><font face="Arial, Helvetica, sans-serif" size="2">Do graphics load quickly and completely?</font></b>
</td><td><font size="2"><font face="Arial, Helvetica, sans-serif">
<input type="radio" name="Completely" value="Yes">Yes  
<input type="radio" name="Completely" value="No">No</font></font></td></tr></table>
<p><br>
<b><font face="Arial, Helvetica, sans-serif" size="3">Help</font></b></p>
<table width="500" border="0" cellspacing="0" cellpadding="0">
<tr><td width="342" height="28" valign="top">
<b><font face="Arial, Helvetica, sans-serif" size="2">Are help instructions easy to find?</font></b></td>
<td width="138" height="28" valign="top"><font size="2"><font face="Arial, Helvetica, sans-serif">
<input type="radio" name="EasyFind" value="Yes">Yes  
<input type="radio" name="EasyFind" value="No">No</font></font></td></tr>
<tr><td width="342">
<b><font face="Arial, Helvetica, sans-serif" size="2">Are help instructions written for kids / teens?</font>
</b></td><td width="138"><font size="2"><font face="Arial, Helvetica, sans-serif">
<input type="radio" name="WrittenK" value="Yes">Yes  
<input type="radio" name="WrittenK" value="No">No</font></font></td></tr></table>
<p> </p>
<table width="700" border="0" cellspacing="10" cellpadding="1"><tr><td width="270"><div align="right">
<input type="submit" name="send" value="Send Evaluation"></div></td><td width="177"> </td>
<td width="207"><div align="left"><input type="reset" name="clear" value="Clear Form"></div></td></tr>
<tr colspan=3><td colspan=3>
<table width="500" border="1" bordercolor="#000000" height="2" align="center" cellpadding="0"
cellspacing="0" bgcolor="#ffffff"><tr><td><font size="1" color="#ffffff">.</font></td></tr></table>
</td></tr><tr><td colspan=3><div align="center">
<font face="Arial, Helvetica, sans-serif" size="1"><b>http://</b></font><br> 
<font face="Arial, Helvetica, sans-serif" size="1"><b>&copy; 2002</b></font>
<font face="Arial, Helvetica, sans-serif" size="2"><a href="mailto:">
<b><font size="1">Contact Webmaster</font></b></a></font></div></td></tr>
</table></form>
</body>
</html>
```

How to Evaluate a Web Site — Perl Script

```perl
#!/usr/local/bin/perl

# ***************************************************************
# ABOVE is where you MUST specify the path to your
# perl interpreter on your Web server.
# Replace /usr/local/bin/perl with your path.
# ***************************************************************

if ($ENV{'REQUEST_METHOD'}eq"GET"){$buffer = $ENV{'QUERY_STRING'};}
    elsif($ENV{'REQUEST_METHOD'}eq"POST"){
        read(STDIN,$buffer,$ENV{'CONTENT_LENGTH'});
    }
$bufferb = $buffer;
#separate the name of the input from its value.
@forminputs = split(/&/, $bufferb);

foreach $forminput (@forminputs)
{
    #separate the name of the input from its value
    ($name, $value) = split(/=/, $forminput);

    #Un-Webify plus signs and %-encoding
    $value =~ tr/+/ /;
    $value =~ s/%([a-fA-F0-9][a-fA-F0-9])/pack("C", hex($1))/eg;

    #stick them in the in array
    $in{$name} = $value;
}
print "Content-type: text/html\n\n";

##############################################
# ABOVE is the required header for a perl script    #
##############################################

##########################################################
# (Below) Email received by library containing user-entered information #
##########################################################

# ***************************************************************
# Here's where you MUST specify the path to your
# email program (probably sendmail) ON your Web server.
# Replace /usr/sbin/sendmail with your path.
# ***************************************************************
```

Group 4—Library Web Site Forms/Surveys

```
open (LMAIL, "I/usr/sbin/sendmail -t");
print LMAIL ("To: $in{LibraryEmail}\n");
print LMAIL ("From: $in{Email}\n");
print LMAIL ("Subject: $in{Form} - patron submission\n");

print LMAIL ("------------------\nPatron information\n\n");


print LMAIL ("Name:\n $in{Name}\n\n");
print LMAIL ("E-mail Address:\n $in{Email}\n\n");
print LMAIL ("Home Address:\n $in{HomeAddr}\n\n");
print LMAIL ("School:\n $in{School}\n\n");
print LMAIL ("Home Phone/Fax:\n $in{HomePhone}\n\n");
print LMAIL ("Teacher's Name:\n $in{Teacher}\n\n");
print LMAIL ("Grade:\n $in{EducationLevel}\n\n");

print LMAIL ("------------------\nSubmitted information \n\n");
print LMAIL ("------------------\nAuthority\n\n");

print LMAIL ("Who created the content of the Web site?\n $in{Created}\n\n");
print LMAIL ("Does the Web site offer a group / organization point-of-view?\n $in{PointOfView}\n\n");
print LMAIL ("Is there a link to the author or group?\n $in{Link}\n\n");
print LMAIL ("Are information sources cited?\n $in{SourcesCited}\n\n");

print LMAIL ("------------------\nCurrency\n\n");

print LMAIL ("When was the Web site last updated?\n $in{Updated}\n\n");
print LMAIL ("Are Web pages dated?\n $in{DatedPages}\n\n");
print LMAIL ("What is the copyright date?\n $in{Copyright}\n\n");
print LMAIL ("Are there dead links on pages?\n $in{Dead}\n\n");

print LMAIL ("------------------\nOrganization\n\n");

print LMAIL ("Can kids / teens easily find the information on this site?\n $in{Organization}\n\n");

print LMAIL ("------------------\nAudience\n\n");

print LMAIL ("Is the subject appropriate for kids / teens?\n $in{Subject}\n\n");
print LMAIL ("Will kids / teens find the text easy to read?\n $in{Read}\n\n");
print LMAIL ("Are the graphics appropriate for kids / teens?\n $in{Graphics}\n\n");

print LMAIL ("------------------\nScope\n\n");

print LMAIL ("What topics are covered?\n $in{Topics}\n\n");
print LMAIL ("Are there links to other similar sites?\n $in{OtherSitesL}\n\n");
```

```
print LMAIL ("-------------------\nUniqueness\n\n");

print LMAIL ("Is the information unique to the Web?\n $in{Unique}\n\n");
print LMAIL ("If no, where else can you find it?\n $in{WhereElse}\n\n");

print LMAIL ("------------------\nFunctionality\n\n");

print LMAIL ("Is the Web site easy to connect to?\n $in{Connect}\n\n");
print LMAIL ("Do Web pages load quickly?\n $in{Quickly}\n\n");
print LMAIL ("Do graphics load quickly and completely?\n $in{Completely}\n\n");

print LMAIL ("------------------\nHelp\n\n");

print LMAIL ("Are help instructions easy to find?\n $in{EasyFind}\n\n");
print LMAIL ("Are help instructions written for kids / teens?\n $in{WrittenK}\n\n");

print LMAIL ("\n.\n");


###############################################
# Email received by the user confirming form submission #
###############################################


# **********************************************
# Here's where you MUST specify the path to your
# email program ON your Web server.
# Replace /usr/sbin/sendmail with your path.
# **********************************************

open (MAIL, "|/usr/sbin/sendmail -t");

# **********************************************
# Here's where you MAY customize the email
# response to the user. You may change any wording
# of the message.
# **********************************************

print MAIL<<toEnd;
To: $in{Email}
From: $in{LibraryEmail}
Subject: $in{Form}

Thanks for completing our form, How to Evaluate a Web Site.

toEnd
    print MAIL ("\n.\n");
```

Group 4—Library Web Site Forms/Surveys

```
#########################################
# Screen response to user after submitting the form  #
#########################################

print ("<html><head><title>$in{Form}</title></head>");
print ("<body bgcolor=\"ffffff\">");

# *************************************************************
# Here's where you MAY change the screen response
# the user sees after submitting the form. You may
# change any wording between the quotation marks.
# *************************************************************

print ("Thanks for completing our form, How to Evaluate a Web Site.");

# *************************************************************
# Here's where you MAY change the name of the link
# back to your main page. You may replace Return
# to our main page with your own wording.
# *************************************************************

print ("<p><center><a href=$in{LibraryURL}>Return to our main page.</a></center>");
print ("</body></html>");
```

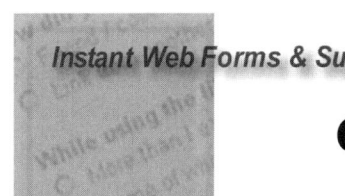

Instant Web Forms & Surveys

Group 5 — Collection Development Forms / Surveys

In this section you'll find one Web-based form and one survey. The form allows students to suggest books, videos, DVDs, and CDs that they'd like to see your library purchase. The survey lets students give your staff feedback on the types of fiction and non-fiction books and magazines they currently read, as well as the types of new materials they would read/listen to if you purchased them.

Recommend an Item
Make it easy for students to suggest a book, videotape, DVD, or CD that they want you to purchase for your library collection. All students have to do is fill out the form and tell you why they think your library should purchase the item. Put a link to this form on your home page or library collections page.

Reading Interests Survey
One way to build your collection is have students help you to identify the types of materials that they read and the genres/subjects that interest them the most. Add a link to this survey periodically to your library collections page or home page.

Recommend an Item

If you'd like the library to purchase a book, videotape, DVD, CD, etc., just fill out the form below and tell us why you think we should buy it.

Name (first, last)

E-mail address

Home address (+ city)

School you attend

Home phone/fax (+ areacode)

Teacher's name

What grade are you in?
○ 3 ○ 4 ○ 5 ○ 6 ○ 7
○ 8 ○ 9 ○ 10 ○ 11 ○ 12

Material type
○ Book ○ Magazine ○ DVD / Videotape ○ Music CD
○ Other (explain)

Age level
○ Young kids ○ Older kids ○ Young adults ○ Teens

Title

Author / Artist

Publisher / Date published

The library should purchase this item because...

[Send Recommendation]   [Clear Form]

http://
© 2002 Contact Webmaster

Recommend an Item — HTML Form

```html
<html>
<head><title>Recommend an Item</title></head>
<body bgcolor="#FFFFFF">
<table width="700" border="1" bordercolor="000000" height="85" bgcolor="ffffff">
<tr valign="middle" align="center"><td>
<p>
<font halign=center color="#000000" face="Arial, Helvetica, sans-serif" size="+3">
<b><i>Recommend an Item</i></b></font></p>
</td></tr></table>
<form method="post" action="http://www.yourLibrary.org/cgi-bin/ca1.pl" name="">
<p> </p>
<p><font face="Arial, Helvetica, sans-serif" size="2"><b>If you'd like the library to purchase a book, videotape, DVD, CD, etc., just fill out the form below <br>and tell us why you think we should buy it.</b></font></p>
<p> </p>
<input type="hidden" name="LibraryEmail" value="you@yourLibrary.org">
<input type="hidden" name="LibraryURL" value="http://www.yourLibrary.org">
<input type="hidden" name="Form" value="Recommend an Item">
<p></p>
<table width="407" border="0" cellspacing="4" cellpadding="1">
<tr><td width="202">
<b><font face="Arial, Helvetica, sans-serif" size="2">Name</font></b><font face="Arial, Helvetica, sans-serif" size="1">  (first, last)</font><br><font face="Arial, Helvetica, sans-serif" size="2">
<input type="text" name="Name" size="25"></font></td>
<td width="189">
<b><font face="Arial, Helvetica, sans-serif" size="2">E-mail address<br></font></b><font face="Arial, Helvetica, sans-serif" size="2"><input type="text" name="Email" size="25"></font></td></tr>
<tr><td width="202" height="2">
<b><font face="Arial, Helvetica, sans-serif" size="2">Home address</font></b><font face="Arial, Helvetica, sans-serif" size="1">  (+ city)</font><br><font face="Arial, Helvetica, sans-serif" size="2">
<input type="text" name="HomeAddr" size="25"></font></td>
<td width="189" height="2">
<b><font face="Arial, Helvetica, sans-serif" size="2">School you attend<br></font></b><font face="Arial, Helvetica, sans-serif" size="2"><input type="text" name="School" size="25"></font></td></tr>
<tr><td width="202" height="2">
<b><font face="Arial, Helvetica, sans-serif" size="2">Home phone/fax</font></b><font face="Arial, Helvetica, sans-serif" size="1">  (+ areacode)</font><br><font face="Arial, Helvetica, sans-serif" size="2"><input type="text" name="HomePhone" size="25"></font></td>
<td width="189" height="2">
<b><font face="Arial, Helvetica, sans-serif" size="2">Teacher's name <br></font></b><font face="Arial, Helvetica, sans-serif" size="2"><input type="text" name="Teacher" size="25"></font></td></tr>
<tr><td width="391" colspan="2" height="48">
<b><font face="Arial, Helvetica, sans-serif" size="2">What grade are you in?</font></b><br><font face="Arial, Helvetica, sans-serif" size="2"></font>
```

```html
<table width="87%" border="0" cellspacing="4" cellpadding="0"><tr><td height="8" width="16%">
<font face="Arial, Helvetica, sans-serif" size="2"><input type="radio" name="EducationLevel" value="3">
3</font></td>
<td height="8" width="16%">
<font face="Arial, Helvetica, sans-serif" size="2"><input type="radio" name="EducationLevel" value="4">
4</font></td>
<td height="8" width="16%">
<font face="Arial, Helvetica, sans-serif" size="2"><input type="radio" name="EducationLevel" value="5">
5</font></td>
<td height="8" width="16%">
<font face="Arial, Helvetica, sans-serif" size="2"><input type="radio" name="EducationLevel" value="6">
6</font></td>
<td height="8" width="36%">
<font face="Arial, Helvetica, sans-serif" size="2"><input type="radio" name="EducationLevel" value="7">
7</font></td></tr>
<tr><td height="2" width="16%">
<font face="Arial, Helvetica, sans-serif" size="2"><input type="radio" name="EducationLevel" value="8">
8</font></td>
<td height="2" width="16%">
<font face="Arial, Helvetica, sans-serif" size="2"><input type="radio" name="EducationLevel" value="9">
9</font></td>
<td height="2" width="16%">
<font face="Arial, Helvetica, sans-serif" size="2"><input type="radio" name="EducationLevel" value="10">
10</font></td>
<td height="2" width="16%">
<font face="Arial, Helvetica, sans-serif" size="2"><input type="radio" name="EducationLevel" value="11">
11</font></td>
<td height="2" width="36%">
<font face="Arial, Helvetica, sans-serif" size="2"><input type="radio" name="EducationLevel" value="12">
12</font>
</td></tr></table>
</td></tr></table>
<p><br>
<b><font face="Arial, Helvetica, sans-serif" size="2">Material type<br></font></b><font face="Arial, Helvetica, sans-serif" size="2">
<input type="radio" name="MaterialType" value="Book">Book   
<input type="radio" name="MaterialType" value="Magazine">Magazine   
<input type="radio" name="MaterialType" value="DVD / Videotape">DVD / Videotape    
<input type="radio" name="MaterialType" value="Music CD">Music CD   <br>
<input type="radio" name="MaterialType" value="Other">Other<font size="3"><b> </b></font><font face="Arial, Helvetica, sans-serif" size="1">(explain)</font> <font size="2"><input type="text" name="MatTypeO" size="15"></font></font></font></p>
<p>
<b><font face="Arial, Helvetica, sans-serif" size="2">Age level<br></font></b>
<font face="Arial, Helvetica, sans-serif" size="2"><input type="radio" name="AgeLevel" value="Young
```

```html
kids">Young kids   </font>
<font face="Arial, Helvetica, sans-serif" size="2"><input type="radio" name="AgeLevel" value="Older kids">Older kids   
<input type="radio" name="AgeLevel" value="Young adults">Young adults   
<input type="radio" name="AgeLevel" value="Teens">Teens</font></p>
<p>
<font face="Arial, Helvetica, sans-serif" size="2"><b><br>Title</b><br><font size="3"><input type="text" name="Title" size="40"></font></font></p>
<p>
<font face="Arial, Helvetica, sans-serif" size="2"><b>Author / Artist</b><br><font size="3"><input type="text" name="Author" size="40"></font></font></p>
<p>
<font face="Arial, Helvetica, sans-serif" size="2"><b>Publisher / Date published</b><br>
<font size="3"><input type="text" name="Publisher" size="40"><br><br><br></font></font></p>
<p>
<font face="Arial, Helvetica, sans-serif" size="2"><b>The library should purchase this item because...</b><br>
</font><font size="3" face="Arial, Helvetica, sans-serif"><textarea name= "ReasonToBuy" cols="40" rows="2"></textarea></font><br></p>
<p> </p>
<table width="700" border="0" cellspacing="10" cellpadding="1">
<tr><td width="313"><div align="right"><input type="submit" name="send" value="Send Recommendation"></div></td>
<td width="134"> </td><td width="207"><div align="left"><input type="reset" name="clear" value="Clear Form"></div></td></tr>
<tr colspan=3><td colspan=3>
<table width="500" border="1" height="2" align="center" cellpadding="0" cellspacing="0" bgcolor="ffffff" bordercolor="000000"><tr><td><font size="1" color="#ffffff">.</font></td></tr></table></td></tr>
<tr><td colspan=3><div align="center">
<font face="Arial, Helvetica, sans-serif" size="1"><b>http://</b></font><br><font size="2"> 
<font face="Arial, Helvetica, sans-serif" size="1"><b>&copy; 2002</b></font></font>
<font face="Arial, Helvetica, sans-serif" size="1"><a href="mailto:">
<b>Contact Webmaster</b></a></font></div></td></tr>
</table></form>
</body>
</html>
```

Recommend an Item — Perl Script

```perl
#!/usr/local/bin/perl

# ***************************************************
# ABOVE is where you MUST specify the path to your
# perl interpreter on your Web server.
# Replace /usr/local/bin/perl with your path.
# ***************************************************

if ($ENV{'REQUEST_METHOD'}eq"GET"){$buffer = $ENV{'QUERY_STRING'};}
    elsif($ENV{'REQUEST_METHOD'}eq"POST"){
        read(STDIN,$buffer,$ENV{'CONTENT_LENGTH'});
    }
$bufferb = $buffer;
#separate the name of the input from its value.
@forminputs = split(/&/, $bufferb);

foreach $forminput (@forminputs)
{
    #separate the name of the input from its value
    ($name, $value) = split(/=/, $forminput);

    #Un-Webify plus signs and %-encoding
    $value =~ tr/+/ /;
    $value =~ s/%([a-fA-F0-9][a-fA-F0-9])/pack("C", hex($1))/eg;

    #stick them in the in array
    $in{$name} = $value;
}
print "Content-type: text/html\n\n";

############################################
# ABOVE is the required header for a perl script    #
############################################


###############################################
# (Below) Email received by library containing user-entered information #
###############################################

# ***************************************************
# Here's where you MUST specify the path to your
# email program (probably sendmail) ON your Web server.
# Replace /usr/sbin/sendmail with your path.
# ***************************************************
```

```
open (LMAIL, "|/usr/sbin/sendmail -t");
print LMAIL ("To: $in{LibraryEmail}\n");
print LMAIL ("From: $in{Email}\n");
print LMAIL ("Subject: $in{Form} - patron submission\n");

print LMAIL ("------------------\nPatron information\n\n");


print LMAIL ("Name:\n $in{Name}\n\n");
print LMAIL ("E-mail Address:\n $in{Email}\n\n");
print LMAIL ("Home Address:\n $in{HomeAddr}\n\n");
print LMAIL ("School:\n $in{School}\n\n");
print LMAIL ("Home Phone/Fax:\n $in{HomePhone}\n\n");
print LMAIL ("Teacher's Name:\n $in{Teacher}\n\n");
print LMAIL ("Grade:\n $in{EducationLevel}\n\n");

print LMAIL ("------------------\nSubmitted information \n\n");
print LMAIL ("Material type:\n $in{MaterialType}\n\n");
print LMAIL ("Other material type:\n $in{MatTypeO}\n\n");
print LMAIL ("Age Level:\n $in{AgeLevel}\n\n");
print LMAIL ("Title:\n $in{Title}\n\n");
print LMAIL ("Author / Artist:\n $in{Author}\n\n");
print LMAIL ("Publisher / Date Published:\n $in{Publisher}\n\n");
print LMAIL ("I think the library should purchase this item because:\n $in{ReasonToBuy}\n\n");
print LMAIL ("\n.\n");

##############################################
# Email received by the user confirming form submission #
##############################################

# ***********************************************
# Here's where you MUST specify the path to your
# email program ON your Web server.
# Replace /usr/sbin/sendmail with your path.
# ***********************************************

open (MAIL, "|/usr/sbin/sendmail -t");

# ***********************************************
# Here's where you MAY customize the email
# response to the user. You may change any wording
# of the message.
# ***********************************************

print MAIL<<toEnd;
```

To: $in{Email}
From: $in{LibraryEmail}
Subject: $in{Form}

Thanks for suggesting that we purchase a new item for our collection.\n\n
We are always looking for new resources to enrich our collections.

toEnd
   print MAIL ("\n.\n");

###
Screen response to user after submitting the form
###

print ("<html><head><title>$in{Form}</title></head>");
print ("<body bgcolor=\"ffffff\">");

***
Here's where you MAY change the screen response
the user sees after submitting the form. You may
change any wording between the quotation marks.
***

print ("Thanks for suggesting that we purchase a new item for our collection.<p>
We are always looking for new resources to enrich our collections.");

***
Here's where you MAY change the name of the link
back to your main page. You may replace Return
to our main page with your own wording.
***

print ("<p> <a href=$in{LibraryURL}>Return to our main page.</a> ");
print ("</body></html>");

Reading Interests Survey

We constantly buy new books and magazines for the library. Help us by filling out this survey.
Let us know the types of books and magazines that you read and the subjects that interest you the most.

What do you most like to read?
○ Fiction books   ○ Non-fiction books   ○ Magazines   ○ Other (explain) [____]

How do you find out about new books / magazines?
○ Friends   ○ Browsing the library shelves   ○ Librarians / Teachers   ○ TV / Radio
○ Web sites   ○ Book reviews   ○ Bookstores   ○ Other

Books

How often do you check out books from the library?
○ 2+ times a week   ○ Once a week   ○ 2+ times a month
○ Once a month   ○ Every few months   ○ 2+ times a year

Why do you read books?
○ I like to   ○ Homework   ○ School assignments
○ Personal research   ○ Just for fun   ○ Other

What types of fiction books do you like to read?
○ Action / Adventure   ○ Book series   ○ Fantasy / Science fiction   ○ Horror / Mystery
○ Jokes / Fun   ○ Books for girls ○ Books for boys   ○ Other

What types of non-fiction books do you like to read?
○ Biographies   ○ Health / Fitness / Fashion   ○ Technology / Computers
○ Science   ○ Sports / Hobbies   ○ Art / Drama / Poetry
○ Other (explain) [____]

What new types of books should the library buy?
[_____]

Magazines

How often do you come to the library to read magazines?
○ Once a day   ○ Every other day   ○ 2+ times a week
○ Once a week   ○ 2+ times a month   ○ Less than once a month

Why do you read magazines at the library?
○ I like to   ○ Homework   ○ School assignments
○ Personal research   ○ Just for fun   ○ Other

Which types of magazines do you like to read?
○ News / Current events   ○ Sports / Hobbies   ○ Science
○ Health / Fitness / Fashion   ○ Technology / Computers   ○ Other

What new magazines should the library buy?

Name (first, last)   **E-mail address**

School you attend   **Gender**
                                ○ Female   ○ Male

What grade are you in?
○ 3   ○ 4   ○ 5   ○ 6   ○ 7
○ 8   ○ 9   ○ 10   ○ 11   ○ 12

[Send Survey]   [Clear Survey]

http://
© 2002 Contact Webmaster

Reading Interests Survey — HTML Form

```
<html>
<head><title>Reading Interests Survey</title></head>
<body bgcolor="#FFFFFF">
<table width="700" border="1" bordercolor="#000000" height="85" bgcolor="#ffffff">
<tr valign="middle" align="center"><td>
<p>
<font halign=center color="#000000" face="Arial, Helvetica, sans-serif" size="+3">
<b><i>Reading Interests Survey</i></b></font></p>
</td></tr></table>
<form method="post" action="http://www.yourLibrary.org/cgi-bin/ca2.pl"><p> </p>
<p>
<font face="Arial, Helvetica, sans-serif" size="2"><b>We constantly buy new books and magazines for the library. Help us by filling out this survey.<br> Let us know the types of books and magazines that you read and the subjects that interest you the most.</b></font></p>
<p> </p>
<input type="hidden" name="LibraryEmail" value="you@yourLibrary.org">
<input type="hidden" name="LibraryURL" value="http://www.yourLibrary.org">
<input type="hidden" name="Form" value="Reading Interests Survey">
<p></p><p>
<b><font face="Arial, Helvetica, sans-serif" size="2">What do you most like to read?<br></font></b>
<font face="Arial, Helvetica, sans-serif" size="2">
<input type="radio" name="Read" value="Fiction books">Fiction books  
<input type="radio" name="Read" value="Non-fiction books">Non-fiction books   
<input type="radio" name="Read" value="Magazines">Magazines   
<input type="radio" name="Read" value="Other">Other <font size="1"> (explain) 
<font size="2"><input type="text" name="ReadO" size="10"></font></font></font></p>
<p>
<b><font face="Arial, Helvetica, sans-serif" size="2">How do you find out about new books / magazines?<br>
</font></b>
<table width="561" border="0" cellspacing="0" cellpadding="0"><tr><td width="100">
<font face="Arial, Helvetica, sans-serif" size="2"><input type="radio" name="FindOut" value="Friends">
Friends</font></td>
<td width="201">
<font face="Arial, Helvetica, sans-serif" size="2"><input type="radio" name="FindOut" value="Browsing the library shelves">Browsing the library shelves</font></td>
<td width="164">
<font face="Arial, Helvetica, sans-serif" size="2"><input type="radio" name="FindOut" value="Librarians / Teachers">Librarians / Teachers</font></td>
<td width="96">
<font face="Arial, Helvetica, sans-serif" size="2"><input type="radio" name="FindOut" value="TV / Radio">
TV / Radio</font></td></tr>
<tr><td width="100">
<font face="Arial, Helvetica, sans-serif" size="2"><input type="radio" name="FindOut" value="Web sites">
```

```html
Web sites</font></td>
<td width="201">
<font face="Arial, Helvetica, sans-serif" size="2"><input type="radio" name="FindOut" value="Book reviews">Book reviews</font></td>
<td width="164">
<font face="Arial, Helvetica, sans-serif" size="2"><input type="radio" name="FindOut" value="Book stores">Bookstores</font></td>
<td width="96">
<font face="Arial, Helvetica, sans-serif" size="2"><input type="radio" name="FindOut" value="Other">Other</font></td></tr></table>
<p>
<br><b><font face="Arial, Helvetica, sans-serif" size="3">Books</font></b></p>
<p>
<font face="Arial, Helvetica, sans-serif" size="2"><b>How often do you check out books from the library?</b>   <br></font>
<table width="541" border="0" cellspacing="0" cellpadding="00"><tr><td width="157">
<font face="Arial, Helvetica, sans-serif" size="2"><input type="radio" name="OftenBooks" value="2+ times a week">2+ times a week</font></td>
<td width="134">
<font face="Arial, Helvetica, sans-serif" size="2"><input type="radio" name="OftenBooks" value="Once a week">Once a week</font></td>
<td width="250">
<font face="Arial, Helvetica, sans-serif" size="2"><input type="radio" name="OftenBooks" value="2+times a month">2+ times a month</font></td></tr>
<tr><td width="157">
<font face="Arial, Helvetica, sans-serif" size="2"><input type="radio" name="OftenBooks" value="Once a month">Once a month</font></td>
<td width="134">
<font face="Arial, Helvetica, sans-serif" size="2"><input type="radio" name="OftenBooks" value="Every few months">Every few months</font></td>
<td width="250">
<font face="Arial, Helvetica, sans-serif" size="2"><input type="radio" name="OftenBooks" value="2+times a year">2+ times a year</font>
</td></tr></table>
<p>
<font face="Arial, Helvetica, sans-serif" size="2"><b>Why do you read books?</b>  <br></font>
<table width="466" border="0" cellspacing="0" cellpadding="0"><tr><td width="157">
<font face="Arial, Helvetica, sans-serif" size="2"><input type="radio" name="WhyReadBooks" value="I like to">I like to</font></td>
<td width="135">
<font face="Arial, Helvetica, sans-serif" size="2"><input type="radio" name="WhyReadBooks" value="Homework">Homework</font></td>
<td width="174">
<font face="Arial, Helvetica, sans-serif" size="2"><input type="radio" name="WhyReadBooks" value="School assignments">School assignments</font></td></tr>
```

```html
<tr><td width="157">
<font face="Arial, Helvetica, sans-serif" size="2"><input type="radio" name="WhyReadBooks" value= "Personal research">Personal research</font></td>
<td width="135">
<font face="Arial, Helvetica, sans-serif" size="2"><input type="radio" name="WhyReadBooks" value= "Just for fun">Just for fun</font></td>
<td width="174">
<font face="Arial, Helvetica, sans-serif" size="2"><input type="radio" name="WhyReadBooks" value= "Other">Other</font>
</td></tr></table>
<p>
<font face="Arial, Helvetica, sans-serif" size="2"><b>What types of fiction books do you like to read?<br>
</b></font>
<table width="729" border="0" cellspacing="0" cellpadding="0"><tr><td width="158">
<font face="Arial, Helvetica, sans-serif" size="2"><input type="radio" name="Fiction" value="Action / Adventure">Action / Adventure</font></td>
<td width="135">
<font face="Arial, Helvetica, sans-serif" size="2"><input type="radio" name="Fiction" value="Book Series">Book series</font></td>
<td width="185">
<font face="Arial, Helvetica, sans-serif" size="2"><input type="radio" name="Fiction" value="Fantasy / Science fiction">Fantasy / Science fiction</font></td>
<td width="251">
<font face="Arial, Helvetica, sans-serif" size="2"><input type="radio" name="Fiction" value="Horror / Mystery"> Horror / Mystery</font></td></tr>
<tr><td width="158" valign="top" height="2">
<font face="Arial, Helvetica, sans-serif" size="2"><input type="radio" name="Fiction" value="Jokes / Fun">Jokes / Fun</font></td>
<td width="135" valign="top" height="2">
<font face="Arial, Helvetica, sans-serif" size="2"><input type="radio" name="Fiction" value="Books for girls">Books for girls</font></td>
<td width="185" valign="top" height="2">
<font face="Arial, Helvetica, sans-serif" size="2"><input type="radio" name="Fiction" value="Books for boys">Books for boys</font></td>
<td width="251" height="2">
<font face="Arial, Helvetica, sans-serif" size="2"><input type="radio" name="Fiction" value="Other"> Other   </font>
</td></tr></table>
<p>
<font face="Arial, Helvetica, sans-serif" size="2"><b>What types of non-fiction books do you like to read?
</b><br></font>
<table width="700" border="0" cellspacing="0" cellpadding="0"><tr><td width="156">
<font face="Arial, Helvetica, sans-serif" size="2"><input type="radio" name="Nonfiction" value= "Biographies">Biographies</font></td>
<td width="235">
```

```html
<font face="Arial, Helvetica, sans-serif" size="2"><input type="radio" name="Nonfiction" value=
"Health / Fitness / Fashion">Health / Fitness / Fashion</font></td>
<td width="309">
<font face="Arial, Helvetica, sans-serif" size="2"><input type="radio" name="Nonfiction" value=
"Technology / Computers">Technology / Computers</font></td></tr>
<tr><td width="156">
<font face="Arial, Helvetica, sans-serif" size="2"><input type="radio" name="Nonfiction" value=
"Science">Science</font></td>
<td width="235">
<font face="Arial, Helvetica, sans-serif" size="2"><input type="radio" name="Nonfiction" value="Sports /
Hobbies">Sports / Hobbies</font></td>
<td width="309">
<font face="Arial, Helvetica, sans-serif" size="2"><input type="radio" name="Nonfiction" value="Art / Drama /
Poetry">Art / Drama / Poetry</font></td></tr>
<tr><td colspan="2">
<font face="Arial, Helvetica, sans-serif" size="2"><input type="radio" name="Nonfiction" value="Other">
Other   <font size="1">(explain)<font size="2">  <input type="text"
name="NonFictionOther" size="10"></font></font></font></td><td width="309"> 
</td></tr></table>
<p>
<font face="Arial, Helvetica, sans-serif" size="2"><b>What new types of books should the library buy?
</b><font size="3"><br><textarea name="NewBooks" cols="40" rows="2"></textarea></font></font></p>
<p><br>
<b><font face="Arial, Helvetica, sans-serif" size="3">Magazines</font></b></p>
<p>
<font face="Arial, Helvetica, sans-serif" size="2"><b>How often do you come to the library to read
magazines?<br></b></font>
<table width="613" border="0" cellspacing="0" cellpadding="0"><tr><td width="136">
<font face="Arial, Helvetica, sans-serif" size="2"><input type="radio" name="OftenNews" value="Once a
day">Once a day</font></td>
<td width="179">
<font face="Arial, Helvetica, sans-serif" size="2"><input type="radio" name="OftenNews" value="Every other
day">Every other day</font></td>
<td width="298">
<font face="Arial, Helvetica, sans-serif" size="2"><input type="radio" name="OftenNews" value="2+ times a
week">2+ times a week</font></td></tr>
<tr><td width="136">
<font face="Arial, Helvetica, sans-serif" size="2"><input type="radio" name="OftenNews" value="Once a
week">Once a week</font></td>
<td width="179">
<font face="Arial, Helvetica, sans-serif" size="2"><input type="radio" name="OftenNews" value="2+ times a
month">2+ times a month</font></td>
<td width="298">
<font face="Arial, Helvetica, sans-serif" size="2"><input type="radio" name="OftenNews" value="Less than once
a month">Less than once a month</font></td></tr></table>
```

```html
<p>
<font face="Arial, Helvetica, sans-serif" size="2"><b>Why do you read magazines at the library?</b>
   <br></font>
<table width="466" border="0" cellspacing="0" cellpadding="0"><tr><td width="157">
<font face="Arial, Helvetica, sans-serif" size="2"><input type="radio" name="WhyReadMags" value=
"I like to">I like to</font></td>
<td width="135">
<font face="Arial, Helvetica, sans-serif" size="2"><input type="radio" name="WhyReadMags" value=
"Homework">Homework</font></td>
<td width="174">
<font face="Arial, Helvetica, sans-serif" size="2"><input type="radio" name="WhyReadMags" value= "School
assignments">School assignments</font></td></tr>
<tr><td width="157">
<font face="Arial, Helvetica, sans-serif" size="2"><input type="radio" name="WhyReadMags" value= "Personal
research">Personal research</font></td>
<td width="135">
<font face="Arial, Helvetica, sans-serif" size="2"><input type="radio" name="WhyReadMags" value=
"Just for fun">Just for fun</font></td>
<td width="174">
<font face="Arial, Helvetica, sans-serif" size="2"><input type="radio" name="WhyReadMags" value=
"Other">Other</font>
</td></tr></table>
<p>
<font face="Arial, Helvetica, sans-serif" size="2"><b>Which types of magazines do you like to read?</b><br>
</font>
<table width="600" border="0" cellspacing="0" cellpadding="0"><tr><td width="202">
<font face="Arial, Helvetica, sans-serif" size="2"><input type="radio" name="Mags" value="News / Current
events">News / Current events</font></td>
<td width="193">
<font face="Arial, Helvetica, sans-serif" size="2"><input type="radio" name="Mags" value="Sports /
Hobbies">Sports / Hobbies</font></td>
<td width="205">
<font face="Arial, Helvetica, sans-serif" size="2"><input type="radio" name="Mags" value="Science">
Science</font></td></tr>
<tr><td width="202">
<font face="Arial, Helvetica, sans-serif" size="2"><input type="radio" name="Mags" value="Health / Fitness /
Fashion">Health / Fitness / Fashion</font></td>
<td width="193">
<font face="Arial, Helvetica, sans-serif" size="2"><input type="radio" name="Mags" value="Technology /
Computers">Technology / Computers</font></td>
<td width="205">
<font face="Arial, Helvetica, sans-serif" size="2"><input type="radio" name="Mags" value="Other">
Other </font>
</td></tr></table>
<p>
```

```html
<font face="Arial, Helvetica, sans-serif" size="2"><b>What new magazines should the library buy?</b><font size="3"><br><textarea name= "AdditionalMagazines" cols="40" rows="2"></textarea>
</font></font></p>
<br><br>
<table width="407" border="0" cellspacing="4" cellpadding="1"><tr>
<td width="202">
<b><font face="Arial, Helvetica, sans-serif" size="2">Name</font></b><font face="Arial, Helvetica, sans-serif" size="1">  (first, last)</font><br><font face="Arial, Helvetica, sans-serif" size="2">
<input type="text" name="Name" size="25"></font></td>
<td width="189">
<b><font face="Arial, Helvetica, sans-serif" size="2">E-mail address<br></font></b><font face="Arial, Helvetica, sans-serif" size="2"><input type="text" name="Email" size="25"></font></td></tr>
<tr><td width="202" height="2">
<b><font face="Arial, Helvetica, sans-serif" size="2">School you attend<br></font></b><font face="Arial, Helvetica, sans-serif" size="2"><input type="text" name="School" size="25"></font></td>
<td width="189" height="2">
<b><font face="Arial, Helvetica, sans-serif" size="2">Gender<br></font></b>
<input type="radio" name="Gender" value="Female"><font face="Arial, Helvetica, sans-serif" size="2">Female
</font>
<input type="radio" name="Gender" value="Male"><font face="Arial, Helvetica, sans-serif" size="2">Male
</font></td></tr>
<tr><td width="391" colspan="2" height="48">
<b><font face="Arial, Helvetica, sans-serif" size="2">What grade are you in?</font></b><br>
<table width="87%" border="0" cellspacing="4" cellpadding="0"><tr><td height="8" width="16%">
<font face="Arial, Helvetica, sans-serif" size="2"><input type="radio" name="EducationLevel" value="3">
3</font></td>
<td height="8" width="16%">
<font face="Arial, Helvetica, sans-serif" size="2"><input type="radio" name="EducationLevel" value="4">
4</font></td>
<td height="8" width="16%">
<font face="Arial, Helvetica, sans-serif" size="2"><input type="radio" name="EducationLevel" value="5">
5</font></td>
<td height="8" width="16%">
<font face="Arial, Helvetica, sans-serif" size="2"><input type="radio" name="EducationLevel" value="6">
6</font></td>
<td height="8" width="36%">
<font face="Arial, Helvetica, sans-serif" size="2"><input type="radio" name="EducationLevel" value="7">
7</font></td></tr>
<tr><td height="2" width="16%">
<font face="Arial, Helvetica, sans-serif" size="2"><input type="radio" name="EducationLevel" value="8">
8</font></td>
<td height="2" width="16%">
<font face="Arial, Helvetica, sans-serif" size="2"><input type="radio" name="EducationLevel" value="9">
9</font></td>
<td height="2" width="16%">
```

Group 5—Collection Development Forms/Surveys

```html
<font face="Arial, Helvetica, sans-serif" size="2"><input type="radio" name="EducationLevel" value="10">
10</font></td>
<td height="2" width="16%">
<font face="Arial, Helvetica, sans-serif" size="2"><input type="radio" name="EducationLevel" value="11">
11</font></td>
<td height="2" width="36%">
<font face="Arial, Helvetica, sans-serif" size="2"><input type="radio" name="EducationLevel" value="12">
12</font>
</td></tr></table>
</td></tr></table>
<p> </p>
<table width="700" border="0" cellspacing="10" cellpadding="1"><tr><td width="222"><div align=
"right"><input type="submit" name="send" value="Send Survey"></div></td><td width="216"> </td>
<td width="216"><div align="left"><input type="reset" name= "clear" value="Clear Survey">/div></td></tr>
<tr colspan=3><td colspan=3>
<table width="500" border="1" bordercolor="#000000" height="2" align="center" cellpadding="0"
cellspacing="0" bgcolor="#ffffff"><tr><td><font size="1" color="#ffffff">.</font></td></tr></table></td></tr>
<tr><td colspan=3><div align="center">
<font face="Arial, Helvetica, sans-serif" size="1"> <b>http://</b></font><br><font size="2"> 
<font face="Arial, Helvetica, sans-serif" size="1"><b>&copy; 2002</b></font></font>
<font face="Arial, Helvetica, sans-serif" size="2"><a href="mailto:">
<b><font size="1">Contact Webmaster</font></b></a></font></div></td></tr>
</table></form>
</body>
</html>
```

Reading Interests Survey — Perl Script

```perl
#!/usr/local/bin/perl

# *************************************************************
# ABOVE is where you MUST specify the path to your
# perl interpreter on your Web server.
# Replace /usr/local/bin/perl with your path.
# *************************************************************

if ($ENV{'REQUEST_METHOD'}eq"GET"){$buffer = $ENV{'QUERY_STRING'};}
    elsif($ENV{'REQUEST_METHOD'}eq"POST"){
        read(STDIN,$buffer,$ENV{'CONTENT_LENGTH'});
    }
$bufferb = $buffer;
#separate the name of the input from its value.
@forminputs = split(/&/, $bufferb);

foreach $forminput (@forminputs)
{
    #separate the name of the input from its value
    ($name, $value) = split(/=/, $forminput);

    #Un-Webify plus signs and %-encoding
    $value =~ tr/+/ /;
    $value =~ s/%([a-fA-F0-9][a-fA-F0-9])/pack("C", hex($1))/eg;

    #stick them in the in array
    $in{$name} = $value;
}
print "Content-type: text/html\n\n";

###############################################
# ABOVE is the required header for a perl script   #
###############################################

#####################################################
# (Below) Email received by library containing user-entered information #
#####################################################

# *************************************************************
#
# Here's where you MUST specify the path to your
# email program (probably sendmail) ON your Web server.
# Replace /usr/sbin/sendmail with your path.
# *************************************************************
```

Group 5—Collection Development Forms/Surveys

```
open (LMAIL, "|/usr/sbin/sendmail -t");
print LMAIL ("To: $in{LibraryEmail}\n");
print LMAIL ("From: $in{Email}\n");
print LMAIL ("Subject: $in{Form} - patron submission\n");

print LMAIL ("------------------\nPatron information\n\n");


print LMAIL ("Name:\n $in{Name}\n\n");
print LMAIL ("E-mail Address:\n $in{Email}\n\n");
print LMAIL ("School:\n $in{School}\n\n");
print LMAIL ("Gender:\n $in{Gender}\n\n");
print LMAIL ("Grade:\n $in{EducationLevel}\n\n");

print LMAIL ("------------------\nSubmitted information \n\n");
print LMAIL ("What do you most like to read?\n $in{Read}\n\n");
print LMAIL ("Other material type:\n $in{ReadO}\n\n");
print LMAIL ("How do you find out about new books / magazines / newspapers?\n $in{FindOut}\n\n");
print LMAIL ("------------------\nBooks \n\n");
print LMAIL ("How often do you check out books from the library?\n $in{OftenBooks}\n\n");
print LMAIL ("Why do you read books?\n $in{WhyReadBooks}\n\n");
print LMAIL ("What types of fiction books do you like to read?\n $in{Fiction}\n\n");
print LMAIL ("Other types of fiction:\n $in{FictionOther}\n\n");
print LMAIL ("What types of non-fiction books do you like to read?\n $in{Nonfiction}\n\n");
print LMAIL ("Other types of non-fiction:\n $in{NonFictionOther}\n\n");
print LMAIL ("What new types of books should the library buy?\n $in{NewBooks}\n\n");
print LMAIL ("------------------\nMagazines \n\n");
print LMAIL ("How often do you come to the library to read magazines?\n $in{OftenNews}\n\n");
print LMAIL ("Why do you read magazines at the library?\n $in{WhyReadNews}\n\n");
print LMAIL ("Which types of magazines do you like to read?\n $in{Mags}\n\n");
print LMAIL ("Other types of magazines:\n $in{MagsOther}\n\n");
print LMAIL ("What new magazines should the library buy?\n $in{AdditionalMagazines}\n\n");
print LMAIL ("\n.\n");

################################################
# Email received by the user confirming form submission #
################################################


# *********************************************************
# Here's where you MUST specify the path to your
# email program ON your Web server.
# Replace /usr/sbin/sendmail with your path.
# *********************************************************
#

open (MAIL, "|/usr/sbin/sendmail -t");
```

```
# *************************************************************
# Here's where you MAY customize the email
# response to the user. You may change any wording
# of the message.
# *************************************************************

print MAIL<<toEnd;
To: $in{Email}
From: $in{LibraryEmail}
Subject: $in{Form}

Thanks for completing our Reading Interests Survey.\n\n

toEnd
    print MAIL ("\n.\n");



#############################################
# Screen response to user after submitting the form  #
#############################################

print ("<html><head><title>$in{Form}</title></head>");
print ("<body bgcolor=\"ffffff\">");

# *************************************************************
# Here's where you MAY change the screen response
# the user sees after submitting the form. You may
# change any wording between the quotation marks.
# *************************************************************

print ("Thanks for completing our Reading Interests Survey.");

# *************************************************************
# Here's where you MAY change the name of the link
# back to your main page. You may replace Return
# to our main page with your own wording.
# *************************************************************

print ("<p><center><a href=$in{LibraryURL}>Return to our main page.</a></center>");
print ("</body></html>");
```

Instant Web Forms & Surveys

Group 6 — Circulation Forms

In this section you'll find three forms. The first two forms allow students to apply for a library card, put a hold on an item, recall an item that has been checked out by another person, and renew a book that has been checked out. The third form lets students tell your staff about specific library materials they can't locate.

Apply for a Library Card
If students haven't found the time to come to the library to get a library card, now they can apply for one on-line. If they are under 18, students must include information so that you can get in touch with their parents/guardians so they can complete the application and/or sign any permission forms. When their library card is ready to pick up, you can contact students via e-mail or phone to let them know where to pick up their new library card. Be sure to put a link to this form on your circulation Web page.

Hold / Recall / Renew
Students can use this form to extend the due date of an item they've already checked out, to ask that an item checked out by another person be returned to the library so that they can use it, or to place a hold on an item that has been returned, or is about to be returned, by another person. You can contact students via e-mail or phone to let them know when they can pick up the item or when a renewed item is due. Put a link to this form on all of your circulation pages.

Report a Missing Book
Make it easy for students to let you know that they can't locate an item that is not checked out. You can also use the information on this form to contact students via e-mail or phone if you locate the item. Place a link to this form on your home page, your circulation page, and your library collections pages.

Apply for a Library Card

If you haven't had the time to come to the library to get a library card, you can now apply for one on-line. Fill in the form below and be sure to check the "I agree" box. Include information about your parent/guardian so that we can contact them to complete your application. We'll send you an e-mail message, or phone you, to let you know when your library card is ready.

Name (first, last)

E-mail address

Home address (+ city)

School you attend

Home phone/fax (+ areacode)

Teacher's name

What grade are you in?
○ 3   ○ 4   ○ 5   ○ 6   ○ 7
○ 8   ○ 9   ○ 10   ○ 11   ○ 12

Date of birth
Month/Day/Year

Gender
○ Female   ○ Male

I will take good care of all the library materials I check out with this card. I will abide by all library rules and regulations. I will pay overdue fines and/or additional charges for library materials that are damaged and/or lost while checked out to me.

☐ I agree

If you are under 18 years old...

Name of parent / legal guardian

Parent / guardian home address (if different than above)

Parent / guardian city/state/zip (if different than above)

Parent / guardian e-mail address (if different than above)

Parent / guardian home phone/fax (if different than above)

[Send Application] [Clear Form]

http://
© 2002 Contact Webmaster

Apply for a Library Card — HTML Form

```
<html>
<head><title>Apply for a Library Card</title></head>
<body bgcolor="#FFFFFF">
<table width="700" border="1" height="85" bgcolor="ffffff">
<tr valign="middle" align="center"><td>
<p>
<font halign=center color="#000000" face="Arial, Helvetica, sans-serif" size="+3">
<b><i>Apply for a Library Card</i></b></font></p>
</td></tr></table>
<form method="post" action="http://www.yourLibrary.org/cgi-bin/cc1.pl"><p> </p>
<p>
<font face="Arial, Helvetica, sans-serif" size="2"><b>If you haven't had the time to come to the library to get a library card, you can now apply for one on-line.<br> Fill in the form below and be sure to check the "I agree" box. Include information about your parent/guardian <br>so that we can contact them to complete your application. We'll send you an e-mail message, or phone you, <br>to let you know when your library card is ready.</b>
</font></p>
<p> </p>
<input type="hidden" name="LibraryEmail" value="you@yourLibrary.org">
<input type="hidden" name="LibraryURL" value="http://www.yourLibrary.org">
<input type="hidden" name="Form" value="Apply for a Library Card">
<p></p>
<table width="407" border="0" cellspacing="4" cellpadding="1">
<tr><td width="202">
<b><font face="Arial, Helvetica, sans-serif" size="2">Name</font></b><font face="Arial, Helvetica, sans-serif" size="1">  (first, last)</font><br><font face="Arial, Helvetica, sans-serif" size="2">
<input type="text" name="Name" size="25"></font></td>
<td width="189">
<b><font face="Arial, Helvetica, sans-serif" size="2">E-mail address<br></font></b><font face="Arial, Helvetica, sans-serif" size="2"><input type="text" name="Email" size="25"></font></td></tr>
<tr><td width="202" height="2">
<b><font face="Arial, Helvetica, sans-serif" size="2">Home address</font>  </b><font face="Arial, Helvetica, sans-serif" size="1">(+ city)</font><br><font face="Arial, Helvetica, sans-serif" size="2"><input type="text" name="HomeAddr" size="25"></font></td>
<td width="189" height="2">
<b><font face="Arial, Helvetica, sans-serif" size="2">School you attend<br></font></b><font face="Arial, Helvetica, sans-serif" size="2"><input type="text" name="School" size="25"></font></td></tr>
<tr><td width="202" height="2">
<b><font face="Arial, Helvetica, sans-serif" size="2">Home phone/fax</font><font face="Arial, Helvetica, sans-serif" size="1"> </font></b><font face="Arial, Helvetica, sans-serif" size="1"> (+areacode)
</font><br><font face="Arial, Helvetica, sans-serif" size="2"><input type="text" name="HomePhone" size="25">
</font></td>
<td width="189" height="2">
<b><font face="Arial, Helvetica, sans-serif" size="2">Teacher's name<br></font></b><font face="Arial,
```

```html
Helvetica, sans-serif" size="2"><input type="text" name="Teacher" size="25"></font></td></tr>
<tr><td width="391" colspan="2" height="48">
<b><font face="Arial, Helvetica, sans-serif" size="2">What grade are you in?</font></b><br><font face="Arial, Helvetica, sans-serif" size="2"></font>
<table width="87%" border="0" cellspacing="4" cellpadding="0"><tr><td height="8" width="16%">
<font face="Arial, Helvetica, sans-serif" size="2"><input type="radio" name="EducationLevel" value="3">
3</font></td>
<td height="8" width="16%">
<font face="Arial, Helvetica, sans-serif" size="2"><input type="radio" name="EducationLevel" value="4">
4</font></td>
<td height="8" width="16%">
<font face="Arial, Helvetica, sans-serif" size="2"><input type="radio" name="EducationLevel" value="5">
5</font></td>
<td height="8" width="16%">
<font face="Arial, Helvetica, sans-serif" size="2"><input type="radio" name="EducationLevel" value="6">
6</font></td>
<td height="8" width="36%">
<font face="Arial, Helvetica, sans-serif" size="2"><input type="radio" name="EducationLevel" value="7">
7</font></td></tr>
<tr><td height="2" width="16%">
<font face="Arial, Helvetica, sans-serif" size="2"><input type="radio" name="EducationLevel" value="8">
8</font></td>
<td height="2" width="16%">
<font face="Arial, Helvetica, sans-serif" size="2"><input type="radio" name="EducationLevel" value="9">
9</font></td>
<td height="2" width="16%">
<font face="Arial, Helvetica, sans-serif" size="2"><input type="radio" name="EducationLevel" value="10">
10</font></td>
<td height="2" width="16%">
<font face="Arial, Helvetica, sans-serif" size="2"><input type="radio" name="EducationLevel" value="11">
11</font></td>
<td height="2" width="36%">
<font face="Arial, Helvetica, sans-serif" size="2"><input type="radio" name="EducationLevel" value="12">
12</font>
</td></tr></table>
</td></tr></table>
<p>
<b><font face="Arial, Helvetica, sans-serif" size="2"><br>Date of birth     
</font></b><font face="Arial, Helvetica, sans-serif" size="2"><br>Month/Day/Year</font><font face= "Arial, Helvetica, sans-serif" size="3"><input type="text" name="DateOfBirth" size="15">  </font></p>
<p>
<b><font face="Arial, Helvetica, sans-serif" size="2">Gender<br></font></b><font face="Arial, Helvetica, sans-serif" size="2">
<input type="radio" name="Gender" value="Female">Female   
<input type="radio" name="Gender" value="Male">Male<br>
```

```html
<br><br></font></p>
<p>
<b><font face="Arial, Helvetica, sans-serif" size="2">I will take good care of all the library materials I check out with this card. I will abide by all library rules <br>and regulations. I will pay overdue fines and/or additional charges for library materials that are damaged <br>and/or lost while checked out to me.</font></b></p>
<p>
                               &\nbsp;      
<input type="checkbox" name="Agreement" value="I agree"><input type="hidden" name= "Agreement">
<font face="Arial, Helvetica, sans-serif" size="2">I agree</font><br>
<br><br></p>
<p>
<b><font face="Arial, Helvetica, sans-serif" size="3">If you are under 18 years old... </font></b> </p><p>
<b><font face="Arial, Helvetica, sans-serif" size="2">Name of parent / legal guardian     </font></b><br><font size="3" face="Arial, Helvetica, sans-serif"><input type="text" name="ParentName" size="40"></font></p>
<p>
<b><font face="Arial, Helvetica, sans-serif" size="2">Parent / guardian home address</font></b>  
<font face="Arial, Helvetica, sans-serif" size="1">(if different than above)</font>     <br><font size="3" face="Arial, Helvetica, sans-serif"><input type="text" name= "ParentStreetAddress" size="40"></font></p>
<p>
<b><font face="Arial, Helvetica, sans-serif" size="2">Parent / guardian city/state/zip</font></b><font face="Arial, Helvetica, sans-serif" size="1"> (if different than above)</font>      <br><font size="3" face="Arial, Helvetica, sans-serif"><input type="text" name= "ParentCityStateZip" size="40"></font></p>
<p>
<b><font face="Arial, Helvetica, sans-serif" size="2">Parent / guardian e-mail address</font></b>
<font face="Arial, Helvetica, sans-serif" size="1"> (if different than above)</font><br><font size="3" face="Arial, Helvetica, sans-serif"><input type="text" name="ParentEmail" size="40"></font></p>
<p>
<b><font face="Arial, Helvetica, sans-serif" size="2">Parent / guardian home phone/fax</font></b>
<font face="Arial, Helvetica, sans-serif" size="1"> (if different than above)</font><br><font size="3" face="Arial, Helvetica, sans-serif"><input type="text" name="ParentPhoneFax" size="40"></font></p>
<p> </p>
<table width="700" border="0" cellspacing="10" cellpadding="1"><tr><td width="269"><div align="right">
<input type="submit" name="send" value="Send Application></div></td><td width="178"> </td>
<td width="207"><div align="left"><input type="reset" name="clear" value="Clear Form"></div></td></tr>
<tr colspan=3><td colspan=3>
<table width="500" border="1" bordercolor="000000" height="2" align="center" cellpadding="0" cellspacing="0" bgcolor="ffffff"><tr><td><font size="1" color="#ffffff">.</font></td></tr></table>
</td></tr><tr><td colspan=3><div align="center">
<font face="Arial, Helvetica, sans-serif" size="1"><b>http://</b></font><br><font size="2"> 
<font face="Arial, Helvetica, sans-serif" size="1"><b>&copy; 2002</b></font></font>
```

```
<font face="Arial, Helvetica, sans-serif" size="2"><a href="mailto:">
<b><font size="1">Contact Webmaster</font></b></a></font></div></td></tr>
</table></form>
</body>
</html>
```

Apply for a Library Card — Perl Script

```perl
#!/usr/local/bin/perl

# ***************************************************************
# ABOVE is where you MUST specify the path to your
# perl interpreter on your Web server.
# Replace /usr/local/bin/perl with your path.
# ***************************************************************

if ($ENV{'REQUEST_METHOD'}eq"GET"){$buffer = $ENV{'QUERY_STRING'};}
    elsif($ENV{'REQUEST_METHOD'}eq"POST"){
        read(STDIN,$buffer,$ENV{'CONTENT_LENGTH'});
    }
$bufferb = $buffer;
#separate the name of the input from its value.
@forminputs = split(/&/, $bufferb);

foreach $forminput (@forminputs)
{
    #separate the name of the input from its value
    ($name, $value) = split(/=/, $forminput);

    #Un-Webify plus signs and %-encoding
    $value =~ tr/+/ /;
    $value =~ s/%([a-fA-F0-9][a-fA-F0-9])/pack("C", hex($1))/eg;

    #stick them in the in array
    $in{$name} = $value;
}
print "Content-type: text/html\n\n";

#################################################
# ABOVE is the required header for a perl script   #
#################################################

#########################################################
# (Below) Email received by library containing user-entered information #
#########################################################

# ***************************************************************
# Here's where you MUST specify the path to your
# email program (probably sendmail) ON your Web server.
# Replace /usr/sbin/sendmail with your path.
# ***************************************************************
```

```
open (LMAIL, "|/usr/sbin/sendmail -t");
print LMAIL ("To: $in{LibraryEmail}\n");

print LMAIL ("From: $in{Email}\n");
print LMAIL ("Subject: $in{Form} - patron submission\n");

print LMAIL ("------------------\nPatron information\n\n");

print LMAIL ("Name:\n $in{Name}\n\n");
print LMAIL ("E-mail Address:\n $in{Email}\n\n");
print LMAIL ("Home Address:\n $in{HomeAddr}\n\n");
print LMAIL ("School:\n $in{School}\n\n");
print LMAIL ("Home Phone/Fax:\n $in{HomePhone}\n\n");
print LMAIL ("Teacher's Name:\n $in{Teacher}\n\n");
print LMAIL ("Grade:\n $in{EducationLevel}\n\n");

print LMAIL ("Date of birth:\n $in{DateOfBirth}\n\n");
print LMAIL ("Gender:\n $in{Gender}\n\n");
print LMAIL ("I agree:\n $in{Agreement}\n\n");

print LMAIL ("Name of parent / legal guardian:\n $in{ParentName}\n\n");
print LMAIL ("Parent / Guardian street address:\n $in{ParentStreetAddress}\n\n");
print LMAIL ("Parent / Guardian city / state / zip:\n $in{ParentCityStateZip}\n\n");
print LMAIL ("Parent / Guardian e-mail:\n $in{ParentEmail}\n\n");
print LMAIL ("Parent / Guardian phone / fax:\n $in{ParentPhone}\n\n");

print LMAIL ("\n.\n");

##############################################
# Email received by the user confirming form submission #
##############################################

# ***********************************************************
# Here's where you MUST specify the path to your
# email program ON your Web server.
# Replace /usr/sbin/sendmail with your path.
# ***********************************************************

open (MAIL, "|/usr/sbin/sendmail -t");

# ***********************************************************
# Here's where you MAY customize the email
# response to the user. You may change any wording
# on the form.
# ***********************************************************
```

```
print MAIL<<toEnd;
To: $in{Email}
From: $in{LibraryEmail}
Subject: $in{Form}

Thanks for applying for a library card \n\n
A librarian will contact you in the next couple of days to let you know when your card will be ready to pick up,
where you can pick it up, and what ID you need to bring along with you.

toEnd
    print MAIL ("\n.\n");


##########################################
# Screen response to user after submitting the form  #
##########################################

print ("<html><head><title>$in{Form}</title></head>");
print ("<body bgcolor=\"ffffff\">");
# ***************************************************************
# Here's where you MAY change the screen response
# the user sees after submitting the form. You may
# change any wording between the quotation marks.
# ***************************************************************

print ("Thanks for applying for a library card <p>
A librarian will contact you in the next couple of days to let you know when your card will be ready to pick up,
where you can pick it up, and what ID you need to bring along with you.");


# ***************************************************************
# Here's where you MAY change the name of the link
# back to your main page. You may replace Return
# to our main page with your own wording.
# ***************************************************************

print ("<p><center><a href=$in{LibraryURL}>Return to our main page.</a></center>");
print ("</body></html>");
```

Hold / Recall / Renew

Use this form to...

1. RENEW an item you've already checked out from the library
2. RECALL an item checked out by another person
3. HOLD an item that has been returned, or is about to be returned, by another person

We'll send you an e-mail, or phone you, to let you know when you can pick up the item.

Name (first, last)

E-mail address

Home address (+ city)

School you attend

Home phone/fax (+ areacode)

Teacher's name

What grade are you in?
○ 3   ○ 4   ○ 5   ○ 6   ○ 7
○ 8   ○ 9   ○ 10   ○ 11   ○ 12

Material type
○ Book   ○ DVD / Videotape   ○ Music CD / tape   ○ Other (explain)

Type of request
○ Hold   ○ Recall   ○ Renew

Title

Author / Artist

Call number

Hold / Recall

I need the item before... (eg. Oct. 4th)

○ Anytime is fine

I need this item for...

Renew

Original due date

Reason the item should be renewed

[Send Request] [Clear Form]

http://
©2002 Contact Webmaster

Hold / Recall / Renew — HTML Form

```
<html>
<head><title>Hold / Recall / Renew</title></head>
<body bgcolor="#FFFFFF">
<table width="700" border="1" bordercolor="#000000" height="85" bgcolor="#ffffff">
<tr valign="middle" align="center"><td>
<p>
<font halign=center color="#000000" face="Arial, Helvetica, sans-serif" size="+3">
<b><i>Hold / Recall / Renew</i></b></font></p>
</td></tr></table>
<form method="post" action="http://www.yourLibrary.org/cgi-bin/cc2.pl"><p> </p>
<p>
<font face="Arial, Helvetica, sans-serif" size="2"><b>Use this form to...<br><br>   
  1. RENEW an item you've already checked out from the library<br>   
  2. RECALL an item checked out by another person<br>      3.HOLD
an item that has been returned, or is about to be returned, by another person<br><br> We'll send you an e-mail,
or phone you, to let you know when you can pick up the item.</b></font></p>
<p> </p>
<input type="hidden" name="LibraryEmail" value="you@yourLibrary.org">
<input type="hidden" name="LibraryURL" value="http://www.yourLibrary.org">
<input type="hidden" name="Form" value="Hold / Recall / Renew">
<p></p>
<table width="407" border="0" cellspacing="4" cellpadding="1">
<tr><td width="202">
<b><font face="Arial, Helvetica, sans-serif" size="2">Name</font></b><font face="Arial, Helvetica, sans-serif"
size="1">  (first, last)</font><br><font face="Arial, Helvetica, sans-serif" size="2">
<input type="text" name="Name" size="25"></font></td>
<td width="189">
<b><font face="Arial, Helvetica, sans-serif" size="2">E-mail address<br></font></b><font face="Arial, Helvetica,
sans-serif" size="2"><input type="text" name="Email" size="25"></font></td></tr>
<tr><td width="202" height="2">
<b><font face="Arial, Helvetica, sans-serif" size="2">Home address</font><font face="Arial, Helvetica, sans-
serif" size="1">  </font></b><font face="Arial, Helvetica, sans-serif" size="1">(+ city)
</font><br><font face="Arial, Helvetica, sans-serif" size="2"><input type="text" name="HomeAddr" size="25">
</font></td>
<td width="189" height="2">
<b><font face="Arial, Helvetica, sans-serif" size="2">School you attend<br></font></b><font face="Arial,
Helvetica, sans-serif" size="2"><input type="text" name="School" size="25"></font></td></tr>
<tr><td width="202" height="2">
<b><font face="Arial, Helvetica, sans-serif" size="2">Home phone/fax</font></b><font face= "Arial, Helvetica,
sans-serif" size="1">  (+ areacode)</font><br><font face= Arial, Helvetica, sans-serif"
size="2"><input type="text" name="HomePhone" size="25"></font></td>
<td width="189" height="2">
<b><font face="Arial, Helvetica, sans-serif" size="2">Teacher's name<br></font></b><font face="Arial,
```

```html
Helvetica, sans-serif" size="2"><input type="text" name="Teacher" size="25"></font></td></tr>
<tr><td width="391" colspan="2" height="48">
<b><font face="Arial, Helvetica, sans-serif" size="2">What grade are you in?</font></b><br><font face= "Arial, Helvetica, sans-serif" size="2"></font>
<table width="87%" border="0" cellspacing="4" cellpadding="0"><tr><td height="8" width="16%">
<font face="Arial, Helvetica, sans-serif" size="2"><input type="radio" name="EducationLevel" value="3">
3</font></td>
<td height="8" width="16%">
<font face="Arial, Helvetica, sans-serif" size="2"><input type="radio" name="EducationLevel" value="4">
4</font></td>
<td height="8" width="16%">
<font face="Arial, Helvetica, sans-serif" size="2"><input type="radio" name="EducationLevel" value="5">
5</font></td>
<td height="8" width="16%">
<font face="Arial, Helvetica, sans-serif" size="2"><input type="radio" name="EducationLevel" value="6">
6</font></td>
<td height="8" width="36%">
<font face="Arial, Helvetica, sans-serif" size="2"><input type="radio" name="EducationLevel" value="7">
7</font></td></tr>
<tr><td height="2" width="16%"><font face="Arial, Helvetica, sans-serif" size="2"><input type="radio" name="EducationLevel" value="8">
8</font></td>
<td height="2" width="16%">
<font face="Arial, Helvetica, sans-serif" size="2"><input type="radio" name="EducationLevel" value="9">
9</font></td>
<td height="2" width="16%">
<font face="Arial, Helvetica, sans-serif" size="2"><input type="radio" name="EducationLevel" value="10">
10</font></td>
<td height="2" width="16%">
<font face="Arial, Helvetica, sans-serif" size="2"><input type="radio" name="EducationLevel" value="11">
11</font></td>
<td height="2" width="36%">
<font face="Arial, Helvetica, sans-serif" size="2"><input type="radio" name="EducationLevel" value="12">
12</font>
</td></tr></table>
</td></tr></table>
<p><br>
<font face="Arial, Helvetica, sans-serif" size="2"><b>Material type<br></b>
<input type="radio" name="MaterialType" value="Book">Book   
<input type="radio" name="MaterialType" value="DVD / Videotape">DVD / Videotape    
<input type="radio" name="MaterialType" value="Music CD / tape">Music CD / tape   
<input type="radio" name="MaterialType" value="Other">Other <font face="Arial, Helvetica, sans-serif" size="1"> (explain)</font> <input type="text" name="MatTypeO" size="15"></font></p><p></p>
<p>
<font face="Arial, Helvetica, sans-serif" size="2"><b>Type of request<br></b>
```

Group 6—Circulation Forms

```html
<input type="radio" name="TypeOfRequest" value="Hold">Hold   
<input type="radio" name="TypeOfRequest" value="Recall">Recall   
<input type="radio" name="TypeOfRequest" value="Renew">Renew</font></p>
<p>
<font face="Arial, Helvetica, sans-serif" size="2"><b>Title</b><br><font size="3"><input type="text" name="Title" size="40"></font></font></p>
<p>
<font face="Arial, Helvetica, sans-serif" size="2"><b>Author / Artist</b><br><font size="3"><input type="text" name="Author" size="40"></font></font></p>
<p>
<font face="Arial, Helvetica, sans-serif" size="2"><b>Call number</b><br><font size="3">
<input type="text" name="CallNumber" size="40"></font></font></p>
<p><br>
<b><font face="Arial, Helvetica, sans-serif" size="3">Hold / Recall</font></b></p>
<p>
<font face="Arial, Helvetica, sans-serif" size="2"><b>I need the item before...<font size="1"> 
</font></b><font face="Arial, Helvetica, sans-serif" size="1"> (eg. Oct. 4th)</font><br>
<font size="3"><input type="text" name="NeedBefore" size="15">     </font>
<font face="Arial, Helvetica, sans-serif" size="1"><input type="radio" name="TimeIssue" value="Time is not an issue"></font>Anytime is fine</font></p>
<p>
<font face="Arial, Helvetica, sans-serif" size="2"><b>I need this item for...</b><br><font size="3">
<textarea name="NeedFor" cols="40" rows="2"></textarea></font></font></p>
<p><br>
<b><font face="Arial, Helvetica, sans-serif" size="3">Renew</font></b></p>
<p>
<font face="Arial, Helvetica, sans-serif" size="2"><b>Original due date</b><br><font size="3">
<input type="text" name="OriginalDueDate" size="10"></font></font></p>
<p>
<font face="Arial, Helvetica, sans-serif" size="2"><b>Reason the item should be renewed</b><br>
<font size="3"><textarea name="ReasonRenew" cols="40" rows="2"></textarea></font></font><br></p>
<p> </p>
<table width="700" border="0" cellspacing="10" cellpadding="1"><tr><td width="241"><div align="right">
<input type="submit" name="send" value="Send Request"></div></td><td width="206"> </td>
<td width="207"><div align="left"><input type="reset" name="clear" value="Clear Form"></div></td></tr>
<tr colspan=3><td colspan=3>
<table width="500" border="1" bordercolor="#000000" height="2" align="center" cellpadding="0" cellspacing="0" bgcolor="#ffffff"><tr><td><font size="1" color="#ffffff">.</font></td></tr></table>
</td></tr><tr><td colspan=3><div align="center">
<font face="Arial, Helvetica, sans-serif" size="1"><b>http://</b></font><br><font size="2"> 
<font face="Arial, Helvetica, sans-serif" size="1"><b>&copy; 2002</b></font>
</font><font face="Arial, Helvetica, sans-serif" size="2"><a href="**mailto:**">
<b><font size="1">Contact Webmaster</font></b></a></font></div></td></tr>
</table></form>
</body>
</html>
```

Hold / Recall / Renew — Perl Script

```perl
#!/usr/local/bin/perl

# ************************************************************
# ABOVE is where you MUST specify the path to your
# perl interpreter on your Web server.
# Replace /usr/local/bin/perl with your path.
# ************************************************************

if ($ENV{'REQUEST_METHOD'}eq"GET"){$buffer = $ENV{'QUERY_STRING'};}
    elsif($ENV{'REQUEST_METHOD'}eq"POST"){
        read(STDIN,$buffer,$ENV{'CONTENT_LENGTH'});
    }
$bufferb = $buffer;
#separate the name of the input from its value.
@forminputs = split(/&/, $bufferb);

foreach $forminput (@forminputs)
{
    #separate the name of the input from its value
    ($name, $value) = split(/=/, $forminput);

    #Un-Webify plus signs and %-encoding
    $value =~ tr/+/ /;
    $value =~ s/%([a-fA-F0-9][a-fA-F0-9])/pack("C", hex($1))/eg;

    #stick them in the in array
    $in{$name} = $value;
}
print "Content-type: text/html\n\n";

###############################################
# ABOVE is the required header for a perl script    #
###############################################


#####################################################
# (Below) Email received by library containing user-entered information #
#####################################################


# ************************************************************
# Here's where you MUST specify the path to your
# email program (probably sendmail) ON your Web server.
# Replace /usr/sbin/sendmail with your path.
# ************************************************************
```

Group 6—Circulation Forms

```
open (LMAIL, "I/usr/sbin/sendmail -t");
print LMAIL ("To: $in{LibraryEmail}\n");

print LMAIL ("From: $in{Email}\n");
print LMAIL ("Subject: $in{Form} - patron submission\n");

print LMAIL ("------------------\nPatron information\n\n");

print LMAIL ("Name:\n $in{Name}\n\n");
print LMAIL ("E-mail Address:\n $in{Email}\n\n");
print LMAIL ("Home Address:\n $in{HomeAddr}\n\n");
print LMAIL ("School:\n $in{School}\n\n");
print LMAIL ("Home Phone/Fax:\n $in{HomePhone}\n\n");
print LMAIL ("Teacher's Name:\n $in{Teacher}\n\n");
print LMAIL ("Grade:\n $in{EducationLevel}\n\n");

print LMAIL ("------------------\nSubmitted information \n\n");
print LMAIL ("Material type:\n $in{MaterialType}\n\n");
print LMAIL ("Other type:\n $in{MatTypeO}\n\n");
print LMAIL ("Type of request:\n $in{TypeOfRequest}\n\n");
print LMAIL ("Title:\n $in{Title}\n\n");
print LMAIL ("Author / Artist:\n $in{Author}\n\n");
print LMAIL ("Call number:\n $in{CallNumber}\n\n");
print LMAIL ("------------------\nHold / Recall\n");
print LMAIL ("I need this item before:\n $in{NeedBefore} $in{TimeIssue}\n\n");
print LMAIL ("I need this item for:\n $in{NeedFor}\n\n");
print LMAIL ("------------------\nRenew\n");
print LMAIL ("Original due date:\n $in{OriginalDueDate}\n\n");
print LMAIL ("Reason the item should be renewed:\n $in{ReasonRenew}\n\n");

print LMAIL ("\n.\n");

#############################################
# Email received by the user confirming form submission #
#############################################

# *********************************************************
# Here's where you MUST specify the path to your
# email program ON your Web server.
# Replace /usr/sbin/sendmail with your path.
# *********************************************************

open (MAIL, "I/usr/sbin/sendmail -t");

# *********************************************************
#
```

```
# Here's where you MAY customize the email
# response to the user. You may change any wording
# on the form.
# ************************************************************

print MAIL<<toEnd;
To: $in{Email}
From: $in{LibraryEmail}
Subject: $in{Form}

Thanks for submitting a hold, recall, renew request. \n\n
A librarian will contact you in the next couple of days to let you know when we might have the item ready for you to pick up.

toEnd
    print MAIL ("\n.\n");




##########################################
# Screen response to user after submitting the form  #
##########################################

print ("<html><head><title>$in{Form}</title></head>");
print ("<body bgcolor=\"ffffff\">");

# ************************************************************
# Here's where you MAY change the screen response
# the user sees after submitting the form. You may
# change any wording between the quotation marks.
# ************************************************************

print ("Thanks for submitting a hold, recall, renew request. <p>
A librarian will contact you in the next couple of days to let you know when we might have the item ready for you to pick up.");

# ************************************************************
# Here's where you MAY change the name of the link
# back to your main page. You may replace Return
# to our main page with your own wording.
# ************************************************************

print ("<p><center><a href=$in{LibraryURL}>Return to our main page.</a></center>");
print ("</body></html>");
```

Report a Missing Item

Let us know if you can't find an item in the library. Just fill out the form below. We'll send an e-mail, or phone you, if we find it. If we can't find it, we'll call or email you if we will buy another copy of the item.

Name (first, last)

E-mail address

Home address (+ city)

School you attend

Home phone/fax (+ areacode)

Teacher's name

What grade are you in?
- ○ 3 ○ 4 ○ 5 ○ 6 ○ 7
- ○ 8 ○ 9 ○ 10 ○ 11 ○ 12

What library resources have you already checked? (select any/all)
○ On-line / card catalog   ○ Shelves   ○ Asked at the circulation desk

Missing item
○ Book   ○ Magazine   ○ DVD / Videotape   ○ Music CD / tape   ○ Other (explain)

Call number

Title

Author / Artist

I need the item before... (eg. Oct. 4th)

○ Anytime is fine

[Send Report]   [Clear Form]

http://

© 2002 Contact Webmaster

Report a Missing Item — HTML Form

```
<html>
<head><title>Report a Missing Item</title></head>
<body bgcolor="#FFFFFF">
<table width="700" border="1" height="85" bgcolor="ffffff">
<tr valign="middle" align="center"><td>
<p>
<font halign=center color="#000000" face="Arial, Helvetica, sans-serif" size="+3">
<b><i>Report a Missing Item</i></b></font></p>
</td></tr></table>
<form method="post" action="http://www.yourLibrary.org/cgi-bin/cc3.pl"><p> </p>
<p>
<font face="Arial, Helvetica, sans-serif" size="2"><b>Let us know if you can't find an item in the library. Just fill out the form below. We'll send an e-mail, or <br>phone you, if we find it. If we can't find it, we'll call or email you if we will buy another copy of the item.</b></font></p>
<p> </p>
<input type="hidden" name="LibraryEmail" value="you@yourLibrary.org">
<input type="hidden" name="LibraryURL" value="http://www.yourLibrary.org">
<input type="hidden" name="Form" value="Report a Missing Item">
<p></p>
<table width="407" border="0" cellspacing="4" cellpadding="1">
<tr><td width="202">
<b><font face="Arial, Helvetica, sans-serif" size="2">Name</font></b><font face="Arial, Helvetica, sans-serif" size="1">  (first, last)</font><br><font face="Arial, Helvetica, sans-serif" size="2">
<input type="text" name="Name" size="25"></font></td>
<td width="189">
<b><font face="Arial, Helvetica, sans-serif" size="2">E-mail address<br></font></b><font face="Arial, Helvetica, sans-serif" size="2"><input type="text" name="Email" size="25"></font></td></tr>
<tr><td width="202" height="2">
<b><font face="Arial, Helvetica, sans-serif" size="2">Home address</font><font face="Arial, Helvetica, sans-serif" size="1">  </font></b><font face="Arial, Helvetica, sans-serif" size="1">(+ city)
</font><br><font face="Arial, Helvetica, sans-serif" size="2"><input type="text" name="HomeAddr" size="25">
</font></td>
<td width="189" height="2">
<b><font face="Arial, Helvetica, sans-serif" size="2">School you attend<br></font></b><font face="Arial, Helvetica, sans-serif" size="2"><input type="text" name="School" size="25"></font></td></tr>
<tr><td width="202" height="2">
<b><font face="Arial, Helvetica, sans-serif" size="2">Home phone/fax</font></b><font face="Arial, Helvetica, sans-serif" size="1">  (+ areacode)</font><br><font face="Arial, Helvetica, sans-serif" size="2">
<input type="text" name="HomePhone" size="25"></font></td>
<td width="189" height="2">
<b><font face="Arial, Helvetica, sans-serif" size="2">Teacher's name<br></font></b><font face="Arial, Helvetica, sans-serif" size="2"><input type="text" name="Teacher" size="25"></font></td></tr>
```

Group 6—Circulation Forms

```html
<tr><td width="391" colspan="2" height="48">
<b><font face="Arial, Helvetica, sans-serif" size="2">What grade are you in?</font></b><br><font face= "Arial, Helvetica, sans-serif" size="2"></font>
<table width="87%" border="0" cellspacing="4" cellpadding="0"><tr><td height="8" width="16%">
<font face="Arial, Helvetica, sans-serif" size="2"><input type="radio" name="EducationLevel" value="3">
3</font></td>
<td height="8" width="16%">
<font face="Arial, Helvetica, sans-serif" size="2"><input type="radio" name="EducationLevel" value="4">
4</font></td>
<td height="8" width="16%">
<font face="Arial, Helvetica, sans-serif" size="2"><input type="radio" name="EducationLevel" value="5">
5</font></td>
<td height="8" width="16%">
<font face="Arial, Helvetica, sans-serif" size="2"><input type="radio" name="EducationLevel" value="6">
6</font></td>
<td height="8" width="36%">
<font face="Arial, Helvetica, sans-serif" size="2"><input type="radio" name="EducationLevel" value="7">
7</font></td></tr>
<tr><td height="2" width="16%">
<font face="Arial, Helvetica, sans-serif" size="2"><input type="radio" name="EducationLevel" value="8">
8</font></td>
<td height="2" width="16%">
<font face="Arial, Helvetica, sans-serif" size="2"><input type="radio" name="EducationLevel" value="9">
9</font></td>
<td height="2" width="16%">
<font face="Arial, Helvetica, sans-serif" size="2"><input type="radio" name="EducationLevel" value="10">
10</font></td>
<td height="2" width="16%">
<font face="Arial, Helvetica, sans-serif" size="2"><input type="radio" name="EducationLevel" value="11">
11</font></td>
<td height="2" width="36%">
<font face="Arial, Helvetica, sans-serif" size="2"><input type="radio" name="EducationLevel" value="12">
12</font>
</td></tr></table>
</td></tr></table>
<p>
<br> <b><font face="Arial, Helvetica, sans-serif" size="2">What library resources have you already checked?
</font></b><font face="Arial, Helvetica, sans-serif" size="1">   (select any/all)
</font><br><font face="Arial, Helvetica, sans-serif" size="2">
<input type="radio" name="OC" value="I've checked on-line / the card catalog">On-line / card catalog
   
<input type="radio" name="S" value="I've checked the shelves">Shelves   
<input type="radio" name="CD" value="I've asked at the circulation desk">Asked at the circulation desk</font>
</p>
<p>
```

```html
<b><font face="Arial, Helvetica, sans-serif" size="2">Missing item<br></font></b><font face="Arial, Helvetica, sans-serif" size="2">
<input type="radio" name="MaterialType" value="Book">Book   
<input type="radio" name="MaterialType" value="Magazine">Magazine   
<input type="radio" name="MaterialType" value="DVD / Videotape">DVD / Videotape    
<input type="radio" name="MaterialType" value="Music CD / tape">Music CD / tape   
<input type="radio" name="MaterialType" value="Other">Other  </font><font face="Arial, Helvetica, sans-serif" size="1">(explain) </font><font face="Arial, Helvetica, sans-serif" size="2">
<input type="text" name="MissingO" size="10"></font></p>
<p>
<font face="Arial, Helvetica, sans-serif" size="2"><b><br>Call number</b><br><font size="3"><input type="text" name="CallNumber" size="40"></font></font></p>
<p>
<font face="Arial, Helvetica, sans-serif" size="2"><b>Title</b></font><br><font face="Arial, Helvetica, sans-serif" size="3"><input type="text" name="Title" size="40"></font></p>
<p>
<font face="Arial, Helvetica, sans-serif" size="2"><b>Author / Artist</b><br><font size="3"><input type="text" name="Author" size="40"><br></font></font></p>
<p><br>
<font face="Arial, Helvetica, sans-serif" size="2"><b>I need the item before... </b><font face= "Arial, Helvetica, sans-serif" size="1"> (eg. Oct. 4th)</font><br><font size="3"><input type="text" name="NeedBefore" size="15">      </font><input type="radio" name= "Deadline" value="Time is not an issue">Anytime is fine</font><br></p>
<p> </p>
<table width="700" border="0" cellspacing="10" cellpadding="1"><tr><td width="217"><div align="right">
<input type="submit" name="send" value="Send Report"></div></td><td width="230"> </td>
<td width="207"><div align="left"><input type="reset" name="clear" value="Clear Form"></div></td></tr>
<tr colspan=3><td colspan=3>
<table width="500" border="1" height="2" align="center" cellpadding="0" cellspacing="0" bgcolor="ffffff"><tr><td><font size="1" color="#ffffff">.</font></td></tr></table></td></tr><tr>
<td colspan=3><div align="center">
<font face="Arial, Helvetica, sans-serif" size="1"><b>http://</b></font><br> 
<font face="Arial, Helvetica, sans-serif" size="1"><b>&copy; 2002</b></font>
<font face="Arial, Helvetica, sans-serif" size="2"><a href="mailto:">
<b><font size="1">Contact Webmaster</font></b></a></font></div></td></tr>
</table></form>
</body>
</html>
```

Group 6—Circulation Forms

Report a Missing Item — Perl Script

```perl
#!/usr/local/bin/perl

# ****************************************************
# ABOVE is where you MUST specify the path to your
# perl interpreter on your Web server.
# Replace /usr/local/bin/perl with your path.
# ****************************************************

if ($ENV{'REQUEST_METHOD'}eq"GET"){$buffer = $ENV{'QUERY_STRING'};}
    elsif($ENV{'REQUEST_METHOD'}eq"POST"){
        read(STDIN,$buffer,$ENV{'CONTENT_LENGTH'});
    }
$bufferb = $buffer;
#separate the name of the input from its value.
@forminputs = split(/&/, $bufferb);

foreach $forminput (@forminputs)
{
    #separate the name of the input from its value
    ($name, $value) = split(/=/, $forminput);

    #Un-Webify plus signs and %-encoding
    $value =~ tr/+/ /;
    $value =~ s/%([a-fA-F0-9][a-fA-F0-9])/pack("C", hex($1))/eg;

    #stick them in the in array
    $in{$name} = $value;
}
print "Content-type: text/html\n\n";

################################################
# ABOVE is the required header for a perl script    #
################################################

#########################################################
# (Below) Email received by library containing user-entered information #
#########################################################

# ****************************************************************
# Here's where you MUST specify the path to your
# email program (probably sendmail) ON your Web server.
# Replace /usr/sbin/sendmail with your path.
# ****************************************************************
#
```

```
open (LMAIL, "|/usr/sbin/sendmail -t");
print LMAIL ("To: $in{LibraryEmail}\n");

print LMAIL ("From: $in{Email}\n");
print LMAIL ("Subject: $in{Form} - patron submission\n");

print LMAIL ("------------------\nPatron information\n\n");

print LMAIL ("Name:\n $in{Name}\n\n");
print LMAIL ("E-mail Address:\n $in{Email}\n\n");
print LMAIL ("Home Address:\n $in{HomeAddr}\n\n");
print LMAIL ("School:\n $in{School}\n\n");
print LMAIL ("Home Phone/Fax:\n $in{HomePhone}\n\n");
print LMAIL ("Teacher's Name:\n $in{Teacher}\n\n");
print LMAIL ("Grade:\n $in{EducationLevel}\n\n");

print LMAIL ("------------------\nSubmitted information \n\n");

print LMAIL ("I have already checked these resources:\n $in{OC}, $in{S}, $in{CD}\n\n");
print LMAIL ("Missing item:\n $in{MaterialType}\n\n");
print LMAIL ("Other type:\n $in{MissingO}\n\n");
print LMAIL ("Call number:\n $in{CallNumber}\n\n");
print LMAIL ("Title:\n $in{Title}\n\n");
print LMAIL ("Author / Artist:\n $in{Author}\n\n");
print LMAIL ("I need this item before:\n $in{NeedBefore} $in{Deadline}\n\n");

print LMAIL ("\n.\n");

############################################
# Email received by the user confirming form submission #
############################################

# ************************************************************
# Here's where you MUST specify the path to your
# email program ON your Web server.
# Replace /usr/sbin/sendmail with your path.
# ************************************************************

open (MAIL, "|/usr/sbin/sendmail -t");

# ************************************************************
# Here's where you MAY customize the email
# response to the user. You may change any wording
# on the form.
# ************************************************************
```

Group 6—Circulation Forms

```
print MAIL<<toEnd;
To: $in{Email}
From: $in{LibraryEmail}
Subject: $in{Form}

Thanks for taking the time to let us know that an item is missing.\n\n
We will contact you as soon as we either locate the item or decide to purchase a replacement copy.

toEnd
    print MAIL ("\n.\n");


##########################################
# Screen response to user after submitting the form  #
##########################################

print ("<html><head><title>$in{Form}</title></head>");
print ("<body bgcolor=\"ffffff\">");

# ***************************************************************
# Here's where you MAY change the screen response
# the user sees after submitting the form. You may
# change any wording between the quotation marks.
# ***************************************************************

print ("Thanks for taking the time to let us know that an item is missing.<p>
We will contact you as soon as we either locate the item or decide to purchase a replacement copy.");

# ***************************************************************
# Here's where you MAY change the name of the link
# back to your main page. You may replace Return
# to our main page with your own wording.
# ***************************************************************

print ("<p><center><a href=$in{LibraryURL}>Return to our main page.</a></center>");
print ("</body></html>");
```

Instant Web Forms & Surveys

Group 7— Miscellaneous Forms / Surveys

In this section you'll find one Web-based form and one survey. The form lets teachers, library staff, and parents confidentially and conveniently report library incidents/accidents, disruptive behavior, or any other problem that you need to be made aware of. The survey lets students give you feedback on the types of library-based programs that they would be interested in attending and getting involved in.

Incident Report *(teachers/librarians/parents)*
Teachers, staff, and parents can help you make the library a more user-friendly and safe place. They can use this nifty online form to alert you to any situation or problem that you need to know and do something about. Put a link to this form on your Web site's reference, circulation, or administration pages.

Kids/YA/Teen Program Interests Survey
Kids and teens often are looking for things to do and get involved in. Use this survey to find out the types of programs and clubs your library can offer them after school, after supper, on weekends, or during the summer. Put a link to this survey periodically on your library's home page.

Incident Report

Teachers / Librarians / Parents

Help us make the library a more safe and friendly place for both kids and adults. Use this form to alert us to any situation or problem that we need to know, and do something, about. We'll keep all your input confidential. If you like, we'll phone you, or send you an e-mail, to let you know how the situation is being addressed.

Name (first, last)

E-mail address

Address (+ city)

Name of school

Phone/Fax (+ areacode)

Grade(s) you teach

I am a...
- ○ Classroom teacher
- ○ Librarian / Media specialist
- ○ School staff / Administrator
- ○ Parent
- ○ Other (explain)

Type of incident
- ○ Disruptive behavior
- ○ Harassment
- ○ Accident / injury
- ○ Theft
- ○ Vandalism
- ○ Other (explain)

Date / time the incident occurred

Date   Time

Specific location where the incident occurred

Describe the incident (give us as many details as you can)

Describe the person(s) involved in the incident

[text area]

[Send Report]   [Clear Form]

http://
© 2002 Contact Webmaster

Incident Report — HTML Form

```
<html>
<head><title>Incident Report</title></head>
<body bgcolor="#FFFFFF">
<table width="700" border="1" bordercolor="#000000" height="85" bgcolor="#ffffff">
<tr valign="middle" align="center"><td>
<p><font halign=center color="#000000" face="Arial, Helvetica, sans-serif" size="5">
<b><i><font size="+3">Incident Report </font></i></b></font></p>
</td></tr></table>
<form method="post" action="http://www.yourLibrary.org/cgi-bin/cm2.pl"><p> </p>
<p>
<font size="2" face="Arial, Helvetica, sans-serif"><b> <i>Teachers / Librarians / Parents</i></b></font></p>
<p><font size="2" face="Arial, Helvetica, sans-serif"><b>Help us make the library a more safe and friendly place for both kids and adults. Use this form to alert us <br>to any situation or problem that we need to know, and do something, about. We'll keep all your input confidential. <br>If you like, we'll phone you, or send you an e-mail, to let you know how the situation is being addressed.</b></font></p>
<p> </p>
<input type="hidden" name="LibraryEmail" value="your@yourlibrary.org">
<input type="hidden" name="LibraryURL" value="http://www.yourLibrary.org">
<input type="hidden" name="Form" value="Incident Report"><p></p>
<table width="426" border="0" cellspacing="4" cellpadding="1">
<tr><td width="202">
<b><font face="Arial, Helvetica, sans-serif" size="2">Name</font></b><font face="Arial, Helvetica, sans-serif" size="1">  (first, last)</font><br><font face="Arial, Helvetica, sans-serif" size="2">
<input type="text" name="Name" size="25"></font></td>
<td width="205">
<b><font face="Arial, Helvetica, sans-serif" size="2">E-mail address<br></font></b><font face="Arial, Helvetica, sans-serif" size="2"><input type="text" name="Email" size="25"></font></td></tr>
<tr><td width="202" height="2">
<b><font face="Arial, Helvetica, sans-serif" size="2">Address</font>  </b><font face="Arial, Helvetica, sans-serif" size="1">(+ city)</font><br><font face="Arial, Helvetica, sans-serif" size="2">
<input type="text" name="Addr" size="25"></font></td>
<td width="205" height="2">
<b><font face="Arial, Helvetica, sans-serif" size="2">Name of school<br></font></b><font face="Arial, Helvetica, sans-serif" size="2"><input type="text" name="School" size="25"></font></td></tr>
<tr><td width="202" height="2">
<b><font face="Arial, Helvetica, sans-serif" size="2">Phone/Fax</font> </b><font face="Arial, Helvetica, sans-serif" size="1"> (+ areacode)</font><br><font face="Arial, Helvetica, sans-serif" size="2">
<input type="text" name="Phone" size="25"></font></td>
<td width="205" height="2">
<b><font face="Arial, Helvetica, sans-serif" size="2">Grade(s) you teach<br></font></b><font face="Arial, Helvetica, sans-serif" size="2"><input type="text" name="Grade" size="25"></font></td></tr>
<tr><td colspan="2" height="42">
<p>
```

Group 7—Miscellaneous Forms/Surveys

```html
<b><font face="Arial, Helvetica, sans-serif" size="2">I am a...</font></b><br>
<table width="100%" border="0" cellpadding="0" cellspacing="4"><tr><td width="51%">
<font face="Arial, Helvetica, sans-serif" size="2"><input type="radio" name="Iama" value="Classroom teacher">Classroom teacher</font></td>
<td width="49%">
<font face="Arial, Helvetica, sans-serif" size="2"><input type="radio" name="Iama" value="Librarian / Media specialist">Librarian / Media specialist</font></td></tr>
<tr>
<td width="51%">
<font face="Arial, Helvetica, sans-serif" size="2"><input type="radio" name="Iama" value="School staff / Administrator">School staff / Administrator</font></td>
<td width="49%">
<font face="Arial, Helvetica, sans-serif" size="2"><input type="radio" name="Iama" value="Parent"> Parent</font></td></tr><tr>
<td colspan="2" height="5">
<font face="Arial, Helvetica, sans-serif" size="2"><input type="radio" name="Iama" value="Other">Other<b><font face="Arial, Helvetica, sans-serif" size="1"> </font></b><font face="Arial, Helvetica, sans-serif" size="1"> (explain)  <font size="2"><input type="text" name="IamaOther" size="15"></font></font></font>
</td></tr></table>
</td></tr></table>
<p>
<b><font face="Arial, Helvetica, sans-serif" size="2"><br>Type of incident<br></font></b><font face= "Arial, Helvetica, sans-serif" size="2">
<input type="radio" name="IncidentType" value="Disruptive behavior">Disruptive behavior    
<input type="radio" name="IncidentType" value="Harassment">Harassment   
<input type="radio" name="IncidentType" value="Accident / injury">Accident / injury   
<input type="radio" name="IncidentType" value="Theft">Theft   
<input type="radio" name="IncidentType" value="Vandalism">Vandalism<br>
<input type="radio" name="IncidentType" value="Other">Other   <font size="1">(explain)
</font><font size="3">  <font size="2"><input type="text" name="IncidentTypeOther" size="10"></font>
</font></font></p>
<p>
<b><font face="Arial, Helvetica, sans-serif" size="2">Date / time the incident occurred<br><font></b><font face="Arial, Helvetica, sans-serif" size="2">Date </font><font face="Arial, Helvetica, sans-serif" size="3">
<input type="text" name="Date" size="15">     </font>
<font face="Arial, Helvetica, sans-serif" size="2">Time</font><font face="Arial, Helvetica, sans-serif" size="3">
<input type="text" name="Time" size="15"></font></p>
<p>
<b><font face="Arial, Helvetica, sans-serif" size="2">Specific location where the incident occurred <br></font>
</b><font face="Arial, Helvetica, sans-serif" size="3"><textarea name="IncidentLocation" cols="40" rows="2">
</textarea></font></p>
<p>
<b><font face="Arial, Helvetica, sans-serif" size="2">Describe the incident  </font></b>
<font face="Arial, Helvetica, sans-serif" size="1">(give us as many details as you can)</font><br>
```

```html
<font face="Arial, Helvetica, sans-serif" size="3"><textarea name="IncidentDescription" cols="40" rows="10">
</textarea></font></p>
<p>
<b><font face="Arial, Helvetica, sans-serif" size="2">Describe the person(s) involved in the incident
<br></font></b><font face="Arial, Helvetica, sans-serif" size="3"><textarea name="DescribePerson" cols="40" rows="2"></textarea></font><br></p>
<p> </p>
<table width="700" border="0" cellspacing="10" cellpadding="1"><tr><td width="228"><div align="right">
<input type="submit" name="send" value="Send Report"></div></td><td width="219"> </td>
<td width="207"><div align="left"><input type="reset" name="clear" value="Clear Form"></div></td></tr>
<tr colspan=3><td colspan=3>
<table width="500" border="1" bordercolor="#000000" height="2" align="center" cellpadding="0" cellspacing="0" bgcolor="#ffffff"><tr><td><font size="1" color="#ffffff">.</font></td></tr></table></td></tr>
<tr><td colspan=3><div align="center">
<font face="Arial, Helvetica, sans-serif" size="1"><b>http://</b></font><br><font size="2"> 
<font face="Arial, Helvetica, sans-serif" size="1"><b>&copy; 2002</b></font></font>
<font face="Arial, Helvetica, sans-serif" size="2"><a href="mailto:">
<b><font size="1">Contact Webmaster</font></b></a></font></div></td></tr>
</table></form>
</body>
</html>
```

Incident Report — Perl Script

```perl
#!/usr/local/bin/perl

# *************************************************************
# ABOVE is where you MUST specify the path to your
# perl interpreter on your Web server.
# Replace /usr/local/bin/perl with your path.
# *************************************************************

if ($ENV{'REQUEST_METHOD'}eq"GET"){$buffer = $ENV{'QUERY_STRING'};}
    elsif($ENV{'REQUEST_METHOD'}eq"POST"){
        read(STDIN,$buffer,$ENV{'CONTENT_LENGTH'});
    }
$bufferb = $buffer;
#separate the name of the input from its value.
@forminputs = split(/&/, $bufferb);

foreach $forminput (@forminputs)
{
    #separate the name of the input from its value
    ($name, $value) = split(/=/, $forminput);

    #Un-Webify plus signs and %-encoding
    $value =~ tr/+/ /;
    $value =~ s/%([a-fA-F0-9][a-fA-F0-9])/pack("C", hex($1))/eg;

    #stick them in the in array
    $in{$name} = $value;
}
print "Content-type: text/html\n\n";

###############################################
# ABOVE is the required header for a perl script    #
###############################################

##################################################
# (Below) Email received by library containing user-entered information #
##################################################

# *************************************************************
# Here's where you MUST specify the path to your
# email program (probably sendmail) ON your Web server.
# Replace /usr/sbin/sendmail with your path.
# *************************************************************
```

```
open (LMAIL, "|/usr/sbin/sendmail -t");
print LMAIL ("To: $in{LibraryEmail}\n");
print LMAIL ("From: $in{Email}\n");
print LMAIL ("Subject: $in{Form} - patron submission\n");

print LMAIL ("-------------------\nPatron information\n\n");


print LMAIL ("Name:\n $in{Name}\n\n");
print LMAIL ("E-mail Address:\n $in{Email}\n\n");
print LMAIL ("Home Address:\n $in{HomeAddr}\n\n");
print LMAIL ("School:\n $in{School}\n\n");
print LMAIL ("Home Phone/Fax:\n $in{HomePhone}\n\n");
print LMAIL ("Teacher's Name:\n $in{Teacher}\n\n");
print LMAIL ("Grade:\n $in{EducationLevel}\n\n");

print LMAIL ("-------------------\nSubmitted information \n\n");

print LMAIL ("Type of incident:\n $in{IncidentType}\n\n");
print LMAIL ("Other type:\n $in{IncidentTypeO}\n\n");
print LMAIL ("Date / Time incident occurred:\n $in{Date} / $in{Time}\n\n");
print LMAIL ("Specific location where the incident took place:\n $in{IncidentLocation}\n\n");
print LMAIL ("Description of the incident\n $in{IncidentDescription}\n\n");
print LMAIL ("Description of the person(s) involved:\n $in{DescribePerson}\n\n");

print LMAIL ("\n.\n");

##############################################
# Email received by the user confirming form submission #
##############################################

# ***********************************************************
# Here's where you MUST specify the path to your
# email program ON your Web server.
# Replace /usr/sbin/sendmail with your path.
# ***********************************************************

open (MAIL, "|/usr/sbin/sendmail -t");

# ***********************************************************
# Here's where you MAY customize the email
# response to the user. You may change any wording
# on the form.
# ***********************************************************
```

```
print MAIL<<toEnd;
To: $in{Email}
From: $in{LibraryEmail}
Subject: $in{Form}

Thanks for taking the time to fill out our Incident Report.

toEnd
   print MAIL ("\n.\n");


###########################################
# Screen response to user after submitting the form  #
###########################################

print ("<html><head><title>Incident Report submitted</title></head>");
print ("<body bgcolor=\"ffffff\">");



# ***************************************************************
# Here's where you MAY change the screen response
# the user sees after submitting the form. You may
# change any wording between the quotation marks.
# ***************************************************************

print ("Thanks for taking the time to fill out our Incident Report.");

# ***************************************************************
# Here's where you MAY change the name of the link
# back to your main page. You may replace Return
# to our main page with your own wording.
# ***************************************************************

print ("<p><center><a href=$in{LibraryURL}>Return to our main page.</a></center>");
print ("</body></html>");
```

Kids / Teens Program Interests Survey

Are you looking for something interesting to do after school, on weekends, or during summer vacation? If so, fill out this short survey to let us know the types of library programs or activities you'd be interested in attending or getting involved with.

Would you attend a library program or activity that interests you?   ○ Yes   ○ No

If yes, what are the best times for these programs or activites? (select any/all)
○ After school   ○ After dinner   ○ Weekends   ○ During the summer

What types of programs / activities would you be interested in? (select any/all)

School
○ Homework help sessions   ○ Writing a research paper
○ Creating a bibliography   ○ Tutoring other students

Library / Reading
○ Helping library staff   ○ Helping young kids use the library
○ Library contests   ○ Cool book discussions (eg. Harry Potter)

Your life
○ Babysitting tips / tricks   ○ Exploring careers
○ Teen topics (eg. peer pressure)   ○ Getting your first job

Computers
○ Computer club   ○ Internet club   ○ Computer skills
○ Web skills   ○ Keypals   ○ Global on-line projects

Arts / Crafts
○ Drawing / Painting   ○ Cool crafts   ○ Holiday arts / crafts
○ Young authors club   ○ Drama club   ○ Poetry club

Fun
○ Computer game tournaments   ○ Board game tournaments   ○ Popcorn and a movie
○ Sports programs   ○ Exercise / Fashion programs   ○ Scavenger hunts

How do you find out about upcoming library programs / activities?
○ Posters, etc.   ○ Friends   ○ Librarians / Teachers   ○ Web site
○ Other (explain) [   ]

How would you like to find out about *future* library programs / activities?
○ E-mail   ○ Web site   ○ Posters, etc.
○ Other (explain) [   ]

Name (first, last)

E-mail address

School you attend

Gender
○ Female ○ Male

What grade are you in?
○ 3   ○ 4   ○ 5   ○ 6   ○ 7
○ 8   ○ 9   ○ 10 ○ 11 ○ 12

[Send Survey]   [Clear Survey]

http://
© 2002 Contact Webmaster

Kids / Teens Program Interests Survey — HTML Form

```
<html>
<head><title>Kids / Teens Program Interests Survey</title></head>
<body bgcolor="#FFFFFF">
<table width="700" border="1" bordercolor="000000" height="85" bgcolor="#ffffff">
<tr valign="middle" align="center">
<td>
<p>
<font halign=center color="#000000" face="Arial, Helvetica, sans-serif" size="+3">
<b><i>Kids / Teens Program Interests Survey</i></b></font></p>
</td></tr></table>
<form method="post" action="http://www.yourLibrary.org/cgi-bin/cm5.pl" name=""><p> </p>
<p>
<font face="Arial, Helvetica, sans-serif" size="2"><b>Are you looking for something interesting to do after school, on weekends, or during summer vacation?<br>If so, fill out this short survey to let us know the types of library programs or activities you'd be interested <br></b>in attending or getting involved with.</b></font><br></p>
<p>
<input type="hidden" name="LibraryEmail" value="you@yourLibrary.org">
<input type="hidden" name="LibraryURL" value="http://www.yourLibrary.org">
<input type="hidden" name="Form" value="Kids / Teens Program Interests Survey"></p>
<p> </p>
<p></p><p>
<font face="Arial, Helvetica, sans-serif" size="2"><b>Would you attend a library program or activity that interests you? </b><font face="Arial, Helvetica, sans-serif" size="2">
<input type="radio" name="Attend" value="Yes">Yes 
<input type="radio" name="Attend" value="No">No  </font></font></p>
<p>
<font face="Arial, Helvetica, sans-serif" size="2"><b>If yes, what are the best times for these programs or activites?   </b><font face="Arial, Helvetica, sans-serif" size="1">(select any/all)</font><br></font>
<table width="549" border="0" cellspacing="0" cellpadding="0">tr><td width="110">
<font face="Arial, Helvetica, sans-serif" size="2"><input type="radio" name="AS" value="Other">
 After school</font></td>
<td width="111">
<font face="Arial, Helvetica, sans-serif" size="2"><input type="radio" name="AD" value="Other">
After dinner</font></td>
<td width="103">
<font face="Arial, Helvetica, sans-serif" size="2"><input type="radio" name="W" value="Other">
Weekends</font></td>
<td width="225">
<font face="Arial, Helvetica, sans-serif" size="2"><input type="radio" name="DS" value="Other">
During the summer</font></td></tr></table>
<p><br>
<b><font face="Arial, Helvetica, sans-serif" size="3">What types of programs / activities would you be interested in?</font></b>  <font face="Arial, Helvetica, sans-serif" size="1">(select any/all)</font>
```

Group 7—Miscellaneous Forms/Surveys

```html
<p>
<b><font face="Arial, Helvetica, sans-serif" size="2">School<br></font></b>
<table width="427" border="0" cellspacing="0" cellpadding="0"><tr><td width="205">
<font face="Arial, Helvetica, sans-serif" size="2"><input type="radio" name="SHHS" value="Homework help sessions">Homework help sessions</font></td>
<td width="222">
<font face="Arial, Helvetica, sans-serif" size="2"><input type="radio" name="SWARP" value="Writing a research paper">Writing a research paper</font></td></tr>
<tr><td width="205">
<font face="Arial, Helvetica, sans-serif" size="2"><input type="radio" name="SCAB" value="Creating a bibliography">Creating a bibliography</font></td>
<td width="222">
<font face="Arial, Helvetica, sans-serif" size="2"><input type="radio" name="STOS" value="Tutoring other students">Tutoring other students</font></td></tr></table>
<p>
<b><font face="Arial, Helvetica, sans-serif" size="2">Library / Reading<br></font></b>
<table width="565" border="0" cellspacing="0" cellpadding="0"><tr><td width="205">
<font face="Arial, Helvetica, sans-serif" size="2"><input type="radio" name="LRHLS" value="Helping library staff">Helping library staff</font></td>
<td width="360">
<font face="Arial, Helvetica, sans-serif" size="2"><input type="radio" name="LRHYKUTL" value="Helping young kids use the library">Helping young kids use the library</font></td></tr>
<tr valign="top"><td width="205">
<font face="Arial, Helvetica, sans-serif" size="2"><input type="radio" name="LRLC" value="Library contests">Library contests</font></td>
<td width="360">
<font face="Arial, Helvetica, sans-serif" size="2"><input type="radio" name="LRCBD" value="Cool book discussions">Cool book discussions  <font face="Arial, Helvetica, sans-serif" size="1">(eg. Harry Potter)</font></font></td></tr></table>
<p>
<b><font face="Arial, Helvetica, sans-serif" size="2">Your life<br></font></b>
<table width="412" border="0" cellspacing="0" cellpadding="0"><tr><td width="207">
<font face="Arial, Helvetica, sans-serif" size="2"><input type="radio" name="YLBTT" value="Babysitting tips / tricks">Babysitting tips / tricks</font></td>
<td width="205">
<font face="Arial, Helvetica, sans-serif" size="2"><input type="radio" name="YLEC" value="Exploring careers">Exploring careers</font></td></tr>
<tr><td width="207">
<font face="Arial, Helvetica, sans-serif" size="2"><input type="radio" name="YLTT" value="Teen topics">
Teen topics<b><font face="Arial, Helvetica, sans-serif" size="2">  </font></b><font face="Arial, Helvetica, sans-serif" size="1">(eg. peer pressure)</font></font></td>
<td width="205">
<font face="Arial, Helvetica, sans-serif" size="2"><input type="radio" name="YLGYFJ" value="Getting your first job">Getting your first job</font></td></tr></table>
<p>
```

```html
<b><font face="Arial, Helvetica, sans-serif" size="2">Computers<br></font></b>
<table width="583" border="0" cellspacing="0" cellpadding="0"><tr><td width="155">
<font face="Arial, Helvetica, sans-serif" size="2"><input type="radio" name="CCC" value="Computer club">Computer club</font></td>
<td width="130">
<font face="Arial, Helvetica, sans-serif" size="2"><input type="radio" name="CIC" value="Internet club">
Internet club</font></td>
<td width="298">
<font face="Arial, Helvetica, sans-serif" size="2"><input type="radio" name="CCS" value="Computer skills">Computer skills</font></td></tr>
<tr><td width="155">
<font face="Arial, Helvetica, sans-serif" size="2"><input type="radio" name="CWS" value="Web skills">
Web skills</font></td>
<td width="130">
<font face="Arial, Helvetica, sans-serif" size="2"><input type="radio" name="CK" value="Keypals">
Keypals</font></td>
<td width="298">
<font face="Arial, Helvetica, sans-serif" size="2"><input type="radio" name="CGOP" value="Global on-line projects">Global on-line projects</font></td></tr></table>
<p>
<b><font face="Arial, Helvetica, sans-serif" size="2">Arts / Crafts<br></font></b>
<table width="449" border="0" cellspacing="0" cellpadding="0"><tr><td width="155">
<font face="Arial, Helvetica, sans-serif" size="2"><input type="radio" name="ACDP" value="Drawing / Painting">Drawing / Painting</font></td>
<td width="130">
<font face="Arial, Helvetica, sans-serif" size="2"><input type="radio" name="ACCC" value="Cool crafts">
Cool crafts</font></td>
<td width="161">
<font face="Arial, Helvetica, sans-serif" size="2"><input type="radio" name="ACHAC" value="Holiday arts / crafts">Holiday arts / crafts</font></td></tr>
<tr><td width="155">
<font face="Arial, Helvetica, sans-serif" size="2"><input type="radio" name="ACYAC" value="Young authors club">Young authors club</font></td>
<td width="130">
<font face="Arial, Helvetica, sans-serif" size="2"><input type="radio" name="ACDC" value="Drama club">
Drama club</font></td>
<td width="161">
<font face="Arial, Helvetica, sans-serif" size="2"><input type="radio" name="ACP" value="Poetry club">
 Poetry club</font></td></tr></table>
<p>
<b><font face="Arial, Helvetica, sans-serif" size="2">Fun<br></font></b>
<table width="594" border="0" cellspacing="0" cellpadding="0"><tr><td width="209">
<font face="Arial, Helvetica, sans-serif" size="2"><input type="radio" name="FCGT" value="Computer game tournaments">Computer game tournaments</font></td>
<td width="204">
```

Group 7—Miscellaneous Forms/Surveys

```html
<font face="Arial, Helvetica, sans-serif" size="2"><input type="radio" name="FBGT" value="Board game tournaments">Board game tournaments</font></td>
<td width="181">
<font face="Arial, Helvetica, sans-serif" size="2"><input type="radio" name="FPAAM" value="Popcorn and a movie">Popcorn and a movie</font></td></tr>
<tr><td width="209">
<font face="Arial, Helvetica, sans-serif" size="2"><input type="radio" name="FSP" value="Sports programs">Sports programs</font></td>
<td width="204">
<font face="Arial, Helvetica, sans-serif" size="2"><input type="radio" name="FEFP" value="Exercise / Fashion programs">Exercise / Fashion programs</font></td>
<td width="181">
<font face="Arial, Helvetica, sans-serif" size="2"><input type="radio" name="FSH" value="Scavenger hunts">Scavenger hunts</font></td></tr></table>
<p> </p>
<p>
<font face="Arial, Helvetica, sans-serif" size="2"><b>How do you find out about upcoming library programs / activities?</b> <br>
<input type="radio" name="Currently" value="Posters, etc.">Posters, etc.  
<input type="radio" name="Currently" value="Friends">Friends   
<input type="radio" name="Currently" value="Librarians / Teachers">Librarians / Teachers   
<input type="radio" name="Currently" value="Web site">Web site<br>
<input type="radio" name="Currently" value="Other">Other   <font size="1">(explain)</font>
<font size="3">   <font size="2">
<input type="text" name="CurrentlyOther" size="10"></font></font></font></p>
<p>
<font face="Arial, Helvetica, sans-serif" size="2"><b>How would you like to find out about <i>future</i> library programs / activities?</b><br>
<input type="radio" name="Future" value="Email ">E-mail  
<input type="radio" name="Future" value="Web site">Web site  
<input type="radio" name="Future" value="Posters, etc.">Posters, etc.<br>
<input type="radio" name="Future" value="Other">Other   <font size="1">(explain)
</font><font size="3">   <font size="2"><input type="text" name="FutureOther" size="10">
</font></font></font><br>
<br><br></p>
<table width="407" border="0" cellspacing="4" cellpadding="1">
<tr><td width="202">
<b><font face="Arial, Helvetica, sans-serif" size="2">Name</font></b><font face="Arial, Helvetica, sans-serif" size="1">  (first, last)</font><br><font face="Arial, Helvetica, sans-serif" size="2">
<input type="text" name="Name" size="25"></font></td>
<td width="189">
<b><font face="Arial, Helvetica, sans-serif" size="2">E-mail address<br></font></b><font face="Arial, Helvetica, sans-serif" size="2"><input type="text" name="Email" size="25"></font></td></tr>
<tr><td width="202" height="2">
<b><font face="Arial, Helvetica, sans-serif" size="2">School you attend<br></font></b><font face="Arial,
```

```html
Helvetica, sans-serif" size="2"><input type="text" name="School" size="25"></font></td>
<td width="189" height="2">
<b><font face="Arial, Helvetica, sans-serif" size="2">Gender<br></font></b>
<input type="radio" name="Gender" value="Female"><font face="Arial, Helvetica, sans-serif" size="2">Female
</font>
<input type="radio" name="Gender" value="Male"><font face="Arial, Helvetica, sans-serif" size="2">Male</font>
</td></tr>
<tr><td width="391" colspan="2" height="48">
<b><font face="Arial, Helvetica, sans-serif" size="2">What grade are you in?</font></b><br>
<font face="Arial, Helvetica, sans-serif" size="2"></font>
<table width="87%" border="0" cellspacing="4" cellpadding="0"><tr><td height="8" width="16%">
<font face="Arial, Helvetica, sans-serif" size="2"><input type="radio" name="EducationLevel" value="3">
3</font></td>
<td height="8" width="16%">
<font face="Arial, Helvetica, sans-serif" size="2"><input type="radio" name="EducationLevel" value="4">
4</font></td>
<td height="8" width="16%">
<font face="Arial, Helvetica, sans-serif" size="2"><input type="radio" name="EducationLevel" value="5">
5</font></td>
<td height="8" width="16%">
<font face="Arial, Helvetica, sans-serif" size="2"><input type="radio" name="EducationLevel" value="6">
6</font></td>
<td height="8" width="36%">
<font face="Arial, Helvetica, sans-serif" size="2"><input type="radio" name="EducationLevel" value="7">
7</font></td></tr>
<tr><td height="2" width="16%">
<font face="Arial, Helvetica, sans-serif" size="2"><input type="radio" name="EducationLevel" value="8">
8</font></td>
<td height="2" width="16%">
<font face="Arial, Helvetica, sans-serif" size="2"><input type="radio" name="EducationLevel" value="9">
9</font></td>
<td height="2" width="16%">
<font face="Arial, Helvetica, sans-serif" size="2"><input type="radio" name="EducationLevel" value="10">
10</font></td>
<td height="2" width="16%">
<font face="Arial, Helvetica, sans-serif" size="2"><input type="radio" name="EducationLevel" value="11">
11</font></td>
<td height="2" width="36%">
<font face="Arial, Helvetica, sans-serif" size="2"><input type="radio" name="EducationLevel" value="12">
12</font></td></tr></table>
</td></tr></table>
<p> </p>
<table width="700" border="0" cellspacing="10" cellpadding="1"><tr><td width="226"><div align="right">
<input type="submit" name="send" value="Send Survey"></div></td><td width="207"> </td>
<td width="221"><div align="left"><input type="reset" name="clear" value="Clear Survey"></div></td></tr>
```

```html
<tr colspan=3><td colspan=3>
<table width="500" border="1" bordercolor="#000000" height="2" align="center" cellpadding="0" cellspacing="0" bgcolor="#ffffff"><tr><td><font size="1" color="#ffffff">.</font></td></tr></table>
</td></tr><tr><td colspan=3><div align="center">
<font face="Arial, Helvetica, sans-serif" size="1"><b>http://</b></font><br> 
<font face="Arial, Helvetica, sans-serif" size="1"><b>&copy; 2002</b></font>
<font face="Arial, Helvetica, sans-serif" size="2"><a href="mailto:">
<b><font size="1">Contact Webmaster</font></b></a></font></div></td></tr>
</table></form>
</body>
</html>
```

Kids / Teens Program Interests Survey — Perl Script

```perl
#!/usr/local/bin/perl

# *************************************************************
# ABOVE is where you MUST specify the path to your
# perl interpreter on your Web server.
# Replace /usr/local/bin/perl with your path.
# *************************************************************

if ($ENV{'REQUEST_METHOD'}eq"GET"){$buffer = $ENV{'QUERY_STRING'};}
    elsif($ENV{'REQUEST_METHOD'}eq"POST"){
        read(STDIN,$buffer,$ENV{'CONTENT_LENGTH'});
    }
$bufferb = $buffer;
#separate the name of the input from its value.
@forminputs = split(/&/, $bufferb);

foreach $forminput (@forminputs)
{
    #separate the name of the input from its value
    ($name, $value) = split(/=/, $forminput);

    #Un-Webify plus signs and %-encoding
    $value =~ tr/+/ /;
    $value =~ s/%([a-fA-F0-9][a-fA-F0-9])/pack("C", hex($1))/eg;

    #stick them in the in array
    $in{$name} = $value;
}
print "Content-type: text/html\n\n";

#################################################
# ABOVE is the required header for a perl script  #
#################################################

#######################################################
# (Below) Email received by library containing user-entered information #
#######################################################

# *************************************************************
# Here's where you MUST specify the path to your
# email program (probably sendmail) ON your Web server.
# Replace /usr/sbin/sendmail with your path.
# *************************************************************
```

Group 7—Miscellaneous Forms/Surveys

```
open (LMAIL, "|/usr/sbin/sendmail -t");
print LMAIL ("To: $in{LibraryEmail}\n");
print LMAIL ("From: $in{Email}\n");
print LMAIL ("Subject: $in{Form} - patron submission\n");

print LMAIL ("------------------\nPatron information\n\n");


print LMAIL ("Name:\n $in{Name}\n\n");
print LMAIL ("E-mail Address:\n $in{Email}\n\n");
print LMAIL ("School:\n $in{School}\n\n");
print LMAIL ("Gender:\n $in{Gender}\n\n");
print LMAIL ("Grade:\n $in{EducationLevel}\n\n");

print LMAIL ("------------------\nSubmitted information \n\n");
print LMAIL ("Would you attend a library program or activity that interests you?\n $in{Attend}\n\n");

print LMAIL ("If yes, what are the best times for these programs or activites?\n $in{AS}, $in{AD}, $in{W}, $in{DS}\n\n");

print LMAIL ("------------------\nWhat Types of Programs / Activities Would You Be Interested In? \n\n");

print LMAIL ("School:\n $in{SHHS}, $in{SWARP}, $in{SCAB}, $in{STOS}\n\n");

print LMAIL ("Library / Reading:\n $in{LRHLS}, $in{LRHYKUTL}, $in{LRLC}, $in{LRCBD}\n\n");

print LMAIL ("Your life:\n $in{YLBTT}, $in{YLEC}, $in{YLTT}, $in{YLGYFJ}\n\n");

print LMAIL ("Computers:\n $in{CCC}, $in{CIC},$in{CCS}, $in{CWS}, $in{CK}, $in{CGOP}\n\n");

print LMAIL ("Arts / Crafts:\n $in{ACDP}, $in{ACCC},$in{ACHAC}, $in{ACYAC}, $in{ACDC}, $in{ACPC}\n\n");

print LMAIL ("Fun:\n $in{FCGT}, $in{FBGT},$in{FPAAM}, $in{FSP}, $in{FEFP}, $in{FSH}\n\n");

print LMAIL ("How do you find out about upcoming library programs / activities?\n $in{Currently}\n\n");
print LMAIL ("Other ways:\n $in{CurrentlyOther}\n\n");

print LMAIL ("How would you like to find out about <i>future</i> library programs / activities?\n $in{Future}\n\n");
print LMAIL ("Other ways:\n $in{FutureOther}\n\n");

print LMAIL ("\n.\n");

################################################
# Email received by the user confirming form submission #
################################################
```

```
# ************************************************
# Here's where you MUST specify the path to your
# email program ON your Web server.
# Replace /usr/sbin/sendmail with your path.
# ************************************************

open (MAIL, "|/usr/sbin/sendmail -t");

# ************************************************
# Here's where you MAY customize the email
# response to the user. You may change any wording
# of the message.
# ************************************************

print MAIL<<toEnd;
To: $in{Email}
From: $in{LibraryEmail}
Subject: $in{Form}

Thanks for completing our Kids / Teens Program Interests Survey.\n\n

toEnd
    print MAIL ("\n.\n");

##########################################
# Screen response to user after submitting the form  #
##########################################

print ("<html><head><title>$in{Form}</title></head>");
print ("<body bgcolor=\"ffffff\">");

# ************************************************
# Here's where you MAY change the screen response
# the user sees after submitting the form. You may
# change any wording between the quotation marks.
# ************************************************

print ("Thanks for completing our Kids / Teens Program Interests Survey.");

# ************************************************
# Here's where you MAY change the name of the link
# back to your main page. You may replace Return
# to our main page with your own wording.
# ************************************************

print ("<p><center><a href=$in{LibraryURL}>Return to our main page.</a></center>");
print ("</body></html>");
```

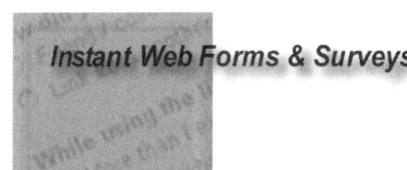

Index

A
Accompanying manual, v, x-xi
Acquisitions forms/surveys, ix, 193–212
Acrobat files, v, x-i
ACTION= attribute, 3, 16, 19
Apply For a Library Card form, ix, 213–222
Ask a Reference Question form, vii, 35–43
Assignment Alert form, vii, 35, 44–52

B
Background skills. See Needed skills
Bibliography, xi-xii
BGCOLOR= attribute, 23
Books, Recommended, ix
Broken link form, viii, 147, 155–161
Button, Radio, 4, 7
Button, Reset, 5, 8
Button, Submit, 3, 5, 8–9

C
CGI-BIN directory, 1–2, 26–27
Checkbox, 5
Circulation forms, ix, 213–234
Citing a Source form, vii, 35, 61–69
Collection Development forms/surveys, ix, 193–212
Colors and forms/surveys, xii, 2, 17, 22–23, 30
Completing required form information, 18–20
    Add the mailto link to the form, 20
    Add the URL to the form, 19–20
    Complete link back to your homepage, 19
    Link up the form and script, 18–19
    Specify the staff e-mail address, 19
Completing required script information, 20–21
    Specify the e-mail program path, 21
    Specify the Perl interpreter path, 20
Computer forms/surveys, viii, 113–146
Cybersurfer Home Survey, viii, 113, 134–145
Cybersurfer Library Survey, viii, 113, 121–133

D
Directories, Server, 1–2, 18–21, 26–27, 30
Downloading files, 1, 17–18, 28–29

E
E-mail and forms/scripts, 2, 11–12, 18–19, 21, 24, 26
Evaluating a Web Site form, ix, 147, 181–191

F
File extensions, 29
File servers. See Servers
File transfer. See FTP
Finding a Class form, vii, 79, 89–96
Fonts and forms/surveys, 2, 17, 22
Form basics, 2–6
Form elements, 3–8
    Checkbox, 5
    Hidden form fields, 5–6, 19
    Multiple line text box, 4, 8
    Radio button, 4, 7
    Reset button, 5, 8
    Single line text box, 3–4
    Submit button, 3, 5, 8–9
Form footer, 8
FORM tag, 3
Forms, HTML (individual)
    Apply for a Library Card form, 216–219
    Ask a Reference Question form, 38–40
    Find a Class form, 90–93
    Get Help Citing a Source form, 63–66
    Get Help Searching the Web form, 55–57
    Get Help With Your Homework form, 72–75
    Hold / Recall / Renew form, 225–227
    Homework Assignment Alert form, 46–49
    How to Evaluate a Web Site form, 183–187
    Incident Report form, 239–241
    Meet With a Librarian form, 82–85
    Recommend an Item form, 195–197
    Report a Broken Link or Problem form, 156–158
    Report a Missing Item form, 232–234
    Reserve a Library Computer form, 115–117
    Sign Our Guest Book form, 163–165
    Suggest a New Web Link form, 149–151
FTP (file transfer), xii, 17–18, 28–29

G
Get Help Citing a Source form, vii, 35, 61–69
Get Help Searching the Web form, vii, 35, 53–60
Get Help With Your Homework form, vii, 35, 70–78
Graphics form, 22–23
Guest Book form, ix, 147, 162–168

H

Header, Perl, 9
Hexidecimal colors, xii, 23
Hidden form fields, 5–6, 19
Hold / Recall / Renew form, ix, 213, 223–230
Home Cybersurfer Survey, viii, 113, 134–145
Homework Assignment Alert form, vii, 35, 44–52
Homework Help form, vii, 35, 70–78
How to Evaluate a Web Site form, ix, 147, 181–191
HTML editing programs, 1
HTML forms
    Introduction, xi-xii, 2–6
    Sample forms, 6–8
    Testing, 25–26, 29, 31
HTML forms (individual). *See* Forms, HTML (individual)

I

Incident Report form, x, 239–241
INPUT tag, 3–5, 7–8
Interpreter, Perl, 1–2, 10, 17–18, 20, 26

K

Kids/Teens Program Interests Survey, xi, 239, 248–258

L

Library Card Application form, ix, 213–222
Library Computer forms/surveys, viii, 113–146
Library Cybersurfer Survey, viii, 113, 121–133
Library Instruction forms/surveys, vii, 79–112
Library Web Site forms/surveys, vii-ix, 147–192
Library Web Site Survey, ix, 147, 169–180
LINUX, 17

M

Mailto link, 8, 19, 30
Meet With a Librarian form, vii, 79–88
METHOD= attribute, 3, 6, 19
Miscellaneous forms/surveys, x, 239–258
Missing Book form, ix, 213, 231–237
Modifying form content, 21–23
    Change form fonts, 22
    Change the color of the header, 22–23
    Change the color of header text, 23
    Make minor changes to text, 22
Modifying Perl scripts, 23–25
    Re-word the e-mail message, 24
    Re-word the link to your homepage, 24–25
    Re-word the screen message, 23–24
Monitor resolutions, 27–28
Multi-line text input box, 4, 8

N

NAME= attribute, 3–5, 7–8
Needed skills, 1–2
New Web Link form, viii, 147–154
NT server, 1, 17–18, 29

P

PDF files, v, x-xi
Perl basics, 9–13
Perl headers, 9–10
Perl interpreter programs, 1–2, 10, 17–18, 20, 26
Perl scripts, xi, 9–13
    Introduction, 9–10
    Sample script, 10–13
    Testing, 26, 29–31
Perl scripts (individual). *See* Scripts, Perl (individual)
Perl variables, 9–10
Preview / Selection Tutorial, x, 17, 28
Print function, 10
Program Interests Survey, x, 239, 248–258
POST attribute, 3, 19

R

Radio button, 4, 7
Reading Interests Survey, ix, 193, 201–212
Recall form, ix, 213, 223–230
Recommend an Item form, ix, 193–200
Reference forms/surveys, vii, 35–78
Reference Question form, vii, 35–43
Renew form, ix, 213, 223–230
Report a Broken Link or Problem form, viii, 147, 155–161
Report a Missing Book form, ix, 213, 231–237
Required form information, 18–20
    Add the mailto link to the form, 20
    Add the URL to the form, 19–20
    Complete link back to your homepage, 19
    Link up the form and script, 18–19
    Specify the staff e-mail address, 19
Required script information, 20–21
    Specify the e-mail program path, 21
    Specify the Perl interpreter path, 20
Reserve a Library Computer form, viii, 113–120
Reset button, 5, 8

S

Sample HTML form, 6–8
Sample Perl script, 10–13
Saving files, 17–28
Screen messages, 10, 12, 23–24, 29–30
Scripts, Perl (individual)   Apply for a Library Card form, 220–222
    Ask a Reference Question form, 41–43

Find a Class form, 94–96
Get Help Citing a Source form, 67–69
Get Help Searching the Web form, 58–60
Get Help With Your Homework form, 76–78
Hold / Recall / Renew form, 228–230
Home Cybersurfer Survey, 142–145
Homework Assignment Alert form, 50–52
How to Evaluate a Web Site form, 188–191
Incident Report form, 240–241
Kids/Teens Program Interests Survey, 256–258
Library Cybersurfer Survey, 130–133
Library Web Site Survey, 177–180
Meet With a Librarian form, 86–88
Reading Interests Survey, 210–212
Recommend an Item form, 198–200
Report a Broken Link or Problem form, 159-161
Report a Missing Book form, 239–241
Reserve a Library Computer form, 118–120
Sign Our Guest Book form, 166–168
Suggest a New Web Link form, 152–154
Training Interests Survey, 102–104
What Do You Want to Learn Survey, 110–112
Searching the Web form, vii, 35, 53–60
Selection Tutorial, x, 17, 28
Servers, 2, 16, 28
    Directories, 1–2, 18–21, 26–27, 30
    Permissions, 2, 26–28
Sign Our Guest Book form, ix, 147, 162–168
Single line text box, 3–4
Skills, Needed, 1–2
Sources for Further Help, xi-xii
Suggest a New Web Link form, viii, 147–154
Submit button, 3, 5, 8–9
Surveys, HTML (individual)
    Home Cybersurfer Survey, 136–141
    Kids/Teens Program Interests Survey, 250–255
    Library Cybersurfer Survey, 123–129
    Library Web Site Survey, 171–176
    Reading Interests Survey, 203–209
    Training Interests Survey, 99–101
    What Do You Want to Learn Survey, 106–109

T

Tags and forms, 2–6
Technical staff, 1–2, 26, 28–29
Teen Program Interests Survey, x, 239, 248–258
Testing forms, 25–26, 29–31
Testing scripts, 26, 29–31
Textarea tag, 4
Text boxes, 3–4, 8
"Thank you" screen/email message, 10, 12, 23–24, 29–30
Training Interests Survey, viii, 79, 97–104
Transferring files. *See* FTP Tutorial, Preview/Selection, x, 17, 28
TYPE= attribute, 3–5, 7–8

U

Uploading files. *See* FTP
UNIX server, xii, 1–2, 12, 18
URLs and forms/surveys, 8, 12, 19, 30
URLs, Recommended, xi-xii

V

VALUE= attribute, 4–5, 9
Variables, Perl, 9–10

W

Web site forms/surveys, viii-ix, 147–192
Web Site Survey, ix, 147, 169–180
What Do You Want to Learn Survey, viii, 79, 105–112

About the Authors

Gail Junion-Metz

As head of her own training and consulting firm, Information Age Consultants, Gail instructs public and school librarians, patrons, teachers, and students of all ages and interests. Gail also likes to write about the Net. She is most widely known for her "Surf For" column, which is featured monthly in *School Library Journal*. Gail has also written a number of Internet books, such as *Internet Coach for Kids: A Guide for Librarians, Teachers, and Parents* and *K–12 Resources on the Internet,* both published by Library Solutions Press. She also co-authored *Using the World Wide Web and Creating Home Pages: A How-To-Do-It Manual for Librarians* and *Creating a Power Web Site: HTML, Tables, Imagemaps, Frames and Forms: A book with Web-Enabled CD-ROM,* both published by Neal-Schuman.

Gail holds a Master of Arts degree in Library Science from the University of Wisconsin, Madison. She is happily married to Ray, also a librarian, has a cool step-son Derrek (her current co-author), and lives in Winfield, Pennsylvania, in the heart of Amish country.

Derrek L. Metz

Derrek is in his third year at Bucknell University where he is majoring in Economics and minoring in Computer Science. He has been working with the Internet and creating Web sites since 1995. Derrek currently holds a Web intern coordinator position for the Alumni, Parents, and Volunteers Office at Bucknell, while also creating and maintaining other campus sites. Last summer he interned at Lombard Risk Management in London, serving on their Web marketing team. Derrek has hopes of continuing his research and affiliation with the Internet's application to the financial and business sectors.

Instant Web Forms & Surveys

How to Launch the CD

Because of the large number of files on the CD and the considerable amount of hard drive space it would take up, we do not recommend that you download the contents of the CD onto your computer. Instead, follow the instructions below to launch the CD from your CD drive any time you want to use it.

Windows Computers
1. Insert the CD into your computer's drive
2. Click on the "Start" button on your taskbar
3. From the "Start" menu, select and click on the RUN option
4. In the "Run" box's "Open": space, type D:/setup.htm then click on the "OK" button
5. This will automatically launch your default Web browser and load the tutorial

MacIntosh Computers
1. Insert the CD into your computer's drive
2. Locate the CD's icon on your desktop and double click on it
3. In the window that displays, locate and double click on the icon for the *setup.htm* file
4. This will automatically launch your default Web browser and load the tutorial